POSTCARD HISTORY SERIES

Marion County

IN VINTAGE POSTCARDS

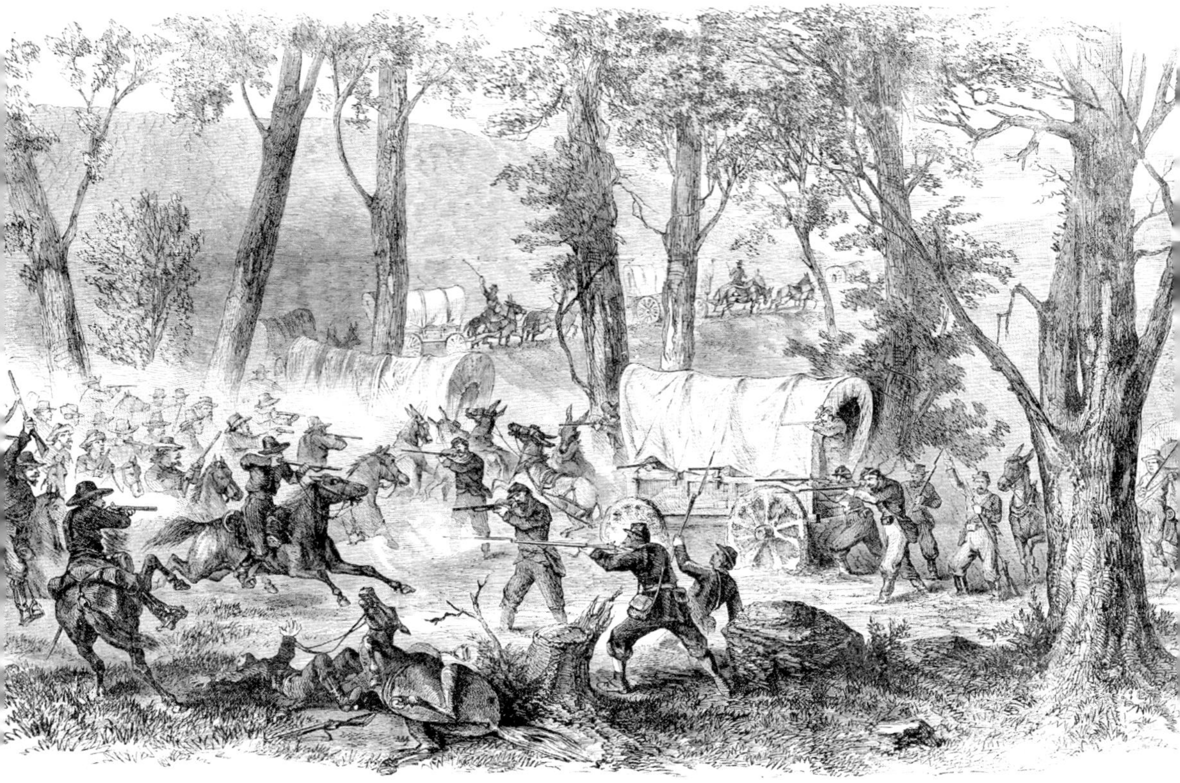

WHEELER'S CONFEDERATE CAVALRY CAPTURING A SUPPLY-TRAIN NEAR JASPER, TENN.
FROM A SKETCH BY J. F. E. HILLEN.

This Civil War sketch is of Confederate general Joseph Wheeler just north of Jasper on Old Anderson Road. In 1883, he and his men completely destroyed a 10-mile-long Union wagon train made up of more than 800 wagons and 4,000 mules. This lithograph first appeared in *Harper's Weekly*.

POSTCARD HISTORY SERIES

Marion County in Vintage Postcards

Billyfrank Morrison

ISBN 978-0-7385-1827-5

Published by Arcadia Publishing
Charleston, South Carolina

Printed in the United States of America

Library of Congress Catalog Card Number: 2005925645

For all general information contact Arcadia Publishing at:
Telephone 843-853-2070
Fax 843-853-0044
E-mail sales@arcadiapublishing.com
For customer service and orders:
Toll-Free 1-888-313-2665

Visit us on the Internet at www.arcadiapublishing.com

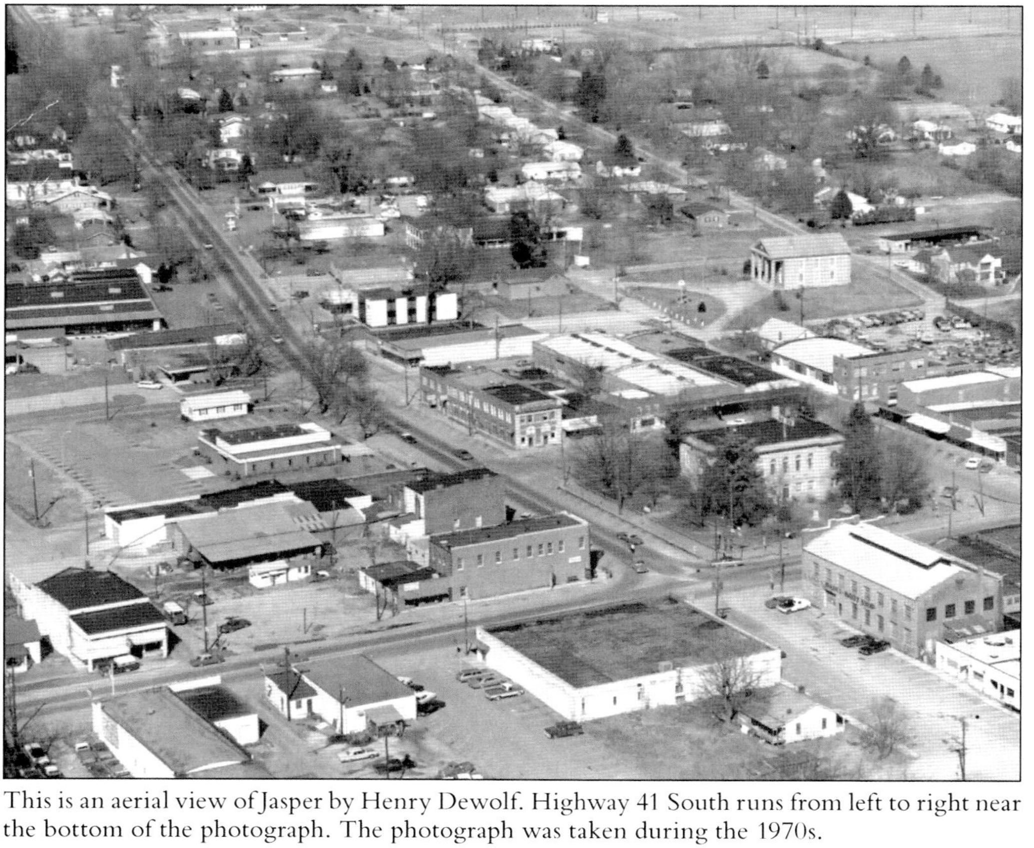

This is an aerial view of Jasper by Henry Dewolf. Highway 41 South runs from left to right near the bottom of the photograph. The photograph was taken during the 1970s.

Contents

ACKNOWLEDGMENTS

I learned from my previous books that you do not write any book without a lot of help. While the shortcomings of the work are mine alone, a number of people provided considerable assistance. I would like to recognize those individuals:

Meredith James Thomas
Lee Mitchell
Nancy Raffo
Jim and Kay Sanders
Randall Sullivan
Gertrude Link
Mitch Kinder
G. I. Brown
Spud Parker
Chili Warren
Barbara Runyon Holloway
Mr. and Mrs. A. J. Gudger
Helen Parton
Ridley Wills II
Billy Simpson
Jim Oliver
Eulene Harris
Pat Morrison
Lee McFarland
Susan Patton
Edwin Z. Kelly Jr.
Tom Allen Morrison
Bob Hookey
William Ray Turner
Karen Tittle
Dean Lay
Bill Lockhart
Carolyn Millhiser
Jo Carlton
Jan Silva
Robert Beene
Mary Nell Grimes
George (Sonny) Rogers

The staff at Arcadia Publishing has been supportive through all my projects. I am particularly appreciative of the help provided by my editor, Adam Latham. Adam is a graduate of the University of the South in Sewanee.

Some acknowledgments are special. Always first in all I do is Evelyn, my wife and consummate assistant. She generously gave of her time to help with anything I asked. Secondly, thanks to my lifelong buddy Bobby Lewis, who helped keep me grounded. He and his beautiful wife, Joanne, always invited me back to Jasper.

Last, but most important, I'd like to pay tribute to my parents, who were born, lived, and died in Marion County. Frank William Morrison Sr. deserves all the credit, or blame, for my interest in collecting postcards. He taught me the value of preserving "old things." Daddy was killed in a robbery attempt near Powell's Crossroads on February 24, 1979. And to my mother, Katherine Viola Jones Morrison, after whom I named my firstborn. Mother instilled in me an early appreciation of art and literature. She died of cancer in 1959 at age 43. Friends and family called her "Purt," which was short for "Pretty." Both now rest in the beautiful Sardis Cemetery in Victoria, Tennessee.

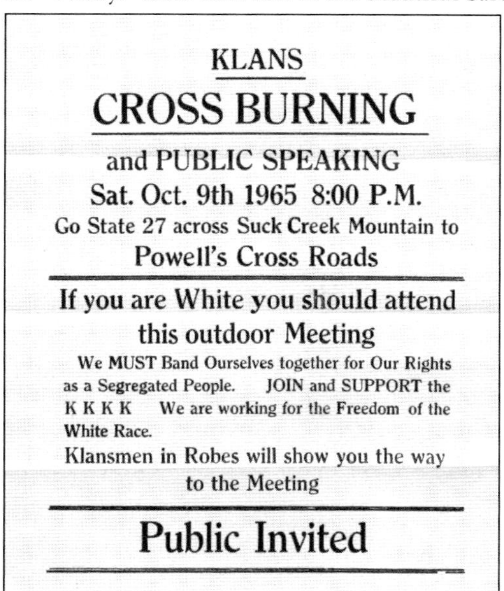

In September 2004, a cross was burned outside the home of the Lilly family in Sequatchie. Johnny Pittman was arrested for a hate crime and pleaded guilty.

FOREWORD

Billyfrank Morrison and I grew up in Marion County, Tennessee—more specifically in the county seat, Jasper. The author grew up on one side of the railroad tracks on what is now Morrison Street in an old church house his father converted to a home in the early 1940s. I grew up on the opposite side on what was then (and is still) Simpson Road. My grandparents built the home I lived in. Jasper was home to our grandparents and our parents. It is our birthplace and where we attended Marion County High School. We are fiercely proud of where we came from and feel an ownership about Marion County.

Billyfrank and I discussed this book when it was still in the planning stages. As a friend of the author and mayor of Jasper, I fully support the preservation of our history in all forms. So when he asked, I eagerly agreed to write this forward to *Marion County in Vintage Postcards*.

While Marion County has a distinct personality, it is the sum of numerous enclaves, each of which influences her. The county is mountains, rivers, a valley, small towns, rural South, and friendly people. Some of the towns (including Jasper) are prospering. Other communities have suffered as a result of disappearing industry (often coal-related). The people of the county are many things, but mostly they are ordinary people living in an extraordinary place.

The more than 200 postcard images that illustrate Morrison's book provide a glimpse into the history of our county. So lean back, relax, and let one of our own give you a tour of our home—Marion County, Tennessee.

—Billy Simpson
Mayor, Jasper, Tennessee

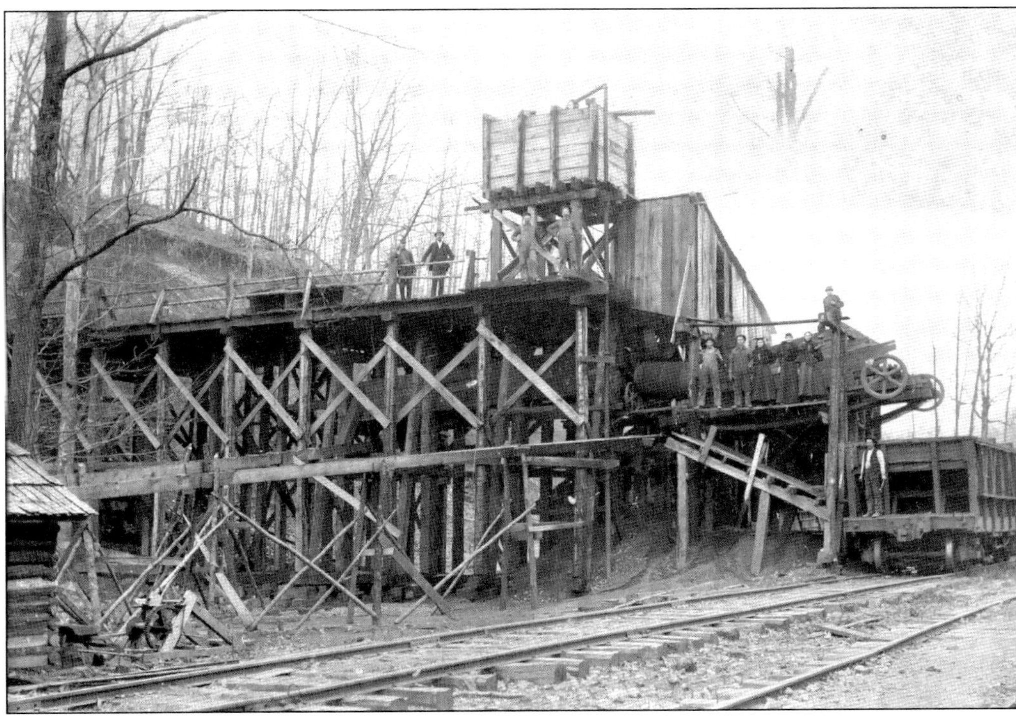

This photograph is of an old tipple at one of the mines in Orme, Tennessee. Based on the way the people are dressed, it must be an occasion of some kind. There are women above the coal car. Two names, D. W. Crawford and Mc D. Dicken, appear on the back of the photograph.

Introduction

This is my third book. My first was of Clarksville, Tennessee, which is where I live. The second was of Fort Campbell, Kentucky, where I worked for many years. But home is where you hang your heart, and mine hangs in Marion County.

Compiling a book on Marion County is part of a personal journey that began more than six decades ago in the prettiest part of the state—Jasper. Writing a book about the county and her people was more than easy. It is, after all, my home—and they are my people.

Each community in Marion County is unique, but none stand alone. They make individual contributions to create an indomitable county. Change in parts of Marion County has been so slow as to be almost imperceptible; in some parts change has come at warp speed. You can see the change—or absence of it—in these vintage postcard images.

As a native, I and Marion County have seen each other at our best and worst. It is the intent of this book to address some of both. I hope that my unique relationships with the area and its residents have enabled me to provide a more intimate and, therefore, more enjoyable account of the county's past. Marion County is in the beautiful Sequatchie Valley, shares the Tennessee River, and is surrounded by the colorful Cumberland Mountains. It abounds with American Indian burial grounds, has passionate memories of a civil war, includes backcountry where outsiders are not warmly received, is home to the Prentice Cooper and Franklin State Forests, and has numerous waterfalls and caves. But mostly, Marion County is, and always has been, home to fiercely independent people.

It is something of a literary tradition to portray such rural areas as breeding grounds for dark secrets, as being economically depressed, as a haven for hard menial work and home to clusters of people who are carving out a lifestyle different from those of other places. Marion County is a contradiction—it is, and is not, all of those.

After all is said and done, this book is about postcards. So, go ahead; take a postcard tour of Marion County, Tennessee.

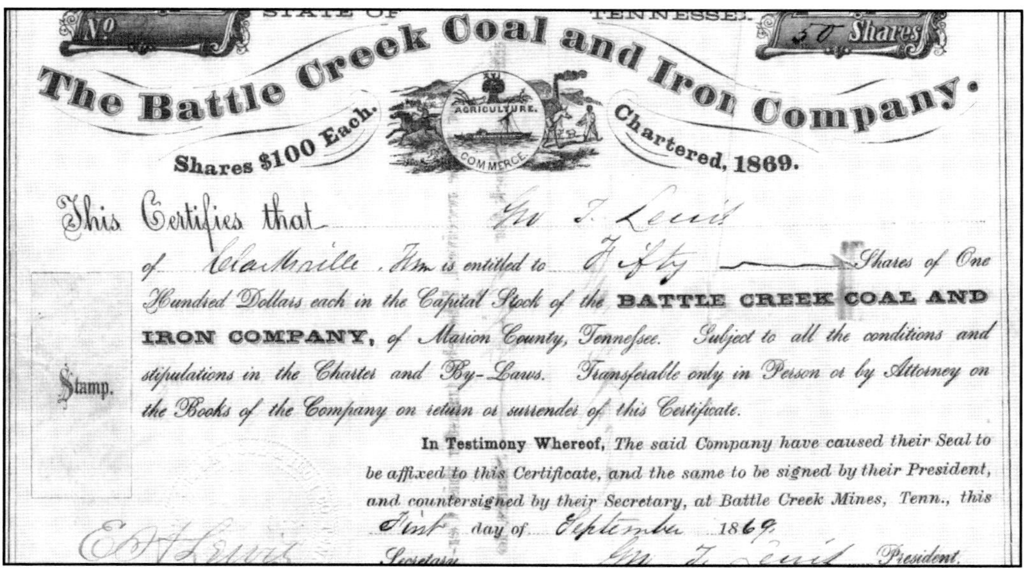
No. STATE OF TENNESSEE. 50 Shares

The Battle Creek Coal and Iron Company.

Shares $100 Each. Chartered, 1869.

AGRICULTURE. COMMERCE

This Certifies that Geo. T. Lewis of Clarksville, Tenn. is entitled to Fifty Shares of One Hundred Dollars each in the Capital Stock of the BATTLE CREEK COAL AND IRON COMPANY, of Marion County, Tennessee. Subject to all the conditions and stipulations in the Charter and By-Laws. Transferable only in Person or by Attorney on the Books of the Company on return or surrender of this Certificate.

Stamp.

In Testimony Whereof, The said Company have caused their Seal to be affixed to this Certificate, and the same to be signed by their President, and countersigned by their Secretary, at Battle Creek Mines, Tenn., this First day of September 1869.

E. H. Lewis, Secretary. Geo. T. Lewis, President.

Coal mining played a significant role in the history of Marion County, but today most of the mines, processing plants, and tipples have been abandoned. The 1940s brought hard times to Marion County, and many families walked along the roads picking up chunks of coal spilled by coal-carrying trucks. During that time, coal was used for heating and/or cooking in most Marion County homes. Few if any families in Marion County were early investors in the coal or iron industry.

One

Jasper
The County Seat

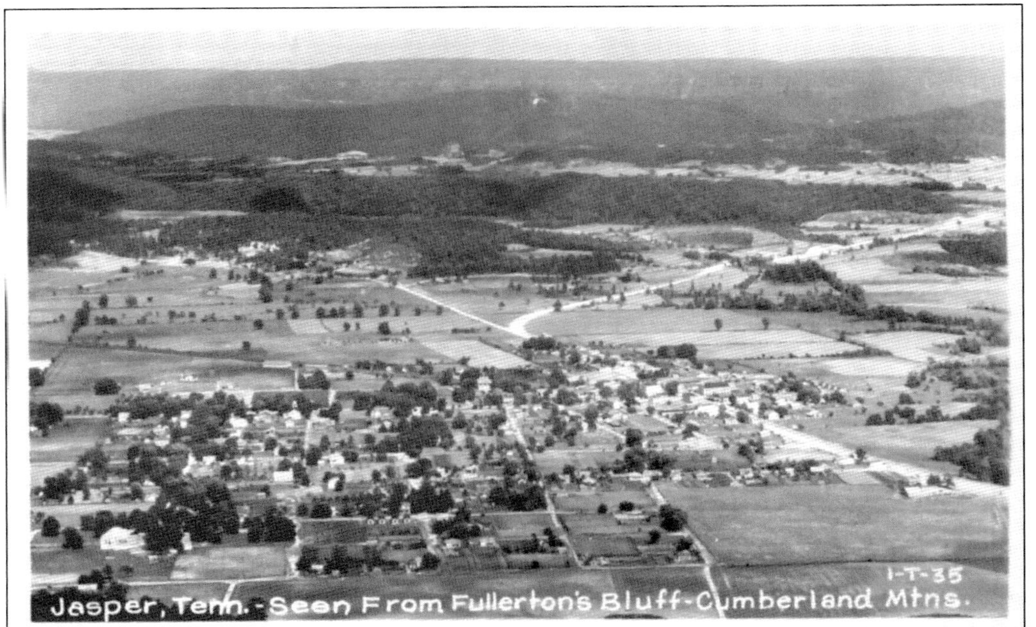

This view of Jasper was taken from Fullerton's Bluff near the settlement of Summertown, where the population would swell to several hundred during summer months but only a few families resided year-round. Prior to the airplane, mountaintops or balloons provided the best vantage points for a photographer.

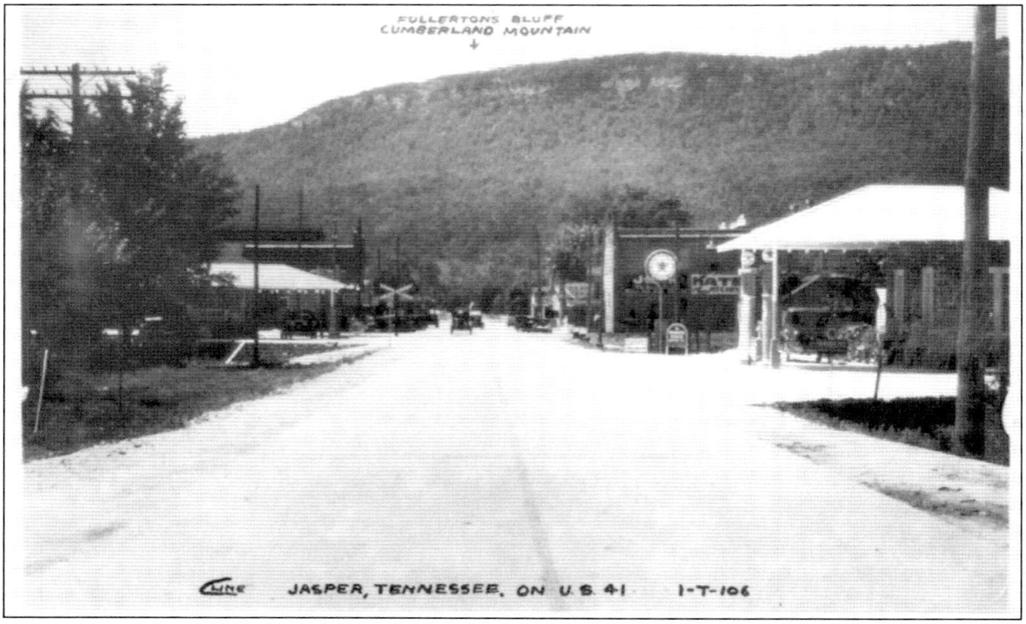

This is in the late 1920s or early 1930s. The Texaco service station on the right was owned and operated by John Moore and later by Tommy Smith and Lester Morrison. On the left is the Gulf service station, owned and operated in the 1940s and 1950s by Bead-Eye Beene (Robert's father). Across the railroad tracks on the right is the Jasper Drug Store with a Kate's Kitchen sign visible on the back of the store. Among the trees in the left front sat Johnson's Boarding House, where Meadow "Siter" Housley lived.

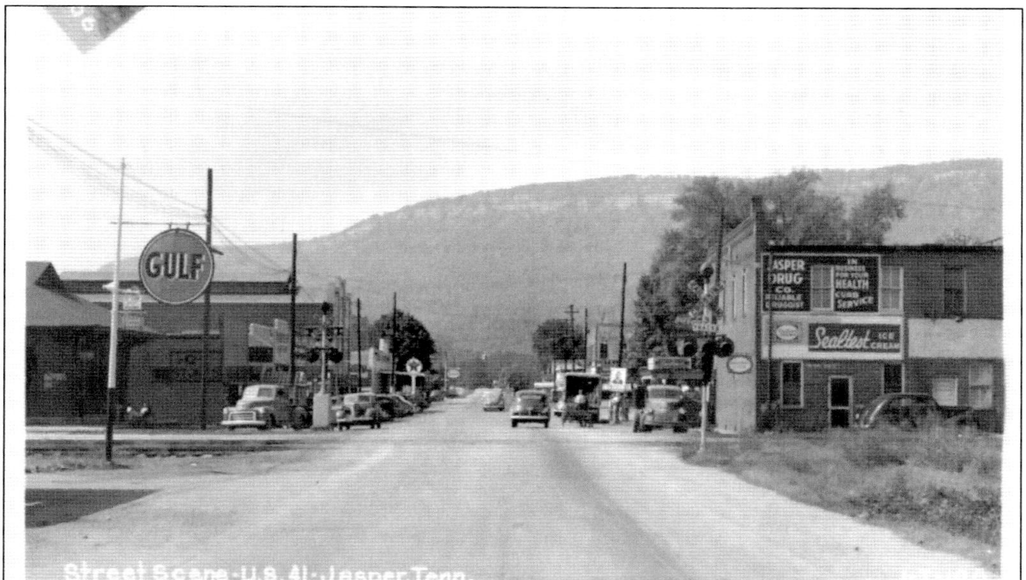

The horse-drawn wagon (center right) is most likely Buck Tanner's. He and Lillian Whiteside resided at the poorhouse on the East Valley Road. William Cline, a Chattanooga photographer, took this real photograph postcard (RPPC) on a Saturday morning. There is a "Dewey for President" sign on a telephone pole on the right. Dewey ran in both the 1944 and 1948 elections.

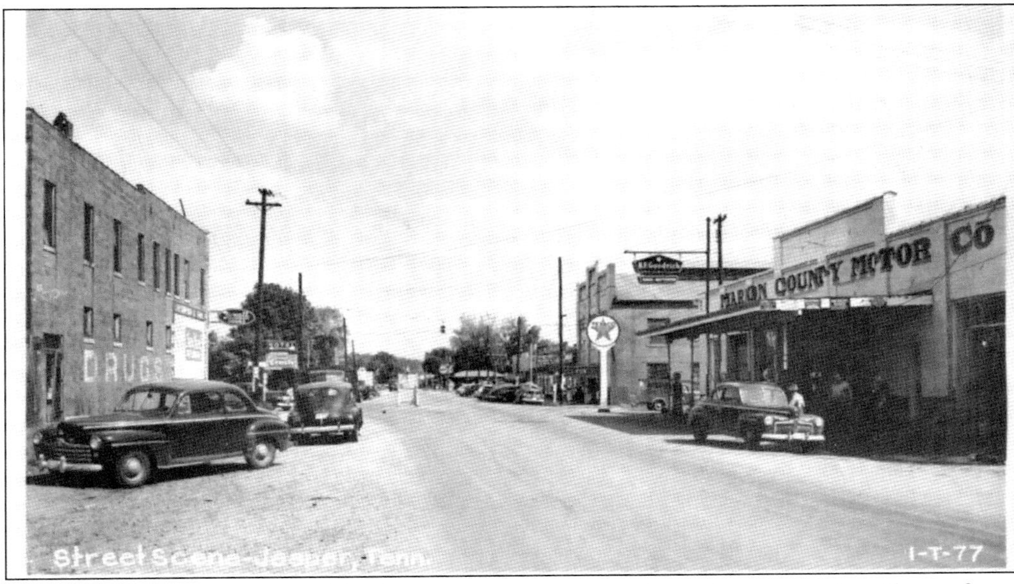

Preceding traffic lights, signs, like the one seen in the street here, directed traffic. The prefix on the automobile license plates is 54—indicating Marion County's ranking among other Tennessee counties in population. The garage building on the right was owned by the Woods family and rented by Bit Garland. Jim Warren, who was employed there, was killed in an auto accident in Sequatchie. J. W. Simpson and Son owned the drugstore on the left.

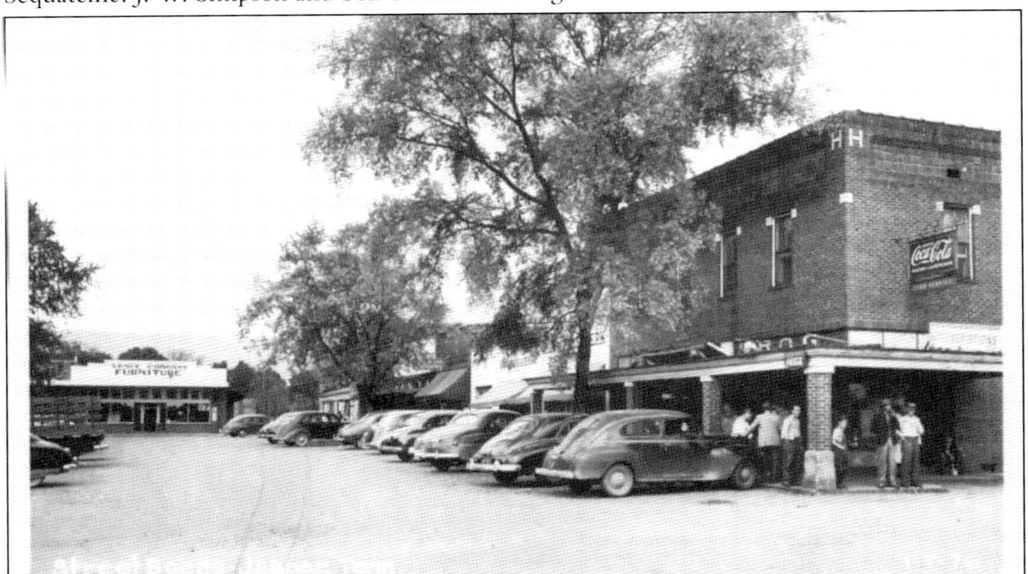

The Jasper Drug Store (lower right) was more than a drugstore—it was a gathering place for the town's men; the Greyhound bus stop; the Quarles (Bill and Eunice) taxi stand; and a gathering place for Marion County High School (MCHS) students. Bobby Condra owns the drugstore building now, and Angie Rogers is a pharmacist there. Vickie Dodson also works there. The "H" in the top corner of the drugstore is for the original owners, the Havrons (Mrs. Braden was a Havron). Vance Furniture Store, seen at the end of the street, is next door to what was the R. D. Gass Hudson Dealership and more recently Cagle's Garage.

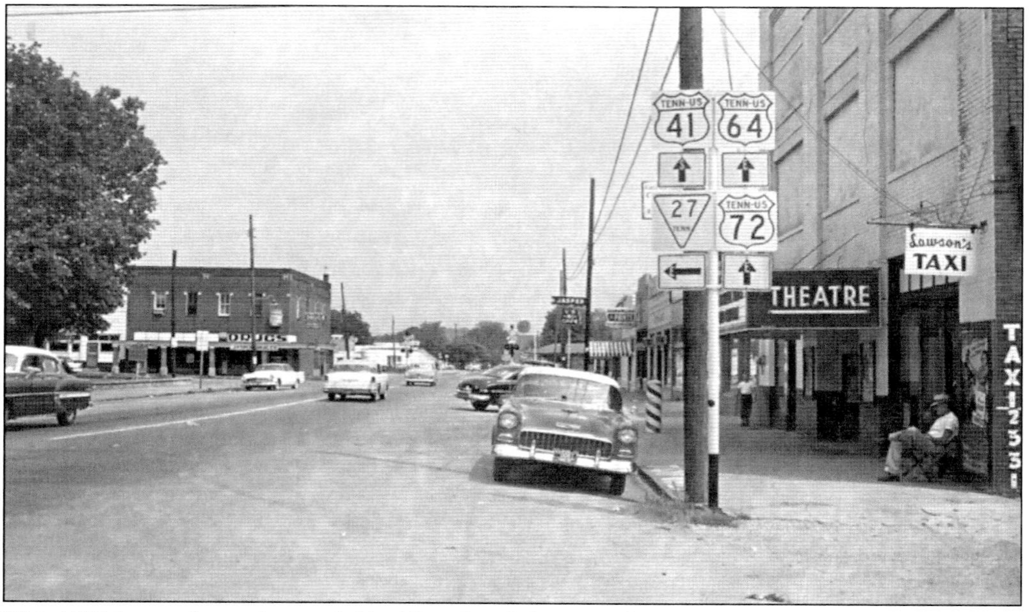

This 1955 image shows Lawson's Taxi Stand and the Fox Theatre. In the 1946 directory, the taxi stand is listed as the Jasper Taxi, with drivers Bill Sr., Bill Jr., Casper, and Haywood Quarles. Dummy Lawson's barbershop (later run by his son Cotton) is visible just beyond the Fox Theatre. According to James Taylor, the man seated is John Teeters, a taxi driver. Cab fare was 25¢ a mile. This card was mailed from Jasper's Otis Phillips to the author, who was serving with the navy at Kingsville, Texas.

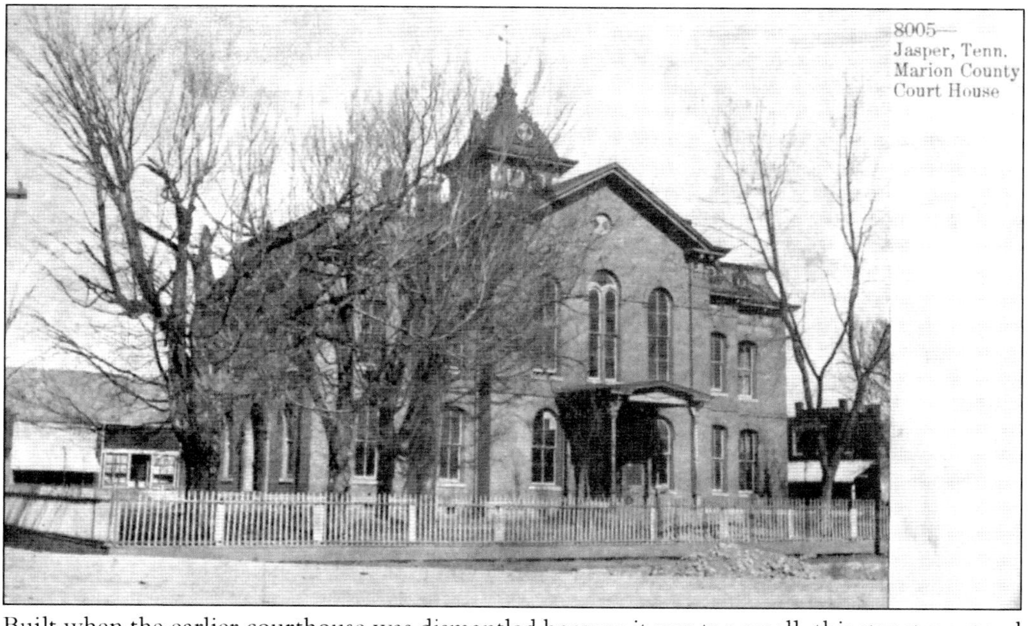

Built when the earlier courthouse was dismantled because it was too small, this structure stood from 1880 until it burned in 1922. Almost all county records were lost in the fire, and Sam Houston Academy was used as a temporary courthouse. This *c.* 1915 card is the earliest known postcard of the courthouse.

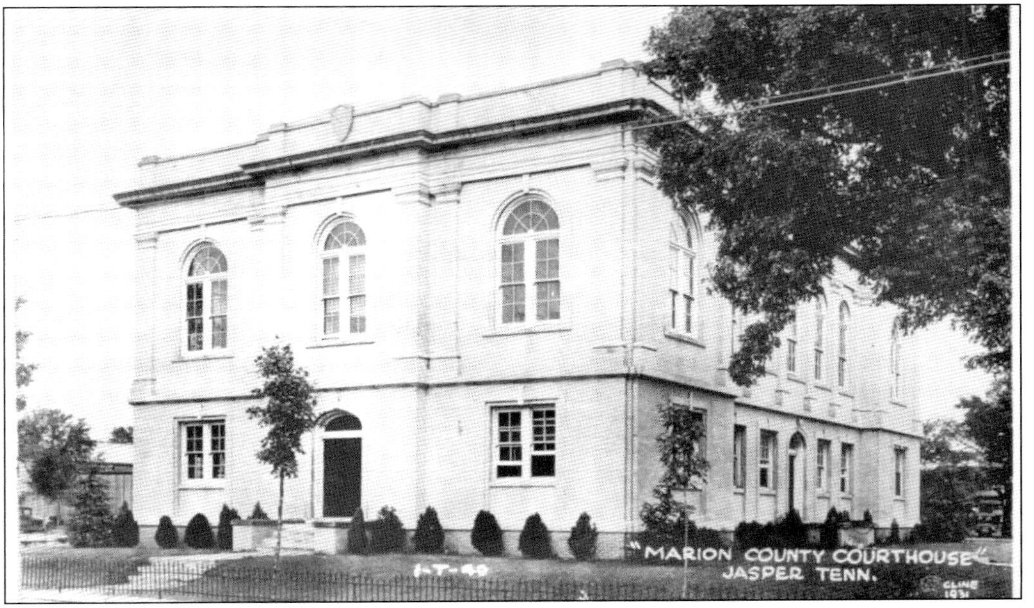

Traditionally the "courthouse square" was the center of social and political activities around the South. Today, in larger communities, courthouses are cold, secure, unfriendly places. The evergreens at the corners of the courthouse are mere shrubs in this postcard. In the late 1950s, boys would climb these trees (see postcard below), get onto the roof of the courthouse, and watch the excitement around the town at night.

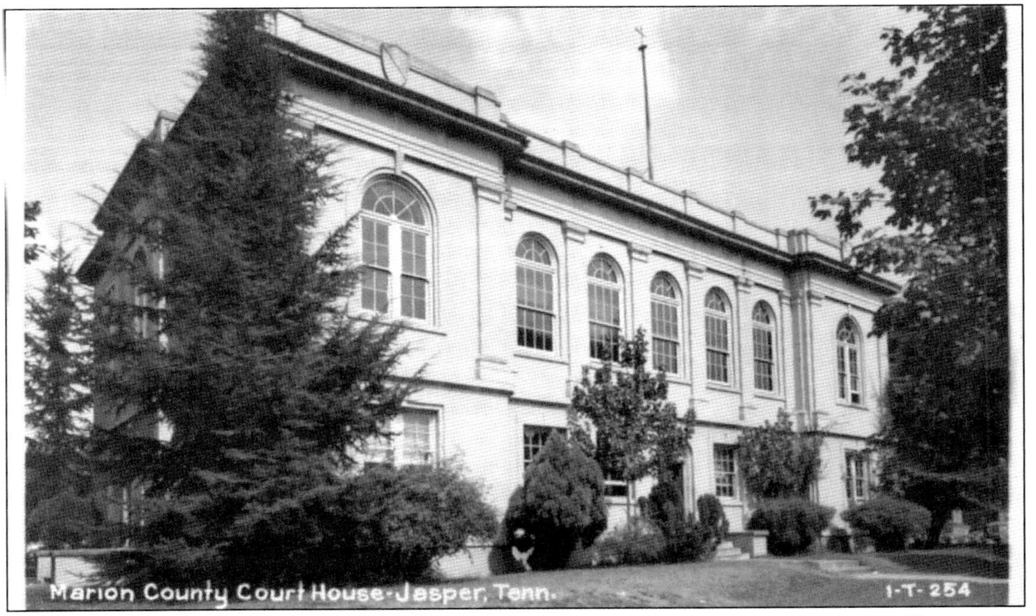

Jim W. Morrison was a local attorney and judge in Jasper and maintained an office in the courthouse. Prior to that, he was deputy sheriff or sheriff for 16 years. He arrested five criminals who were executed (hanged). This image, *c.* 1940, shows no monuments on the lawn. Jasper native Jim Warren's architectural firm did the recent renovation of the courthouse. Among those serving in the courthouse today are Debbie Pittman and Winfred Haggard.

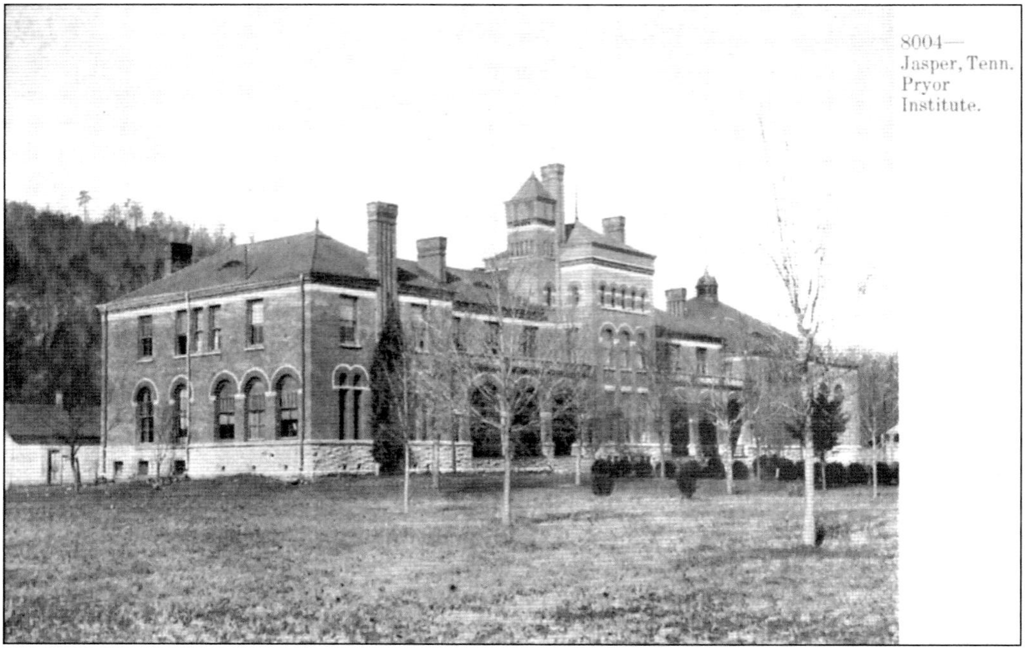

Marion County's mother school, the Pryor Institute, was founded in 1887 and, until 1910, was the only school in the county comparable to a high school. Some students commuted on Valley Train, while other boarded at the school. Its approximately 120 students came from seven states. Originally the school had living quarters for the school president and 60 boarding students. All that remains to indicate this beautiful place was ever there is the street named for it.

Postmarked at the Jasper Post Office in 1898, this cover has math work on the backside. "Where we walk to school each day,/ Indian children used to play./ All across our native land,/ Where the shops and houses stand/ And the trees were very tall;/ And there were no streets at all;/ Not a church and not a steeple,/ Only woods and Indian People."

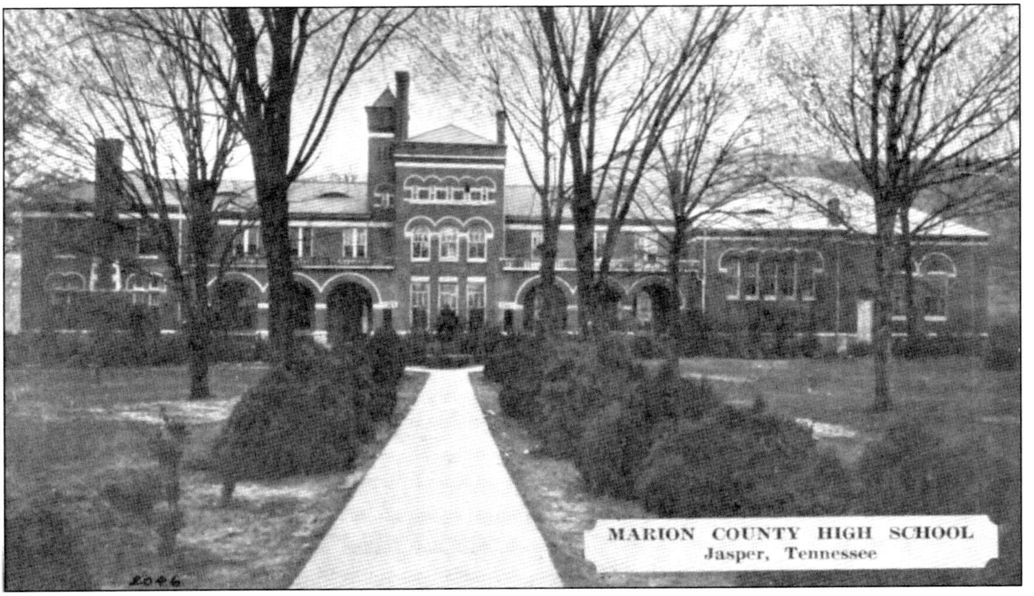

The school would not look much different in 1958 when Nancy Holloway, Suzie Dawson, Eva Pearl Cash, Gladys Rogers, and Mary Nell Grimes graduated. All five girls still live in Jasper. Graduates Eddie Brown, Bill Baker, and Eric Westmoreland all went on to play professional football. MCHS students Angie Raffo and Sandy Kirk played college volleyball and softball, respectively. In 1979, the building was converted to a middle school. "On the city's western border/ Reared against the sky,/ Proudly stood our Alma Mater/ As the years go by."

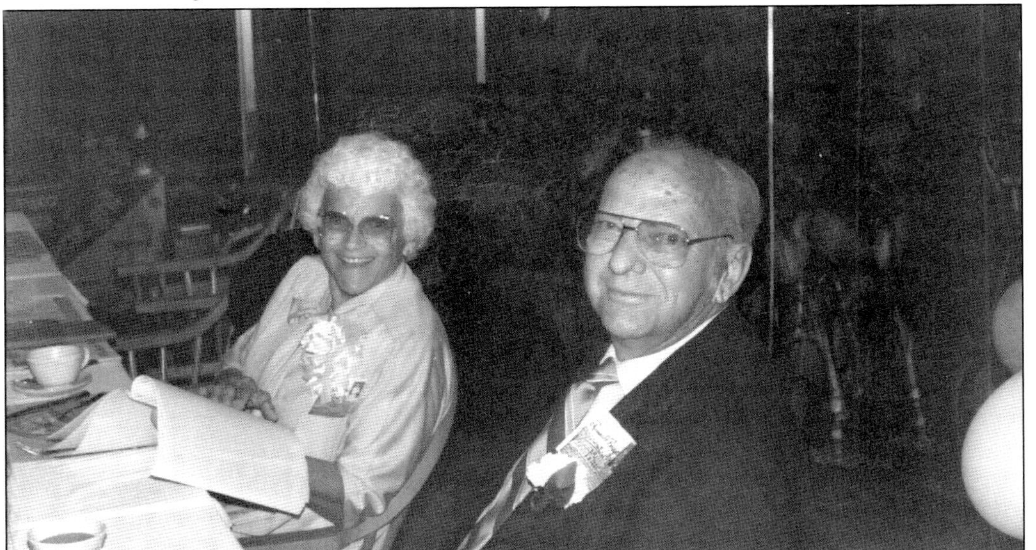

Mr. Russell Priest was principal at MCHS from 1955 until 1977. Mrs. Mary T. Adams taught there from 1948 until 1989. They are shown here attending a reunion of the class of 1958. Another MCHS teacher, Mrs. Gertrude Link, once told Mr. Priest, "No teacher should have to have Billy Simpson for two periods." In 2004, she voted for Billy for a second term as Jasper's mayor. Like their longtime friend the Most Reverend G. A. McGrew, they all had the skills of good teachers and the hearts of good preachers.

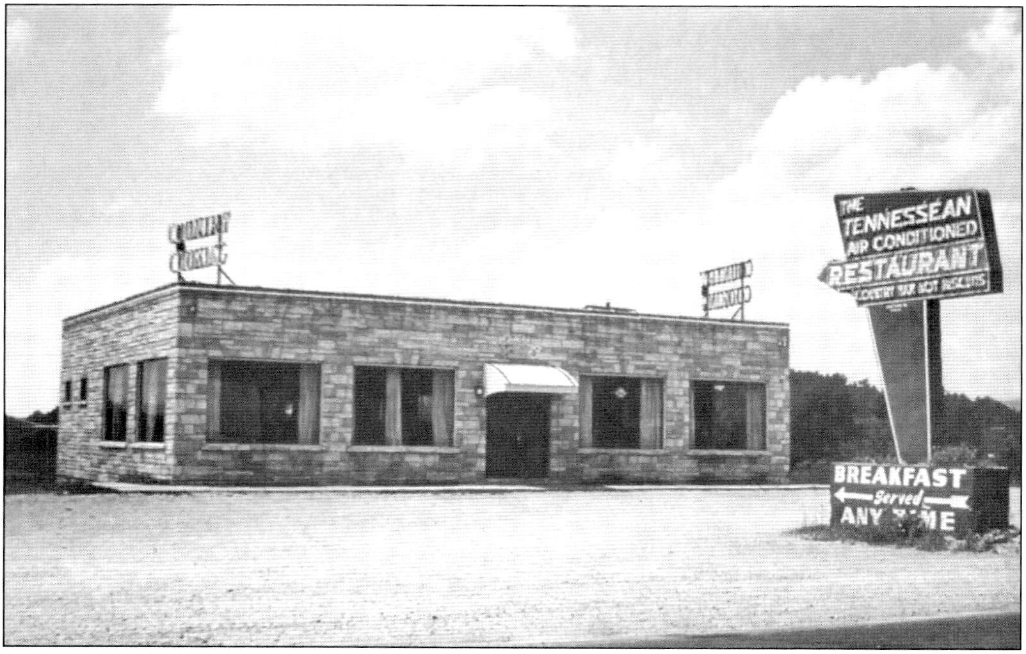

Doris Lee Turner's family owned this establishment. Doris was a good friend of John Acuff, who eventually bought the business. He turned it into a short-lived eatery known as Farmer John's Restaurant.

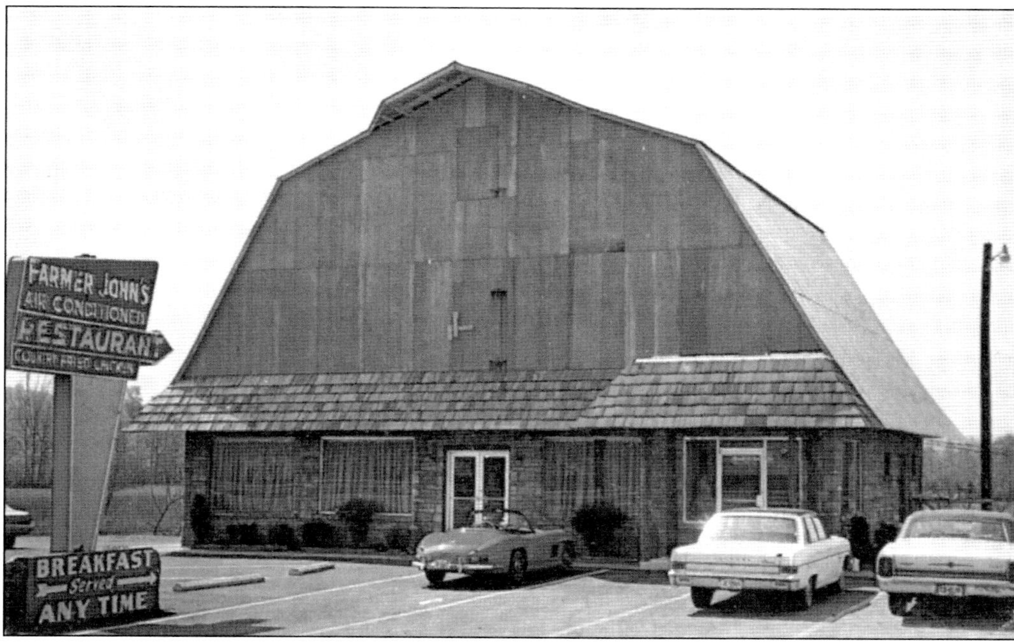

Sue Case Collins managed this 1970s restaurant for a time. It was then sold to Citizen State Bank, and the "barn-like" upper portion was removed. In 1992, Deb Hooper turned it into Deb's Flower Bank.

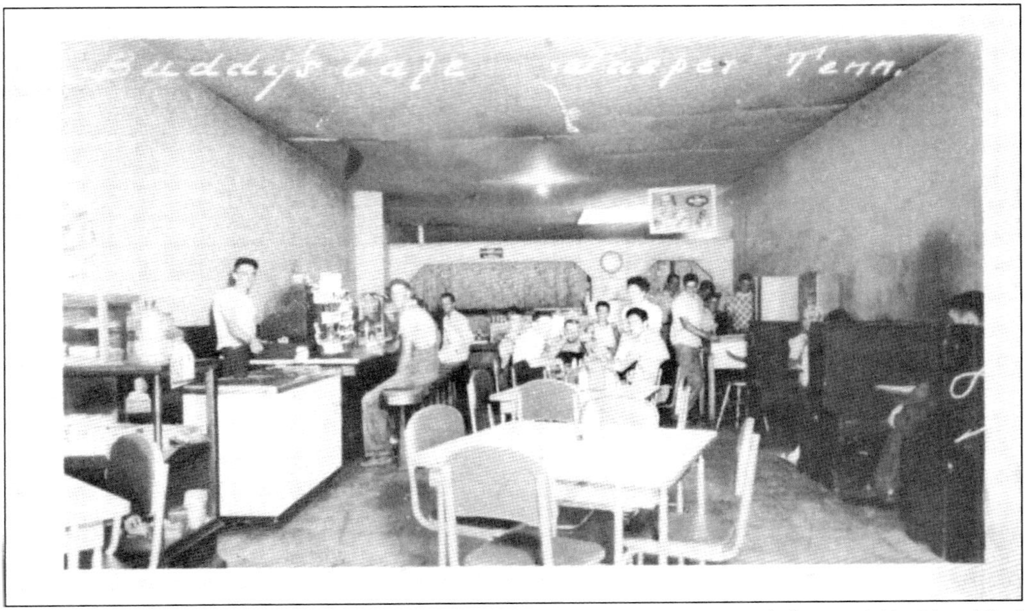

This black-and-white card of the interior of Buddy's Café was printed about 1942. Identified among those eating at Buddy's is "Whistle Breeches" Webb (nearest at the bar). That is Mack Lowery behind the counter. The boys in the back right are playing a pinball machine. During this time, all games won on the pinball machine could be "cashed in" at the rate of a nickel per game. In 2005, Maximum Sports is located here.

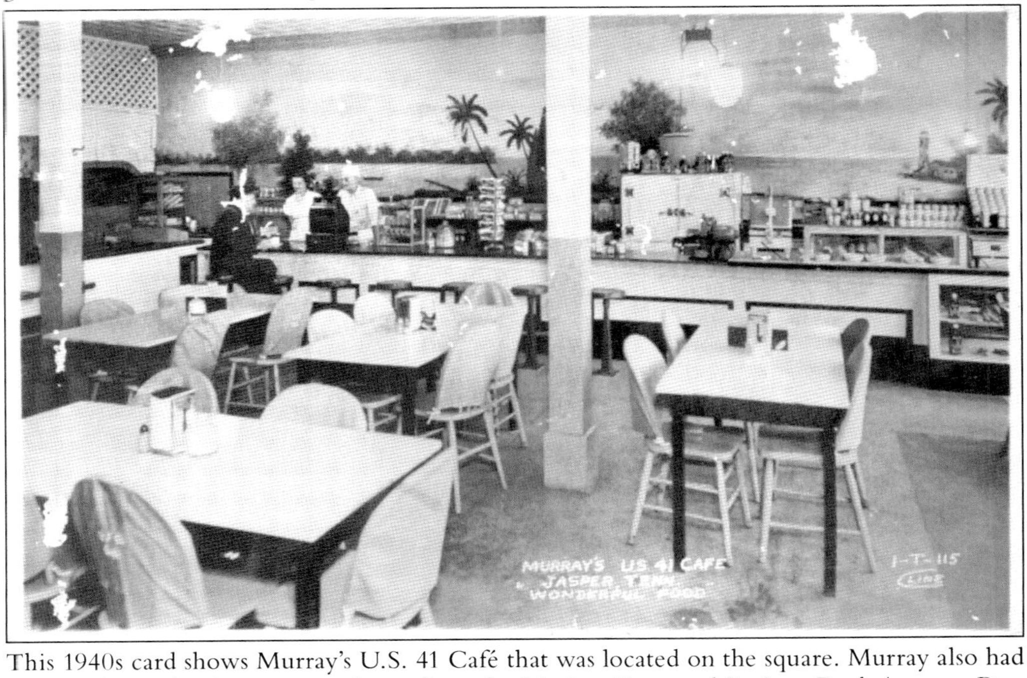

This 1940s card shows Murray's U.S. 41 Café that was located on the square. Murray also had a tavern located a door or two down from the Marion Trust and Savings Bank (next to Roy Layne's Shoe Shop), where many of the town's men would drink a drink or two. The café was later owned or operated by the Lowery and Haynes families.

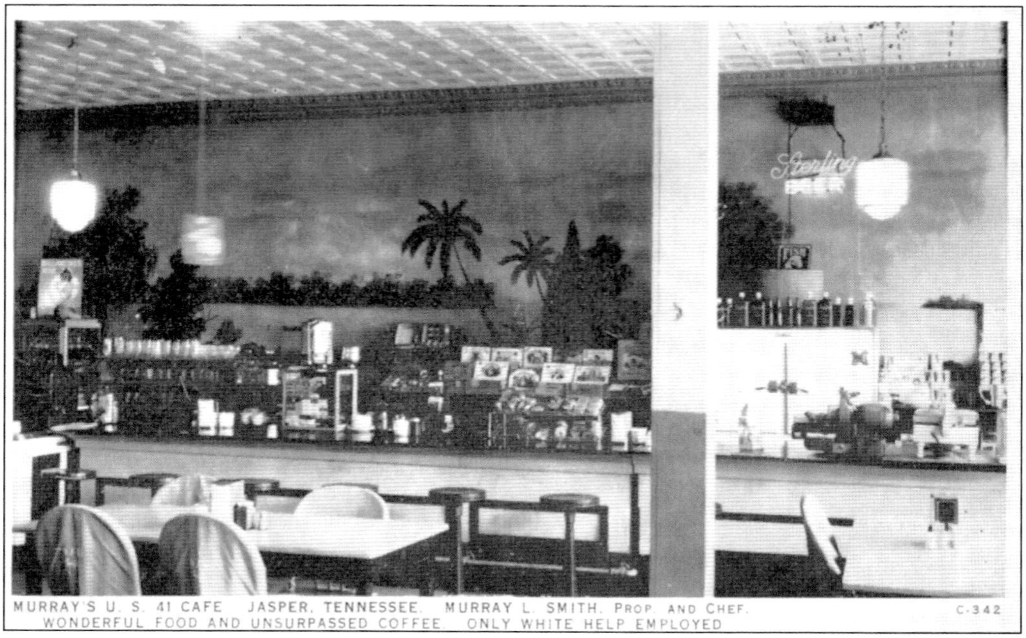

This page contains two similar white-bordered postcards of Murray's. Like many in Jasper, Meredith James, former MCHS football queen, has only a vague recollection of the place. The tropical scene is apparent in all three postcards. Sam and Iva Pearl Featherstone ran this Grade A café for a number of years. The kitchen was to the left. It is believed that Miss Murray was a cook at Jasper's schools. Note the narrative on the card.

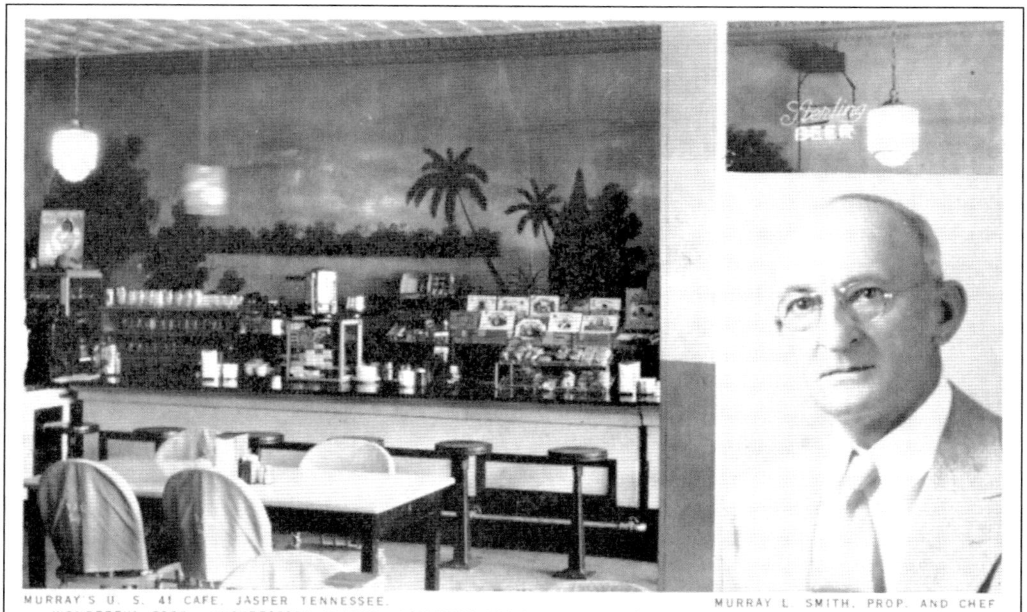

This card includes an inset of proprietor and chef Murray L. Smith. There is a Sterling Beer sign visible above Murray and approximately 12 boxes of cigars behind the counter. This is a white-border card (which were printed 1915–1930). The white border saved ink.

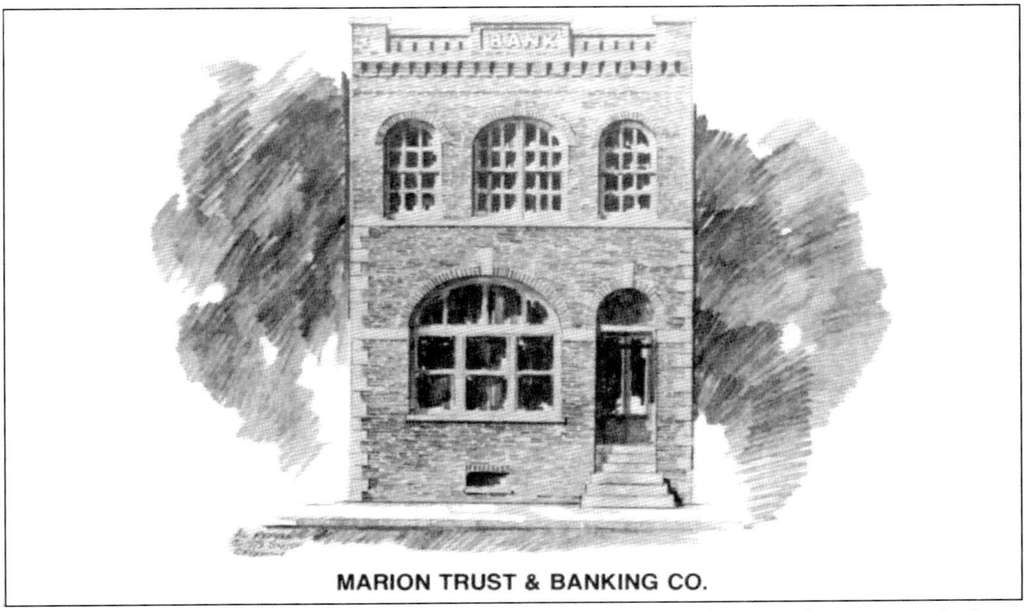

Established in 1904, the bank operated at the same location until 1989. This is one of a four-card set created for the bicentennial celebration in 1986. Barbara Runyon Holloway presented the four cards to the author in 2003. In 1946, D. M. (Todie) Hall was the bank's cashier; Miss Maggie Hall was assistant cashier, and Mrs. Ruby Hornsby bookkeeper and teller. In the 1940s, there was an open-air theater between the bank and Vance's Furniture Store. The bank building is now the law office of Leiderman and Cameron.

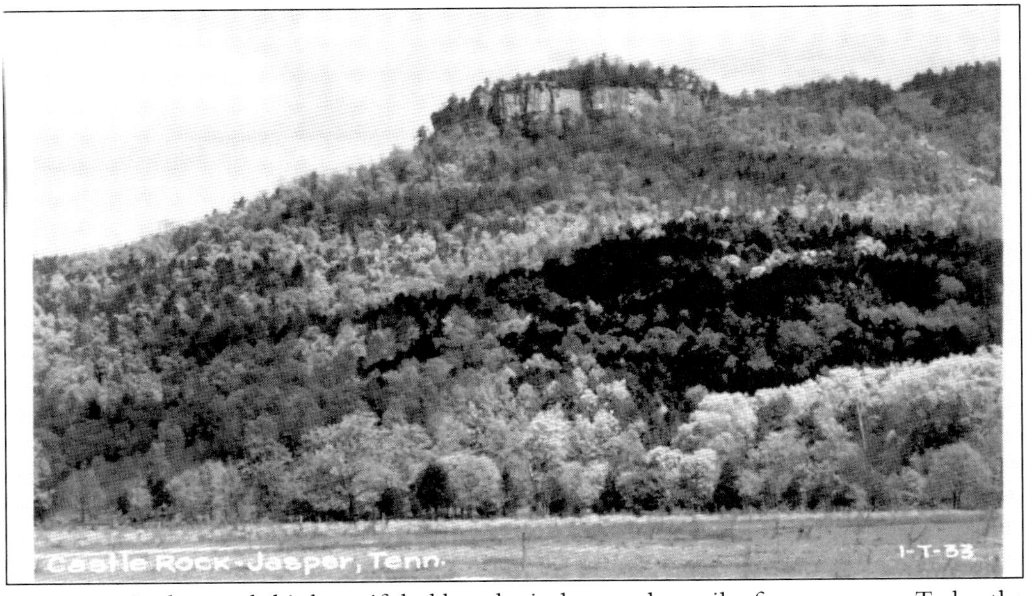

Tennessee Coal owned this beautiful old geological anomaly until a few years ago. Today the county's mountainsides are being recklessly plundered, and rock quarries are a reminder of what happens when men betray their responsibility as stewards to our natural treasures. Only a radical rethinking of our relationship with the valley can preserve it for future generations. Willie P. Price (school custodian) lived halfway up to Castle Rock.

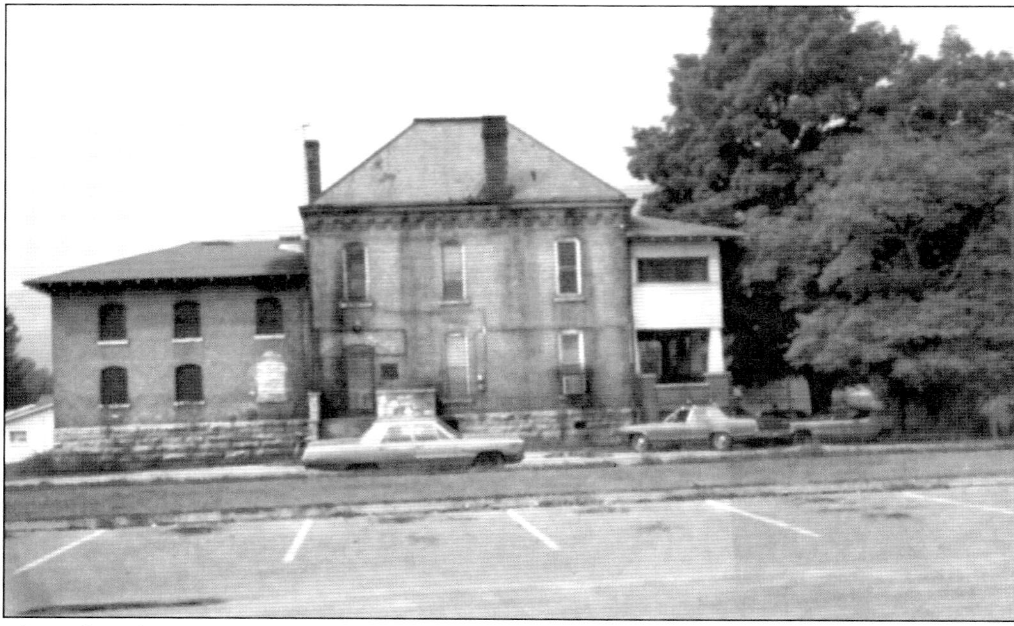

This jail is where "Little Skipper" Phillips died. In 1974, a new jail was built in the same location at a cost of $207,000. Between 1973 and 1978, a total of 59 prisoners were sent from this jail to state prisons. Sheriff Jim Morrison lived there, and his son Dan was born here. Little Homer Dawson brought Ray Millard here when he caught him drag racing. Nappy Pryor immediately released Ray so he could return to Sequatchie.

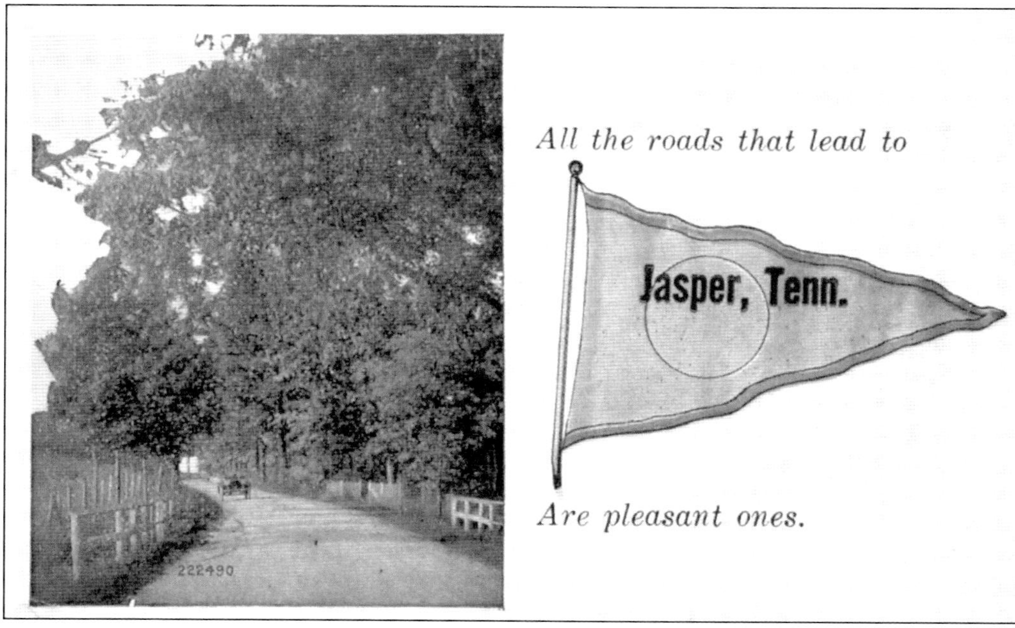

In the early 1900s, these generic cards were common. They were viewed as unattractive and did not have a good survival rate. The name "Peter Turney" is written on the back of the card. Turney was a colonel in the Confederate army's 1st Tennessee Infantry. He was also governor of Tennessee from 1893 to 1897.

Two

Hale's Bar Dam, Haletown, and Guild

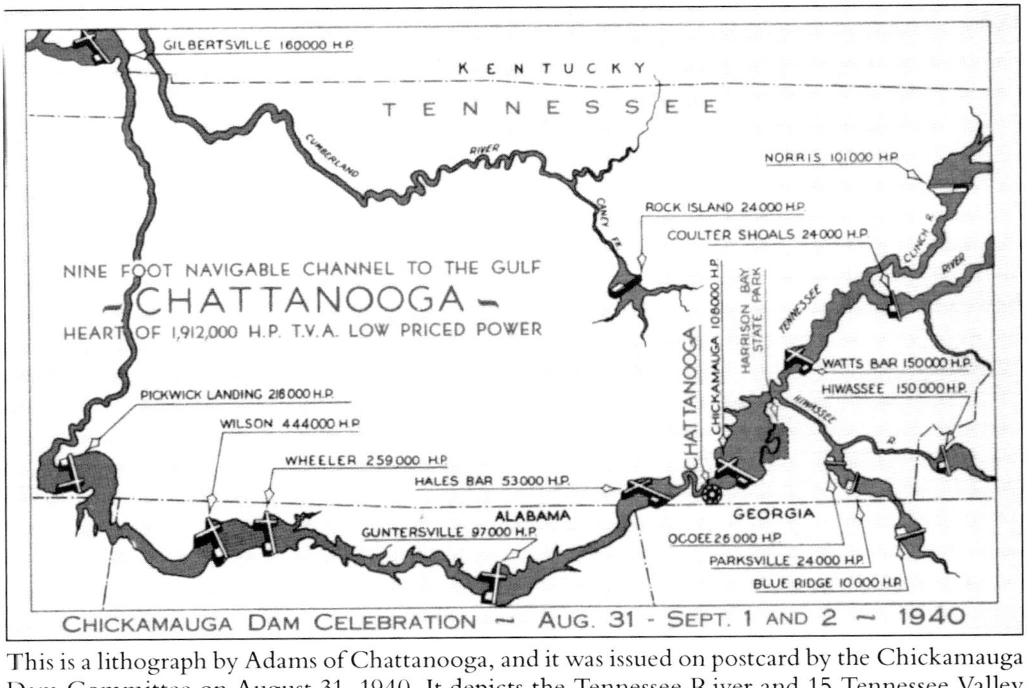

This is a lithograph by Adams of Chattanooga, and it was issued on postcard by the Chickamauga Dam Committee on August 31, 1940. It depicts the Tennessee River and 15 Tennessee Valley Authority (TVA) dams, including Hales Bar Dam. This is a linen postcard (printed 1930–1944), albeit an unusual one. For a time, the Tennessee River provided drinking water, though the best drinking water was found in the Whiteside communities of Scratch Ankle and Egypt Holler.

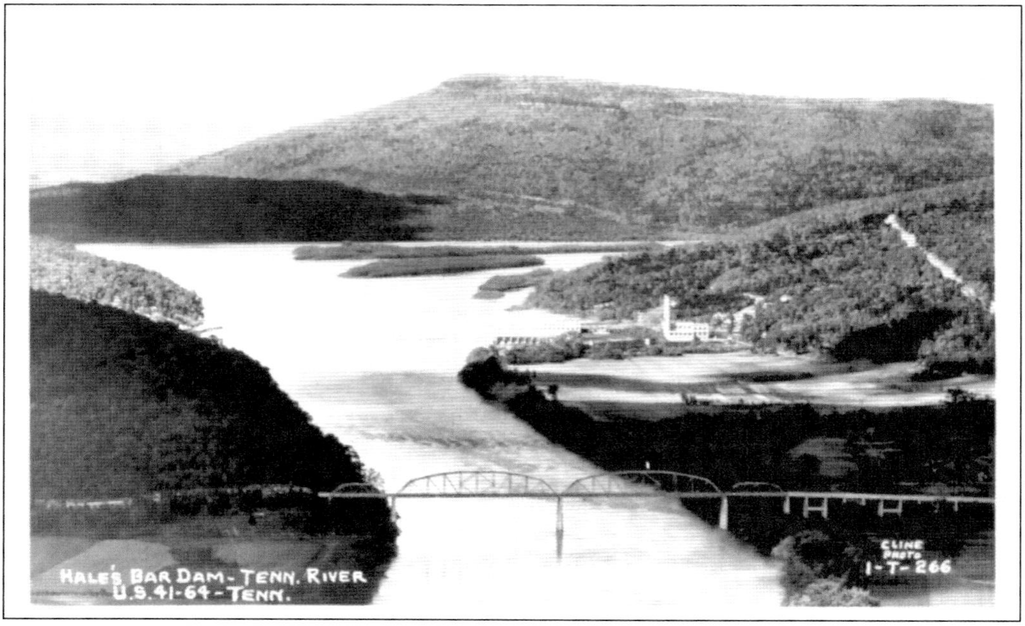

This appears to be a true aerial view of the bridge and dam looking north from below the bridge. The Hales Bar powerhouse is conspicuous, and U.S. 41 can be seen snaking around the mountains toward Chattanooga. Today there is a huge wound growing in the mountain in the center, as stone is quarried from the mountainside. Bennett Lake is just upstream and to the left, and Jasper is the light area between the mountains at upper left.

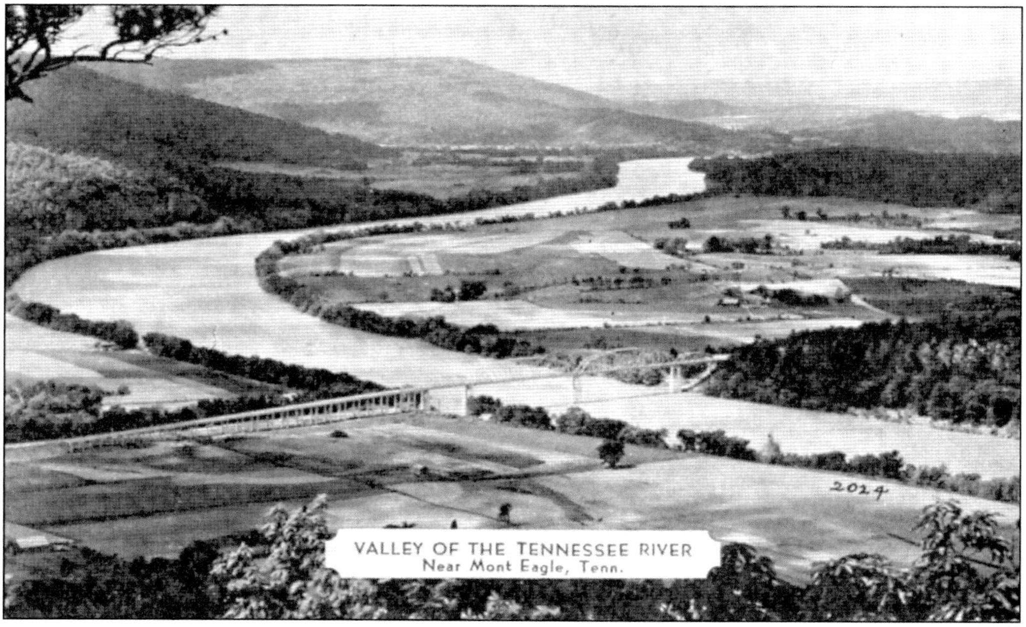

In 1838, during the forced removal of American Indians from Tennessee, the river was, due to a drought, too low for navigation. The river is responsible for many Marion County floods (in 1867, 1886, 1900, 1911, 1917, and 2004). The dam assuaged flooding but by no means eliminated it. In 1940, the river was frozen, allowing cars and horse-drawn wagons to be driven onto it.

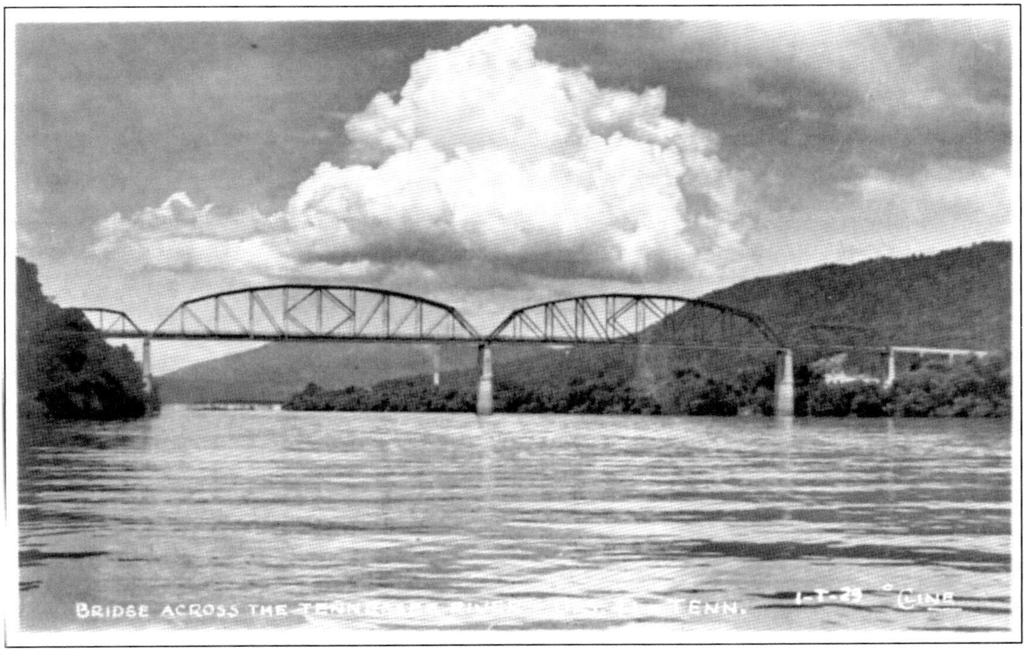

The Marion Memorial Bridge spans the Tennessee River and was originally a toll bridge. It was "floated" in 1968 so engineers could raise it 37 feet to accommodate river traffic. In 1958, during a quintessential testosterone moment brought on by a dare, the author jumped from the bridge. The Battle of Bridgeport occurred just south of here. Today there are plans to demolish the bridge.

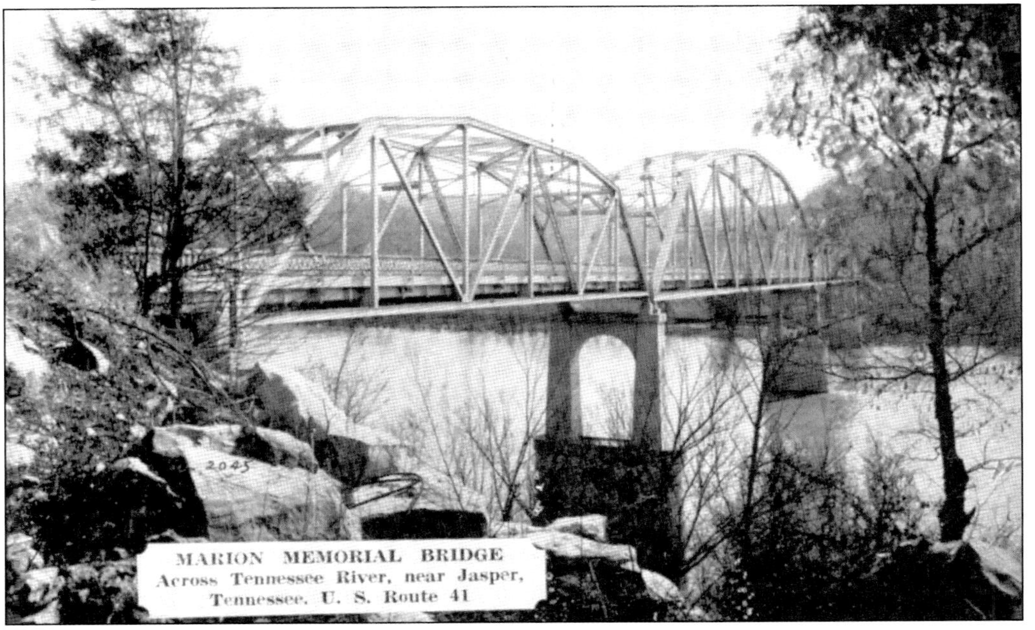

There was once a parking area at the left of the photograph for travelers who wanted to climb onto large rocks for a better view or to take pictures. The TVA changed all that and the bluffs. Two movies were filmed near here. One, *Light in Forest*, was filmed near Bennett Lake.

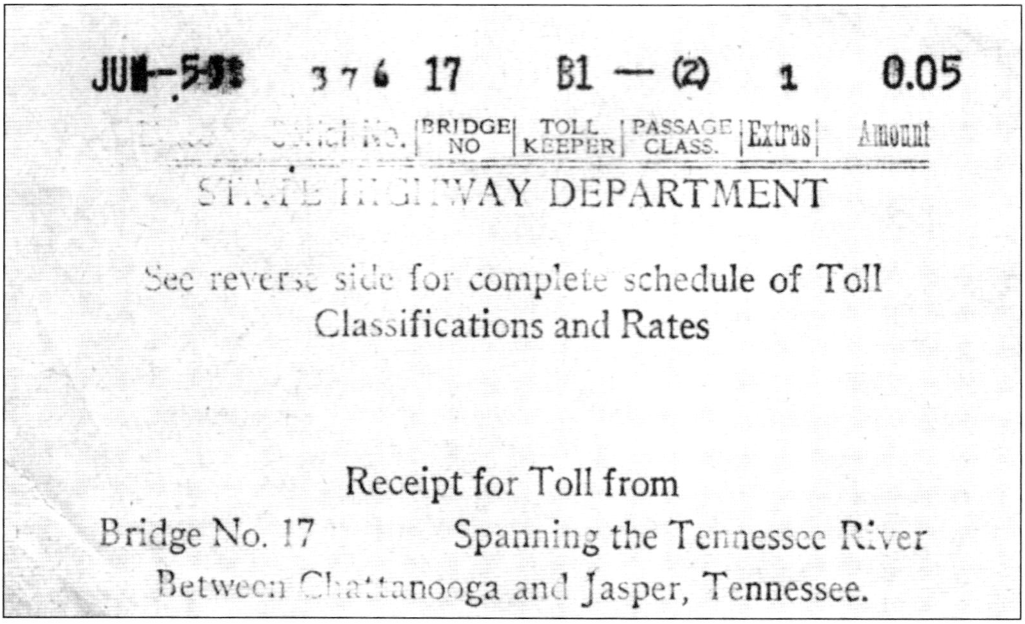

JUN-5-53	376	17	B1 — (2)	1		0.05
Date	Serial No.	BRIDGE NO	TOLL KEEPER	PASSAGE CLASS.	Extras	Amount

STATE HIGHWAY DEPARTMENT

See reverse side for complete schedule of Toll Classifications and Rates

Receipt for Toll from

Bridge No. 17 Spanning the Tennessee River

Between Chattanooga and Jasper, Tennessee.

This is a June 1953 5¢ toll receipt from the State Highway Department for crossing Bridge No. 17 (Marion Memorial Bridge). Many continued to take Rankin's Ferry across the river because it was less expensive. The back of the receipt has a list of toll fees. Circus animals are 25¢ each and domestic animals 2¢ each. Motorcycles are a quarter. In 1953, a quarter meant something very different than it does today.

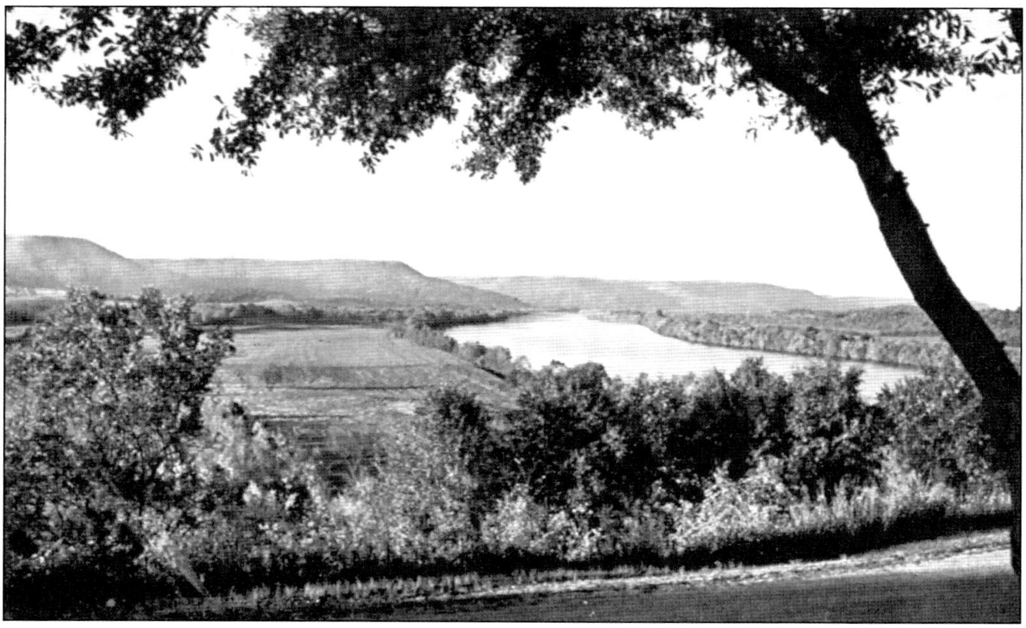

Taken from Battery Hill, this view of the river looks south toward Nickajack Cave and South Pittsburg. It was also near here that a Nashville-bound party (including 15-year-old Rachel Donelson) was attacked by a Cherokee war party. Rachel survived to become the wife of Andrew Jackson.

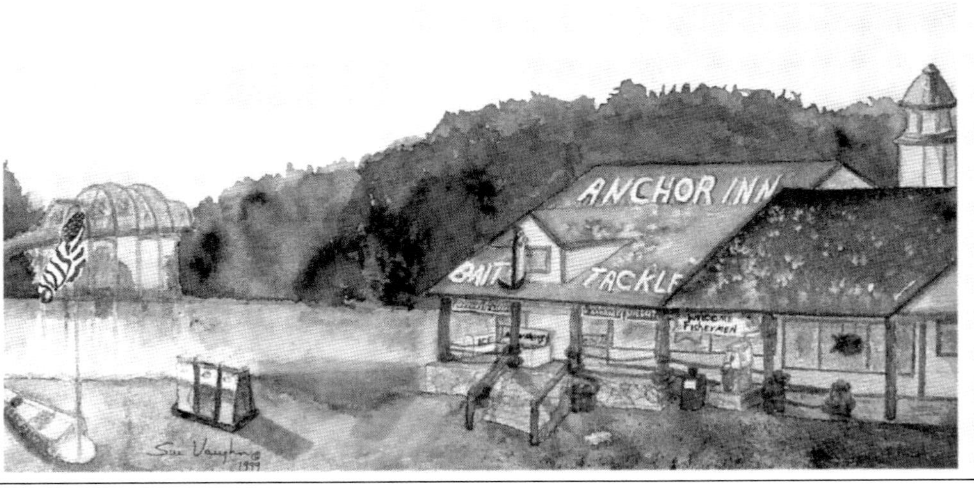

This is a modern card of the Anchor Inn in Guild and is from a watercolor by Sue Vaughn. Terry Cardin owned this property, though the TVA owned most riverfront property. A few hundred yards to the east is the Haletown Post Office, which, for reasons not known, is designated "Guild" Post Office. The post office was previously Henry Lee Bible's restaurant, where Elvis ate on two occasions. Once he ordered a quart of moonshine that was promptly delivered to him.

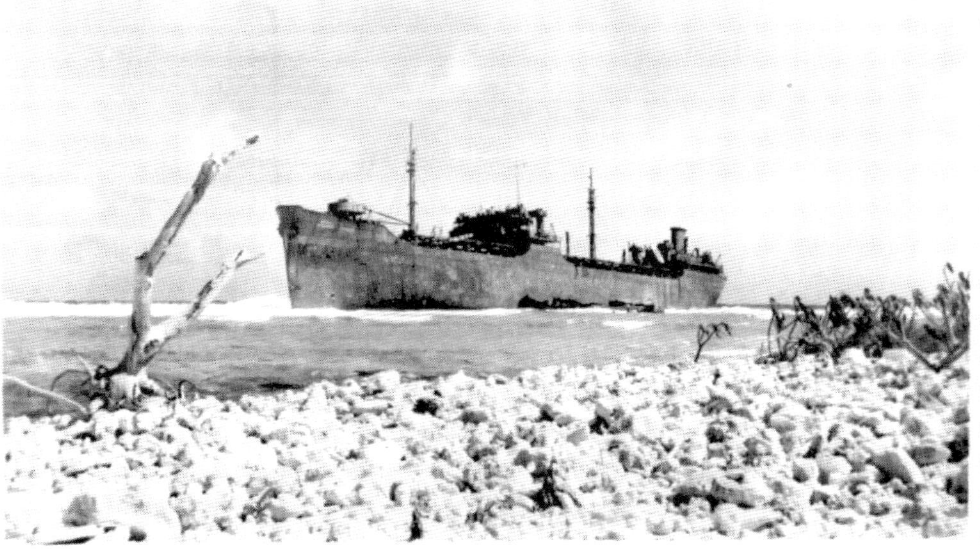

USS Nickajack Trail - Japtan Island

The Nickajack Trail begins in Murfreesboro and comes through Battle Creek to the Nickajack Cave area. The USS *Nickajack Trail* was 300 miles from Eniwetok on March 30, 1946, when she was diverted to refuel the *Sakawa* and *Nagato*. Those ships were on their way to Bikini Atoll for the testing of atomic bombs when their sailors mutinied. The ship ran aground and was lost. Nickajack Cave has been known by many names, including Nick-O-Jack and the American Indian name Ani-Kusati-Yi.

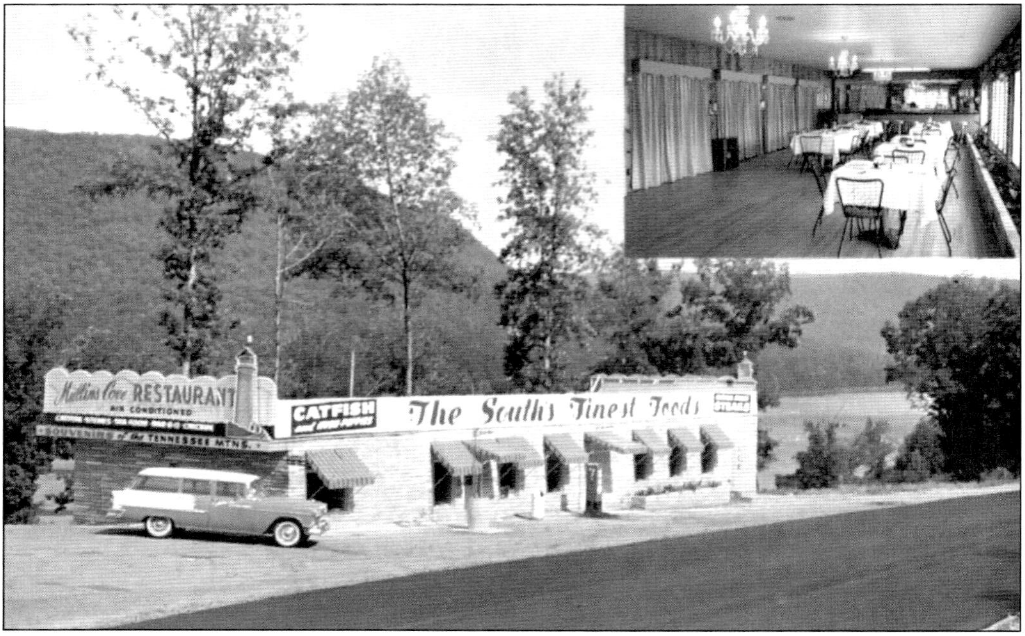

Mullins Cove Restaurant and Sky Room is located between Guild and Chattanooga. In days gone by, it featured dining and dancing with a view. There was an area to fish from and motel accommodations. Bill and Evelyn Glover opened the restaurant around 1955. More recent owners/operators were Paul and Yoyo Frederick. Paul passed away, and his daughter Angela Watson owns it today.

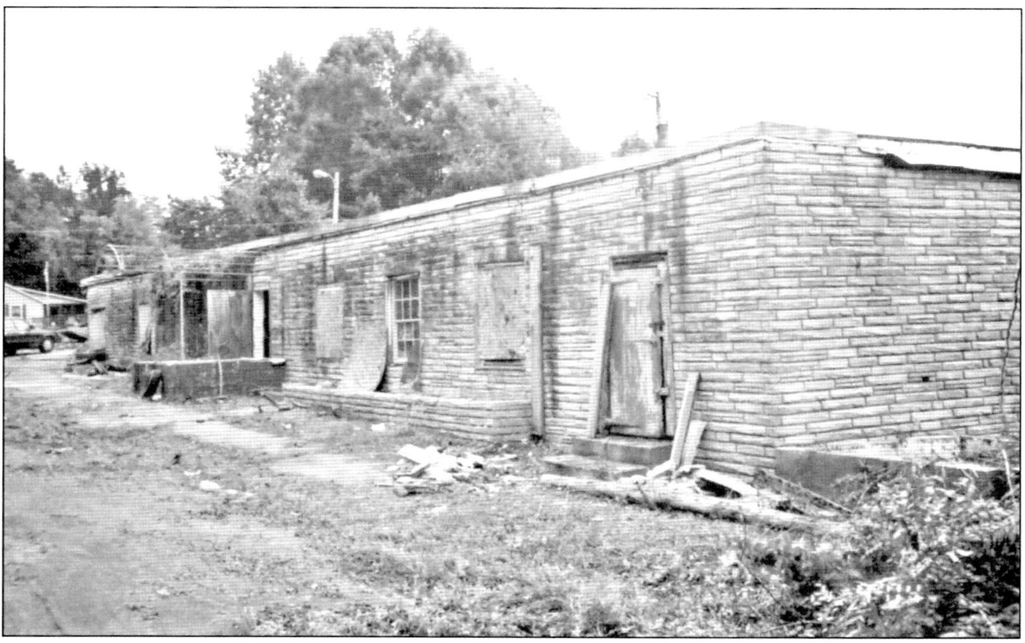

Today the Mullins Cove Restaurant has fallen into a state of disuse. In 1880, across the river along Mullins Cove Road, the community of Shake Rag (a mining town) had more than 30 structures. Today Shake Rag and the Sky Room are mostly history.

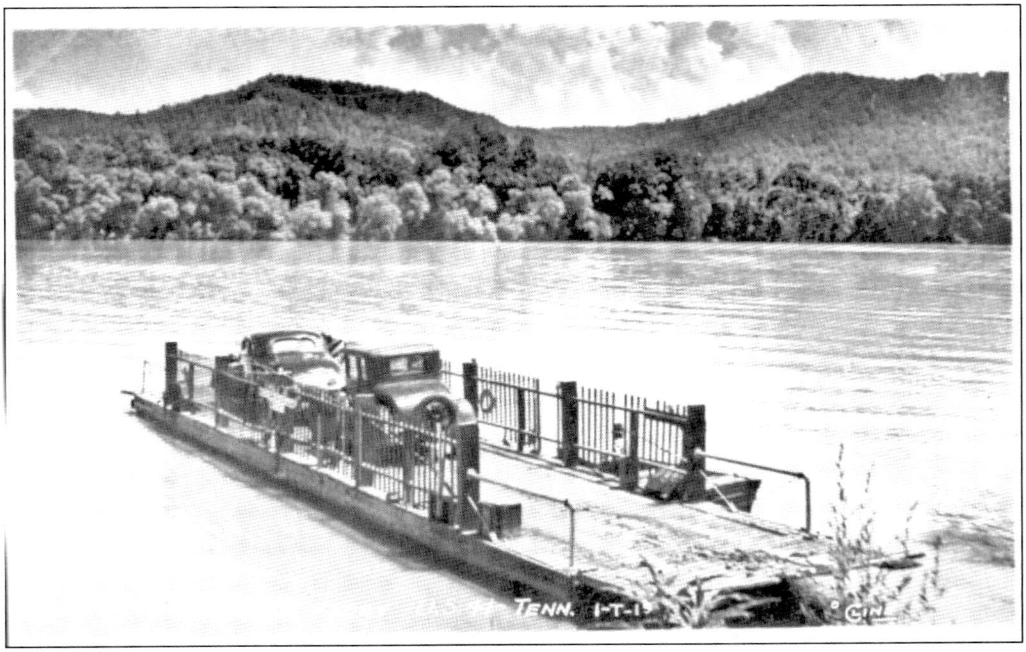

Here is an early RPPC of Rankin's Ferry, with two vehicles that appear to be an A-model Ford and a 1932 Ford. Surprisingly there is a life preserver on the far side of the ferry. There is also a man in a small boat tethered to the ferry.

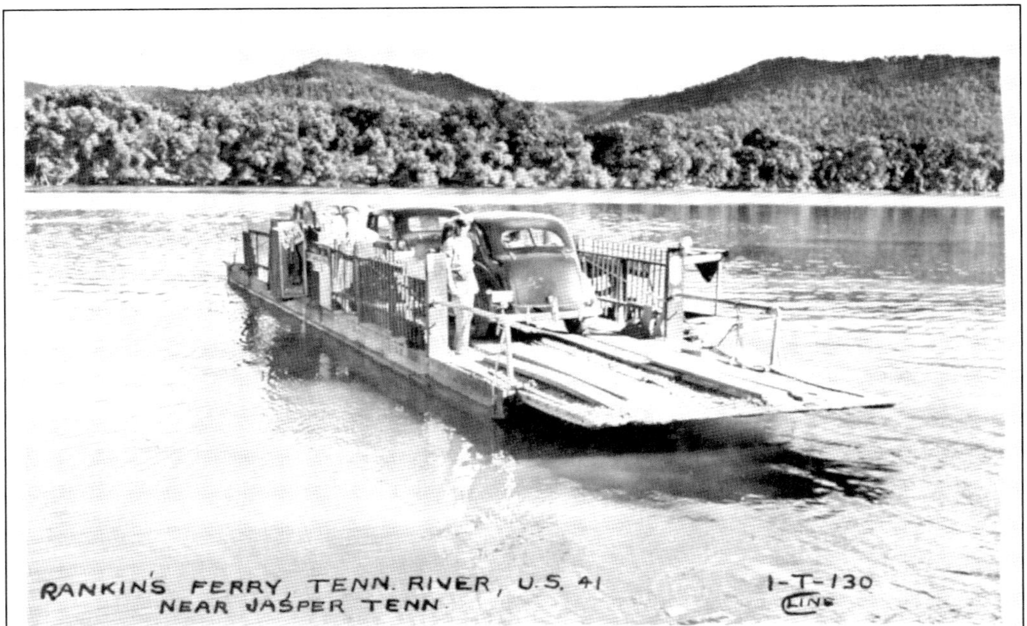

There are four different postcards of Rankin's Ferry, first operated in 1914, known to exist. All are RPPCs by Cline, and one is a night view. This is a 1939 view showing three automobiles (among them, a 1941 Pontiac, nearest, and a 1939 or 1940 Chevrolet), the uniformed ferry captain, and a coke machine that hangs over the left side of the ferry.

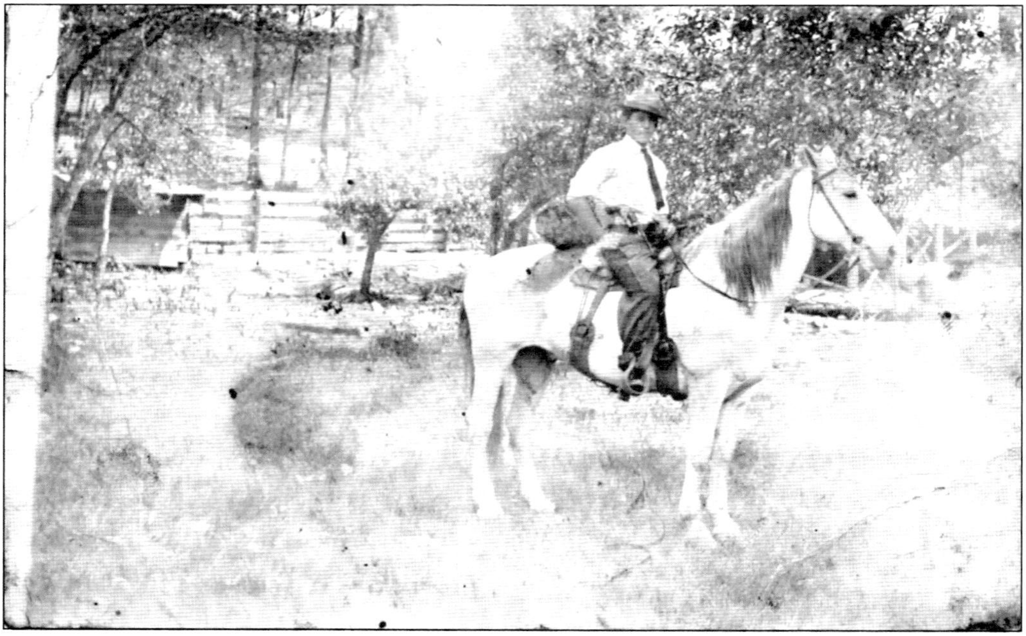

This is a RPPC of John Burnette (often spelled without the "e") of Jasper. John is the half brother of Laura Louisa Burnette. The photograph was taken near the Hales Bar Lock and Dam sometime before 1937. Note the pistol tucked into Burnette's waistband.

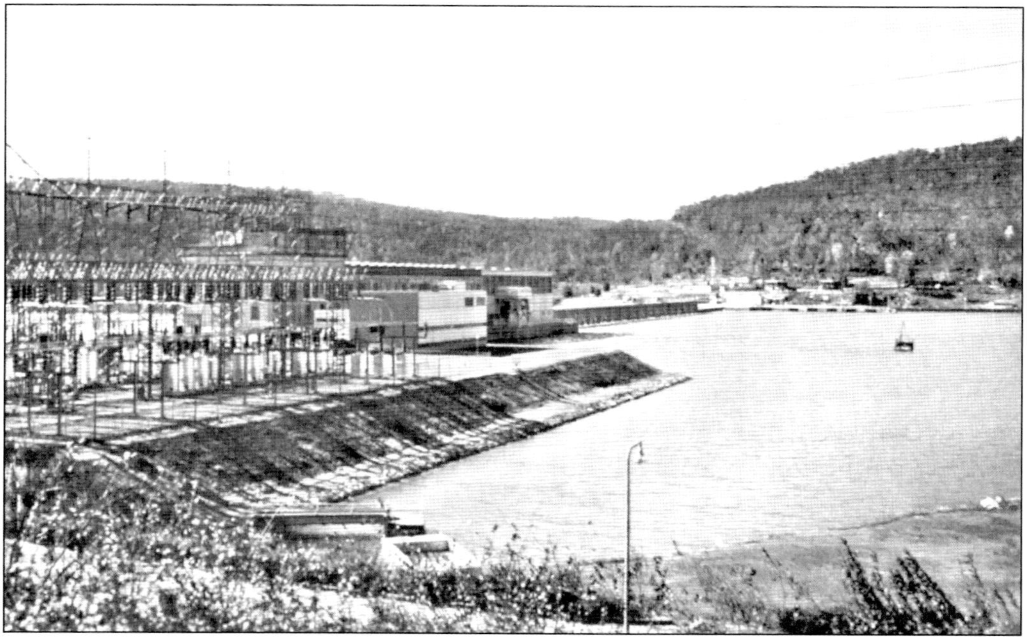

This is the Hale's Bar Dam power station. In 1933, just three percent of farms in the TVA area had electrification—by 1950, that number had grown to 82 percent. Part of the price of electricity was the displacement of 14,400 families. TVA fixed the price in land acquisitions, and if that price was not accepted, the state condemned the property. The dam was raised in May 1949, and two new generators were installed from 1951 to 1952. The trees indicate it is early fall.

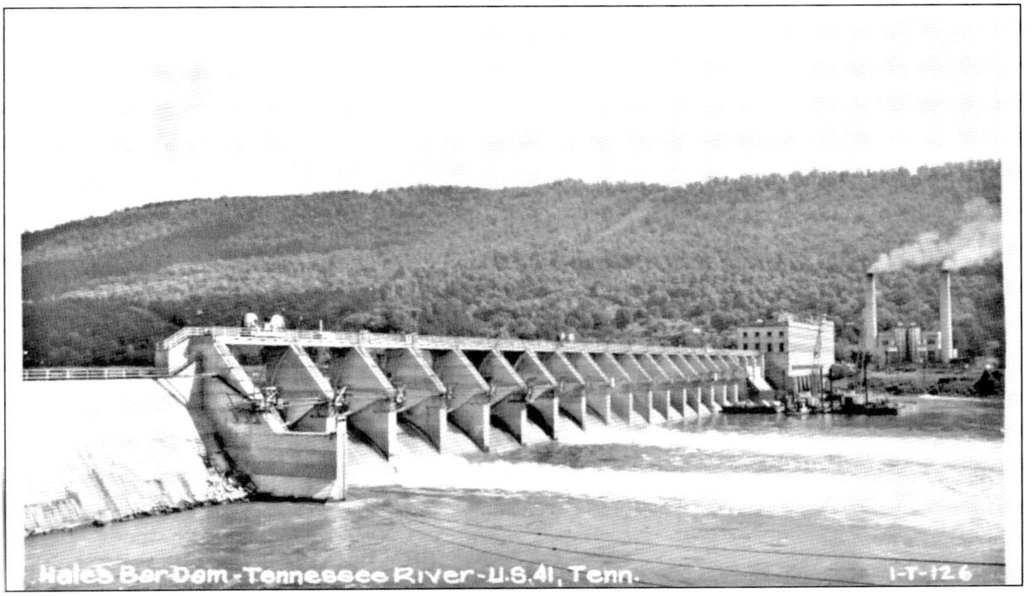

The TVA intended to provide flood control, improve navigation, create recreational areas, and generate electricity. Just as TVA's river projects were nearing completion, along came World War II with "new missions." Power was needed to manufacture aluminum for airplanes, and the Secret City (Oak Ridge) needed power for its infamous Manhattan Project. Later it would be said, "The TVA could help build the atomic bomb but couldn't save the snail darter." The tiny fish brought the TVA's Tellico project to a halt.

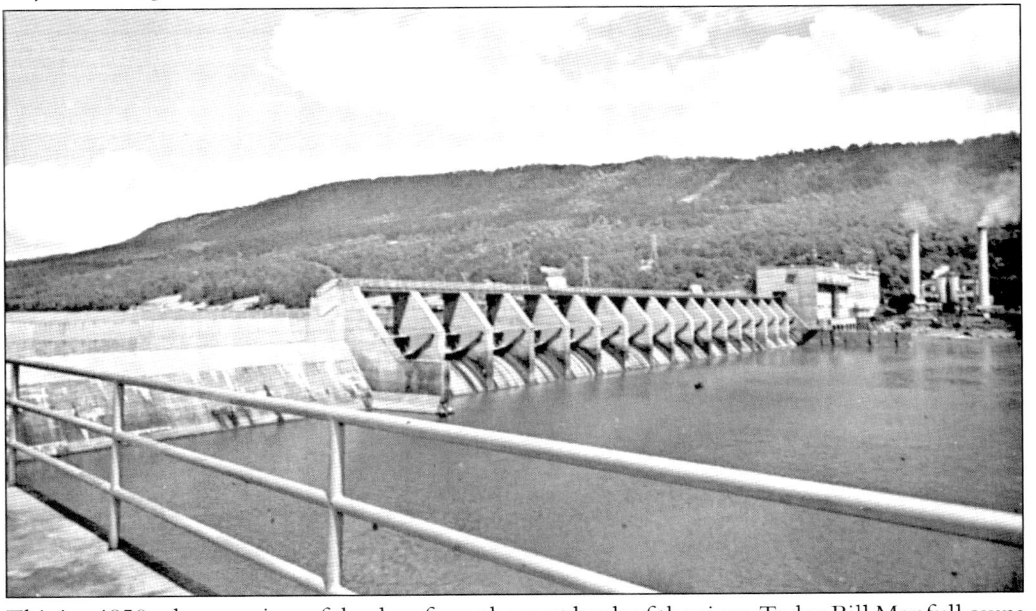

This is a 1950s chrome view of the dam from the west bank of the river. Today Bill Manfull owns the property, and Barbara Hines manages it. The Nickajack Resort, Marina, and Lighthouse Grill (a misnomer—it should be Hales Bar) are owned/operated by Susan and Larry Patton. In 1933, R. J. Hoge Sr. caught a 154-pound Mississippi catfish just below the lock. The spillway consisted of 17 separate 40-ton sections that were brought there by barge.

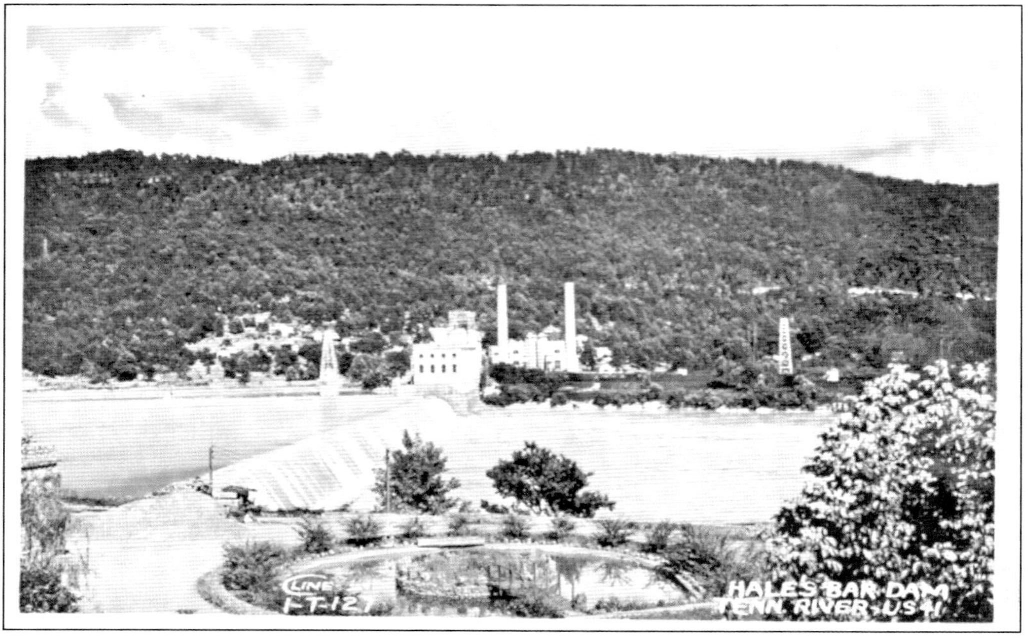

Postcards provide great historical representation of the past. In the foreground of this card is the fishpond and circular drive, both long gone. The dam was 33 miles by river and 8 miles by road from Chattanooga, cost $11 million, and was seven years in constructing. The lock was 60 feet high and 300 feet long.

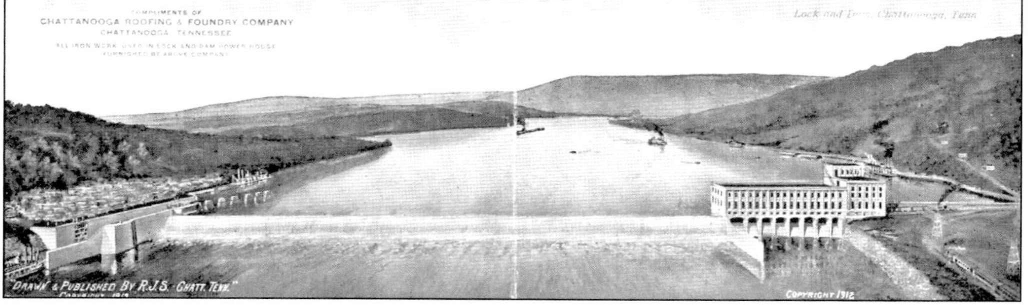

Two Chattanoogans, C. E. James and J. C. Guild, secured a contract to build the dam and founded the Tennessee River Power Company in 1905. Anthony Brady was the major investor. In a test case in the June 1916 session of circuit court in Marion County, the Chattanooga and Tennessee River Power Company was held responsible for an epidemic of malaria along the river and ordered to pay plaintiff Tom Lawson damages of $3,000. In 1905, George Hale owned this property. This is a rare bi-fold card of the dam.

Looking west (from the Guild side), Hales Bar Village, known as "the Camp," is visible on the west bank. The Camp would be abandoned in 1941. Jasper's Junior Hale attended the Hale's Bar Lock and Dam School in the 1930s. The lockmaster's house can be seen on the far side of the river. Beyond that are the four Herner Cabins that had to be moved to higher ground when the area was flooded. Susan Patton lives in Cabin #4 today.

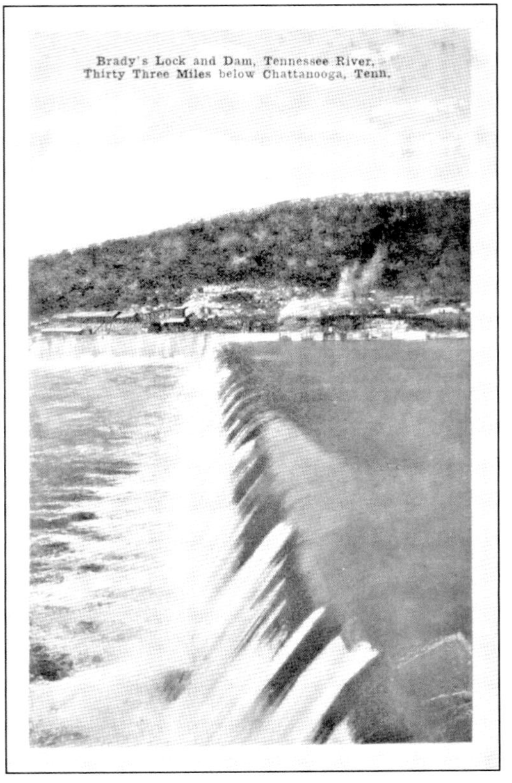

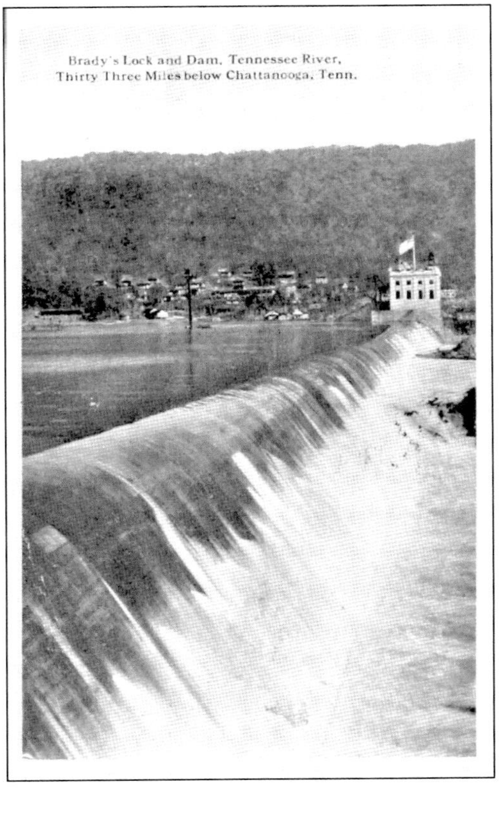

Looking east beyond the powerhouse is Guild (established in 1907 by J. C. Guild). The community contained private schools, a hotel, a nurse station, a theater, and housing for black laborers. A Baptist preacher on a houseboat bound for New Orleans remained tied up above the dam for more than a month waiting to be the first vessel through. This 1917 card identifies the dam as Anthony N. Brady's Dam, which, for a time, it was.

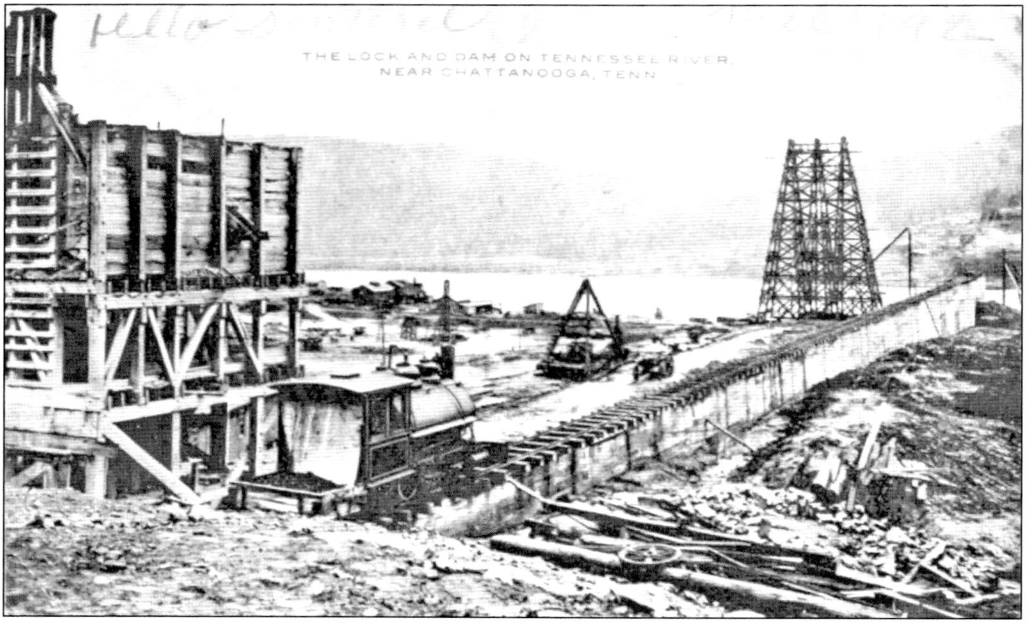

The dam was started in 1905. This 1908 card shows a steam engine on a section of track. Between 1905 and 1913, five contractors who had agreed to the project quit because of its magnitude and the probability of it not working. It was operational from November 1, 1913, through March 11, 1968.

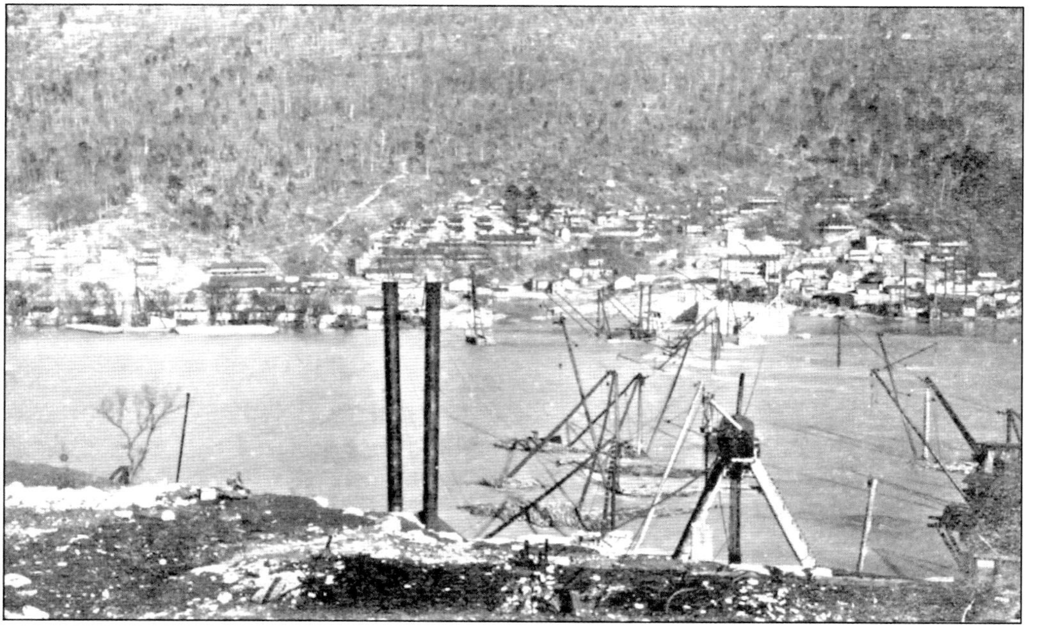

Builders constructed three tunnels here. One tunnel, which was under the dam, schoolchildren would travel through. When two people passed in the tunnel, they had to turn sideways. Tunnels became impassable during rain or when the river was up. Only the spiral stairwell leading to the tunnel survives today. Another tunnel ran to an auxiliary building, and the third tunnel ran under the road and up the hill toward U.S. 41. The purpose of that lengthy tunnel is unknown.

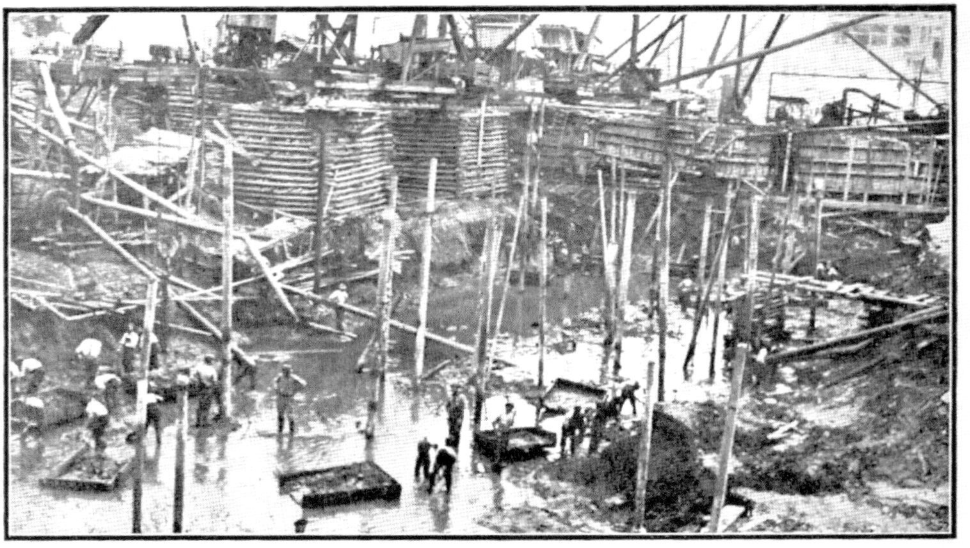

EXCAVATING FOR DAM, HALE'S BAR, GUILD, TENN.

This sepia-colored card shows the excavation and coffers being built. Because the dam leaked constantly, workers around the log rib cofferdams, steam engines, and stiff leg derricks wore high wading boots. Daisy Daffron and Windy Bill Jones, both of Jasper, worked here in 1912.

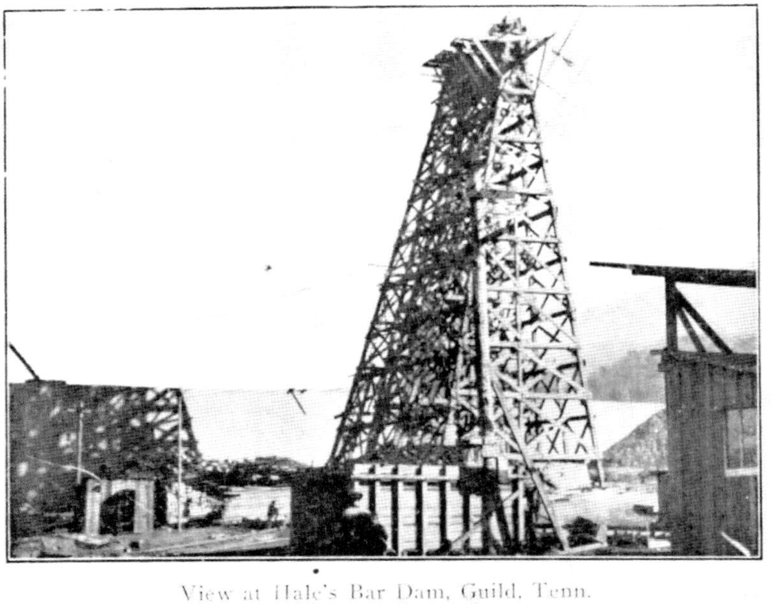

View at Hale's Bar Dam, Guild, Tenn.

This wooden constructed tower is a smoke stack being erected in 1908. This card was sent to Miss Irene Adams of Jasper and was mailed while traveling on the "Pik and Chatt RR." The message asks, "Well how did you enjoy that melon? Are you a going to South Pittsburg Monday?" At the peak of construction, more than 3,500 workers were involved in the dam project.

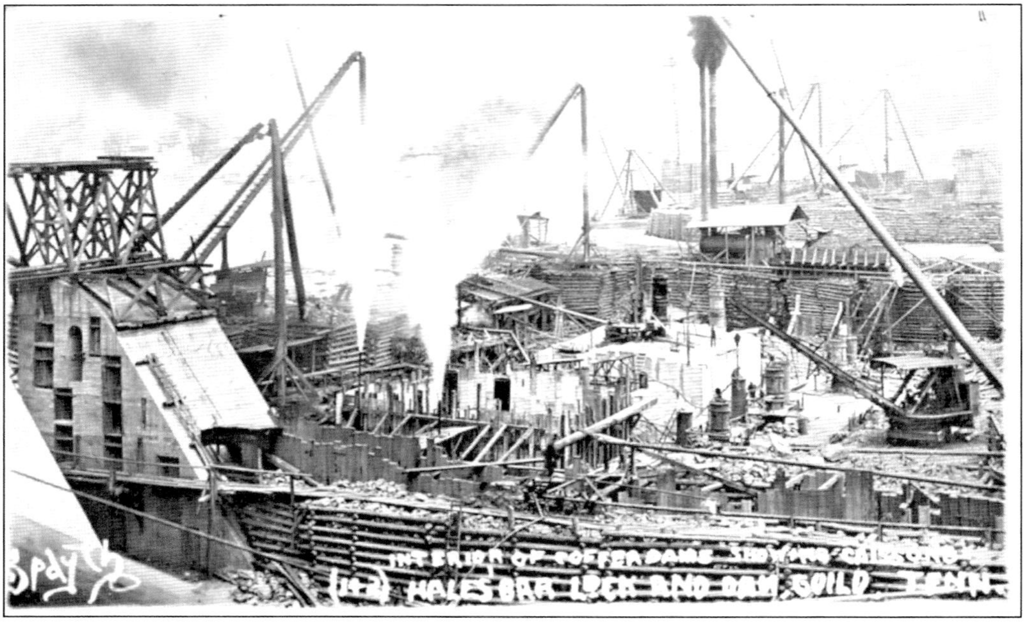

This is one of a series of RPPCs made by Spayth. The first cofferdam was built in 1906 by W. J. Oliver; the first caisson was built in 1907 and the last in 1913. In 1916, Looney McNabb and Riley Jones were on the "Rag Gang" that dumped barge loads of rags and mattresses into the river to try and stop the dam leakage that would eventually overwhelm all efforts and bring about the demise of Hale's Bar Dam. These men earned $1.60 a day.

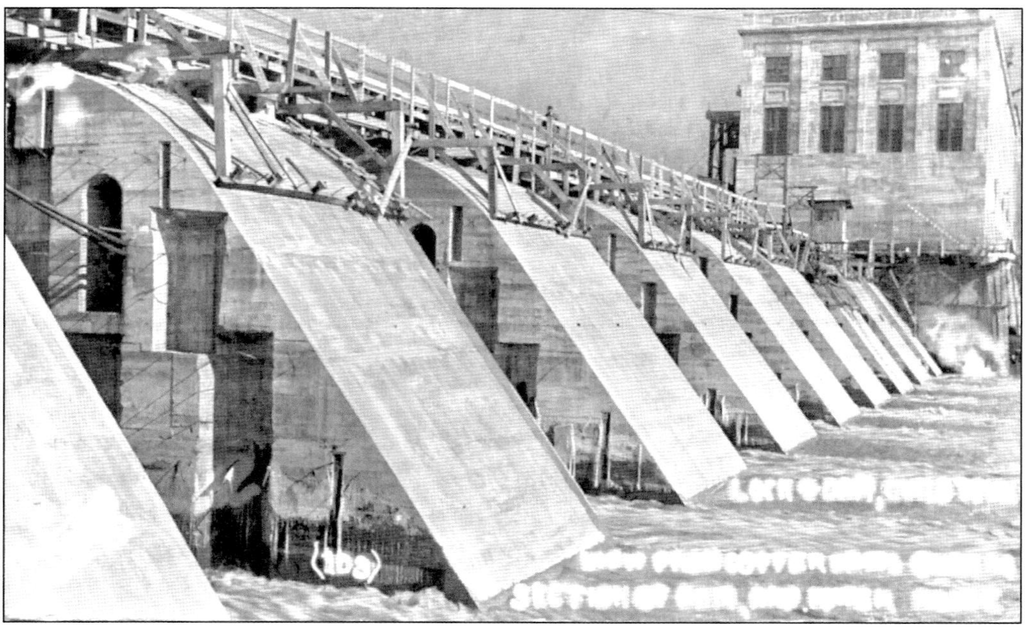

Another RPPC by Spayth shows the dam and powerhouse. A worker is seen crossing the walk at center. The powerhouse was completed in 1910 and upgraded from 1950 through 1953. In 1968, the hydroelectric steam-generating plant was dismantled and moved to Tim's Ford. The dam and 200-foot twin smokestacks were demolished.

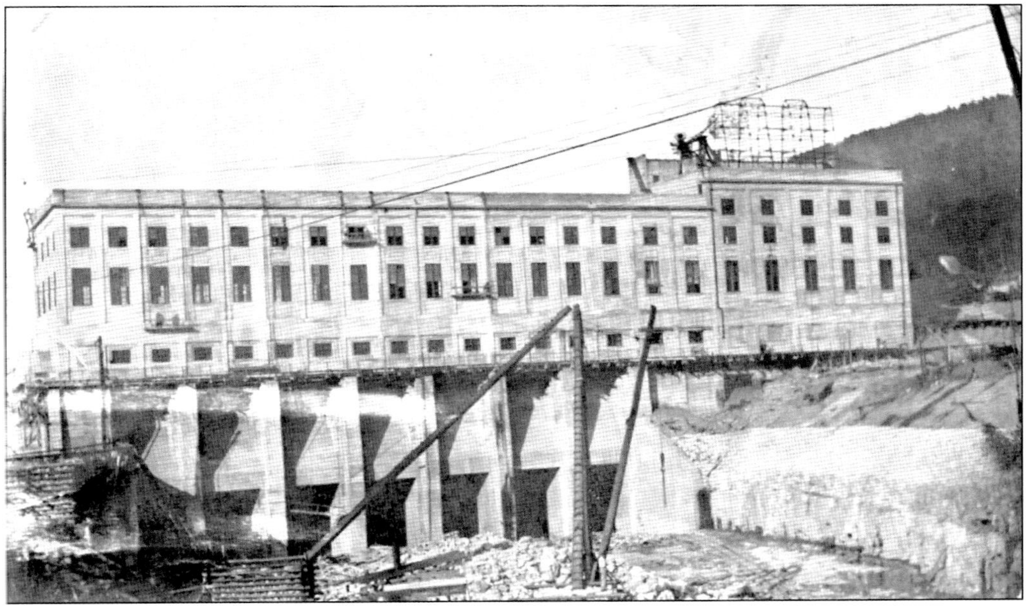

Workers on scaffolds can be seen hanging from the powerhouse. Completed in 1912, the powerhouse had machinery installed in 1913, and the grouting and caisson began sinking the same year. There were seven powerhouse bays, each housing two-turbine units. Under the seven arches were the generators that created electricity. The Nashville, Chattanooga and St. Louis (NC & St L) "Dam" Railroad branch line ran to the powerhouse. Today the structure stands powerless, silent, and unwanted.

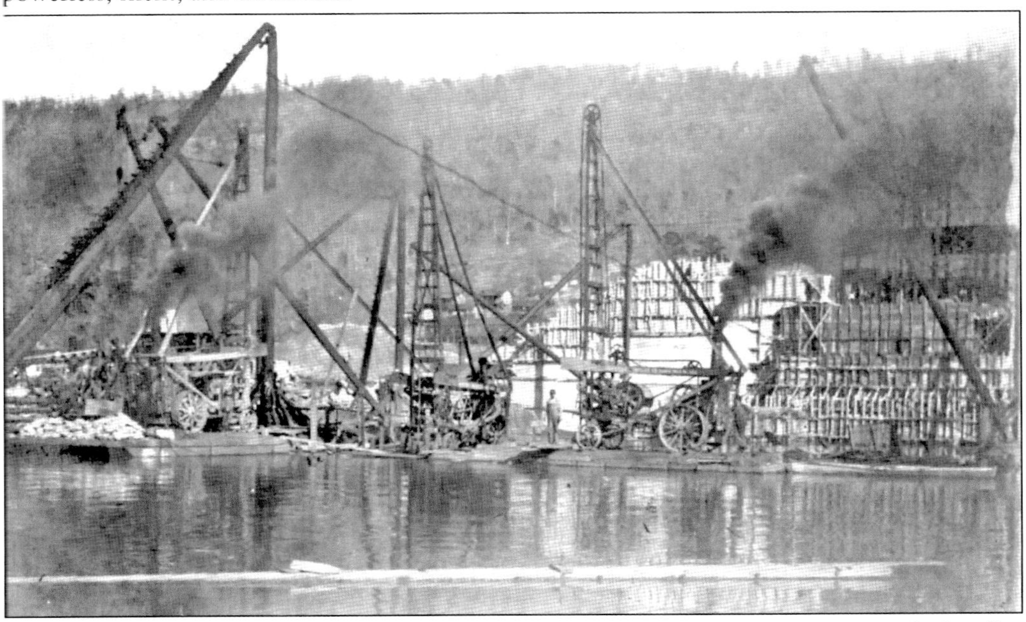

This card is postmarked 1910. The message asks if Ed had "ever seen these on water before." It must be assumed he speaks of the steam-driven pile driver (or steam derricks and steam-hoisting engines) that has "Keystone—Driller Co. Beaver Falls, PA" painted on the boom. Brothers Brown and Riley Jones worked on these in 1913.

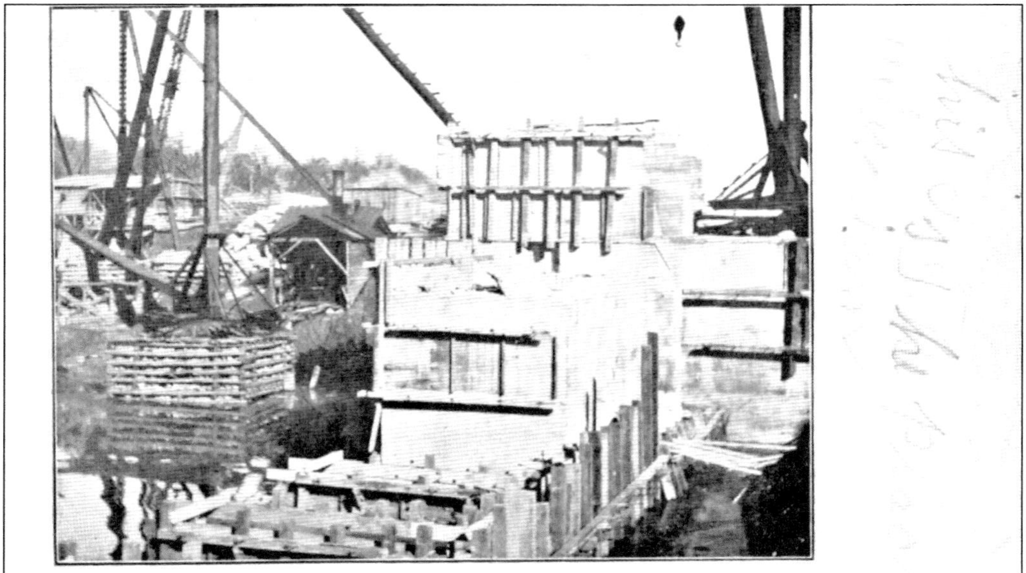

View at Hale's Bar Dam, Guild, Tenn.

Postmarked in Guild, Tennessee, and mailed to Miss Ester Burchard in Dayton, Tennessee, this card shows concrete forms that were poured as the dam was built a section at a time. Men worked 50 feet below the riverbed surface, so an area around the dam had to be pumped dry. The lock's walls were 58 feet tall and the dam 57 feet tall. The head of the water (the height it falls) was 40 feet.

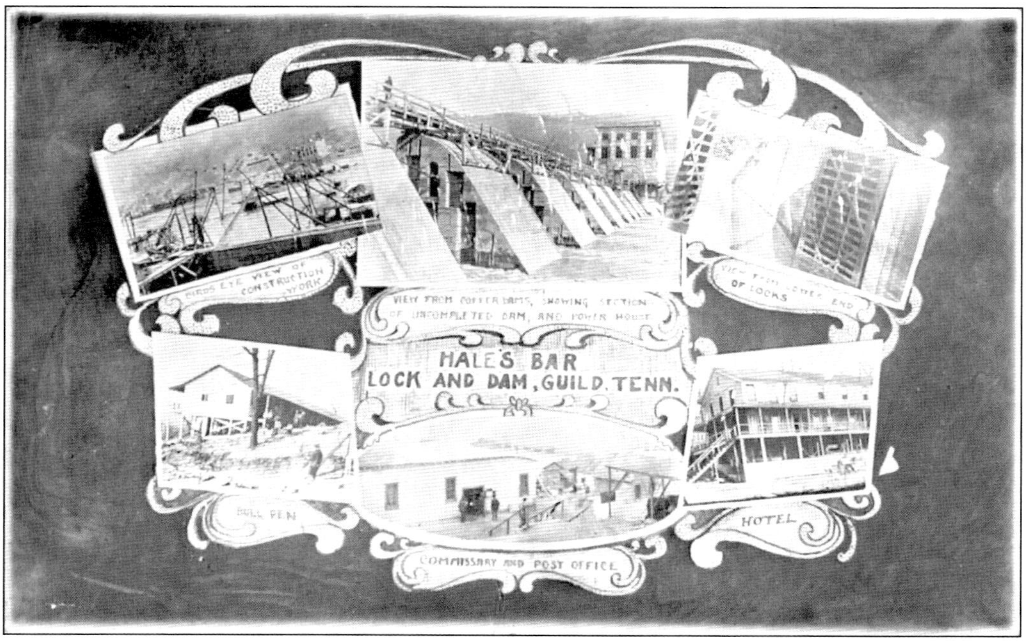

Starting top left and preceding clockwise is construction work looking toward the powerhouse; from the cofferdams showing uncompleted dam sections; a view from the lower end of the locks; the old hotel; the commissary and post office; and the Bull Pen. Mitch Kinder of Cleveland provided this card.

Three

South Pittsburg and Kimball

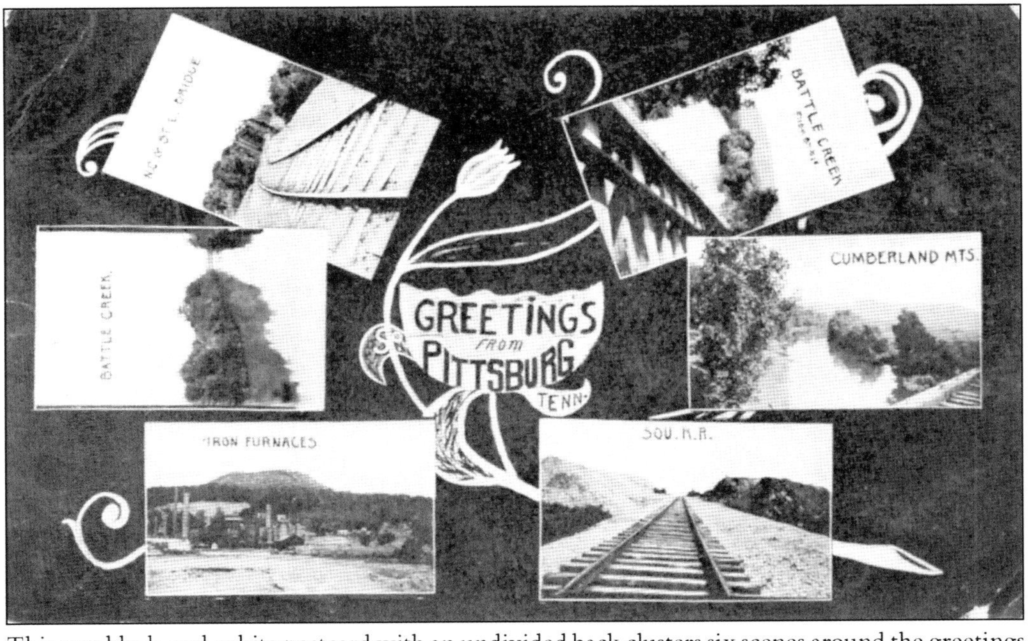

This rare black-and-white postcard with an undivided back clusters six scenes around the greetings from South Pittsburg. These cards were printed in the early 1900s. The Southern Railroad was known as the "Old Southern Grade." She was never completed as the result of signing a franchise with the NC & St L. There are remnants of the construction efforts near the mouth of Battle Creek. In 1907, several men were killed when a steel section slipped from its mooring.

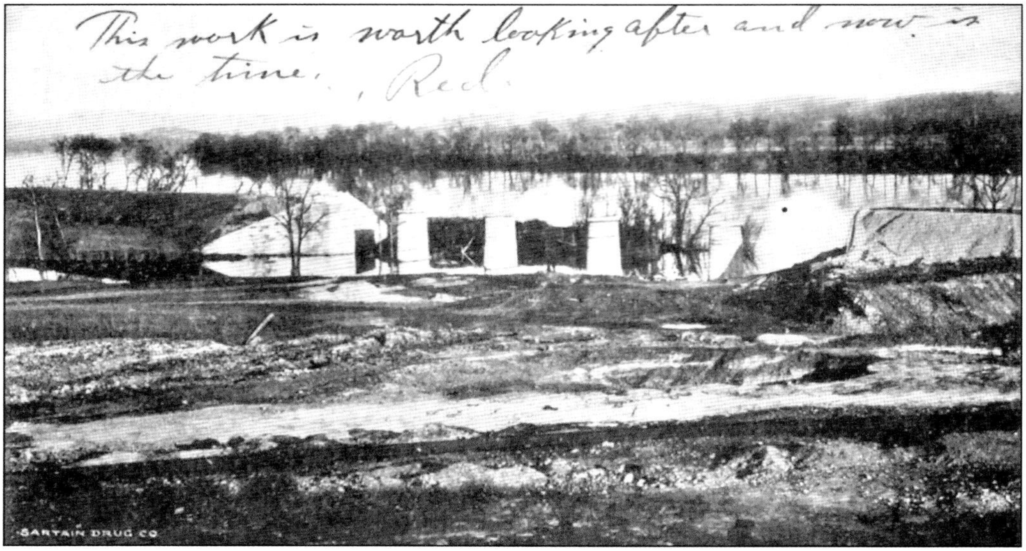

This is from the old Battle Creek Railroad Bridge looking up the creek toward present-day Kimball. The approaches and piers shown here are still standing and at one time had track across them. There was also a tipple built here, and there are the remains of an Irish Navy house on Ferry Road near this site. The card, printed by Sartain Drug Co., was sent from R. N. King and reads, "Here is where S. P. Smith is doing work for the 'Phoenix.' "

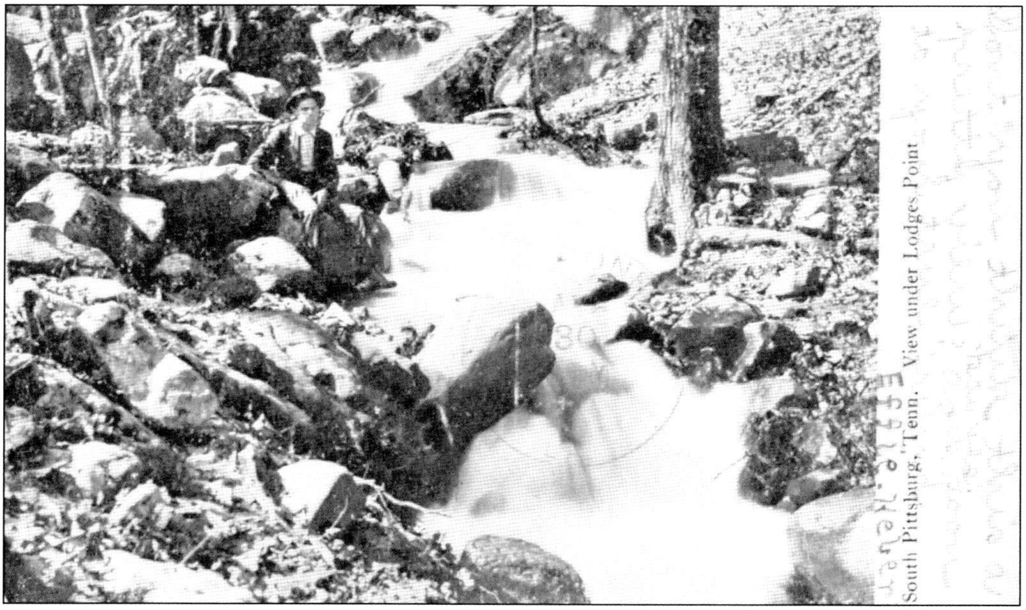

This 1908 postcard may be Cleavets Spring, or Cleavets may be a mineral water found here. Carolyn Millhiser owns Lodge's Point today, and it was her great-grandfather, Joseph Lodge, who started Lodge Manufacturing (cast-iron cookware). When Carolyn's father, C. R. "Dick" Kellerman, was a child, the family would spend summers at Lodge's Point. C. R. Kellerman Sr. would carry milk or bread up from the valley, depending on the signal from home—a white sheet on the line for milk or a blue blanket for bread. The Joseph Lodge extended family of children and grandchildren summered over at cottages on the point until about 1920.

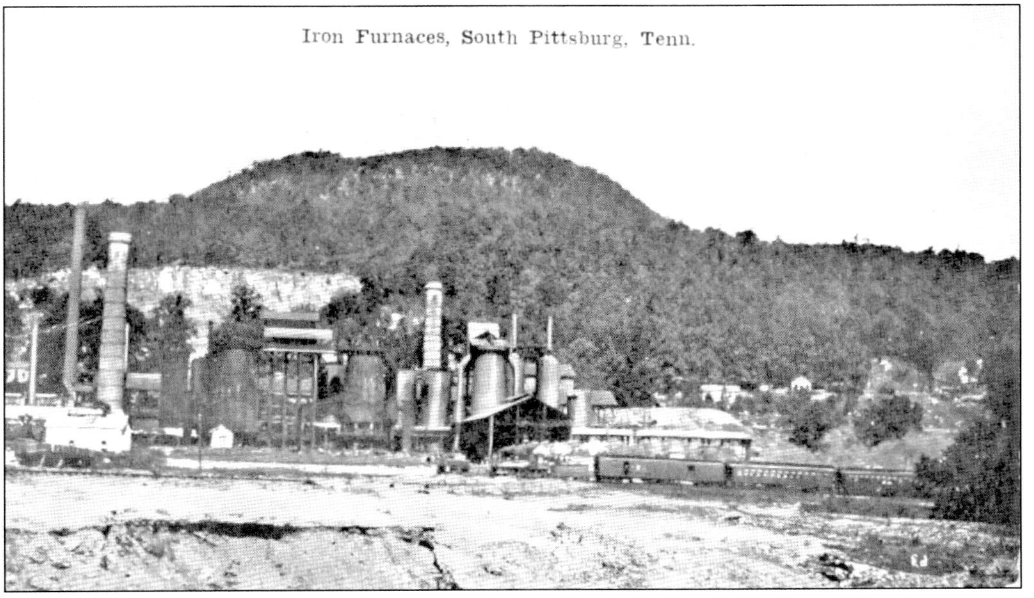

The iron furnaces are gone now but were once a mainstay in South Pittsburg. The site can still be located but is difficult to see because of overgrowth. Coburn Town Road was to the right and led to a flat area on the mountain that overlooked Dixie Lee Junction. Coburn Town was named for Bob Hookey's grandfather. The message on the cards says, "This place is surrounded by mountains and roads are so rough it would be hard to walk home."

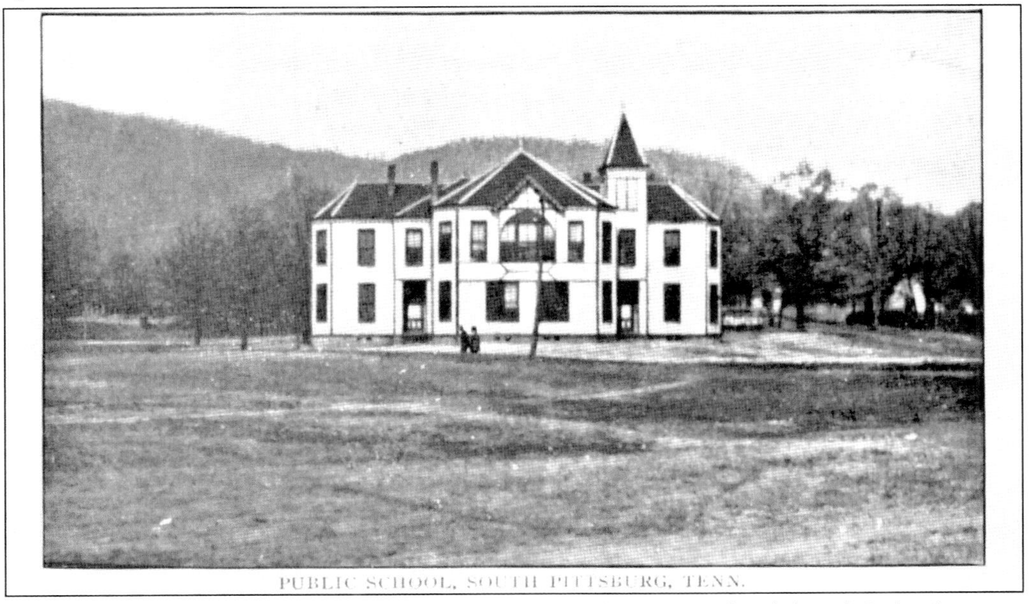

This was South Pittsburg's first public school, located at the corner of Eighth and Cedar Avenues. The city of South Pittsburg had its own school system at one time. Beginning in the early 1900s, it was a 10-room frame building with grades 1 through 10. Before it ceased operations, under the leadership of Principal Wilson New, it offered four years of high school in 1923 and 1924. Later Courtesy Court would be built on this spot. It, too, is gone. The new brick school at Elm and Eighth replaced it.

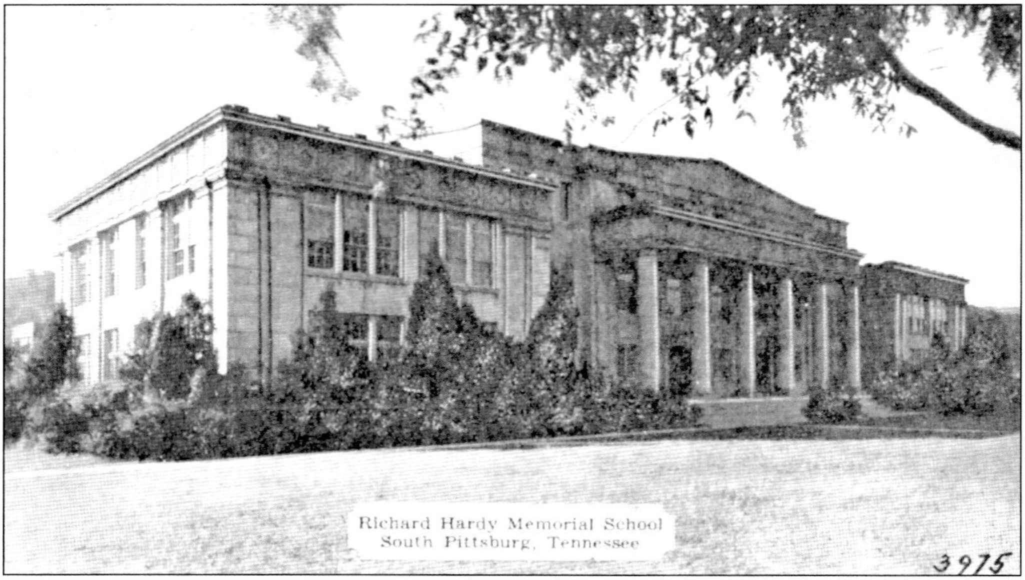

Built around 1926 by Dixie Portland Cement Company at the cost of $243,000 and maintained as a memorial to World War I soldiers, the school was a dream fulfilled for Richard Hardy. It replaced the old Dixie Memorial School (old Red Brick Schoolhouse) and was actually located in Richard City. An addition built onto the back of the building is not visible in this view. This was originally Dixie Portland Memorial School, and seats in the school still carry the initials "DP" on them.

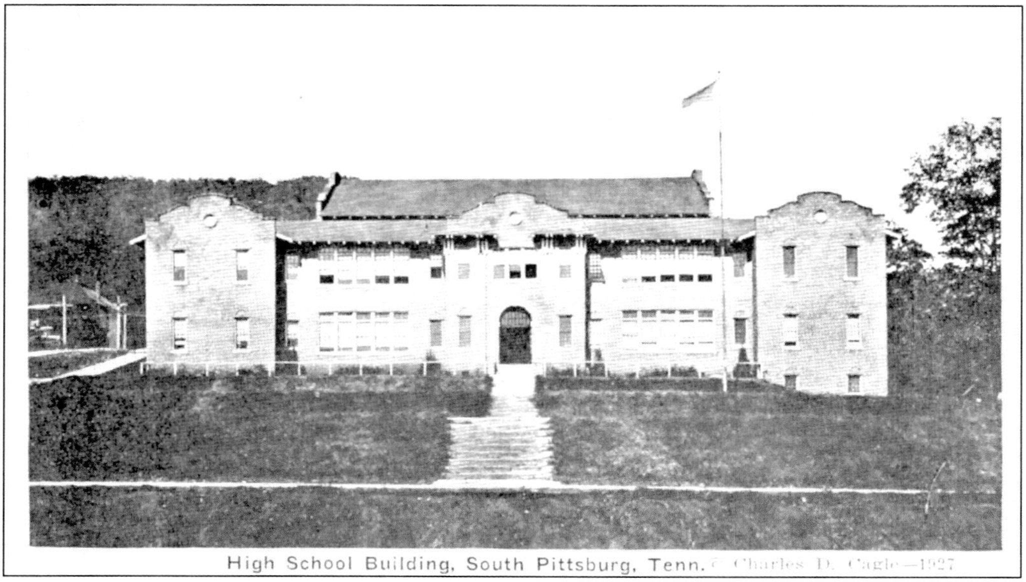

This building was razed in 1966, and the new school sits on this same site. The music room was in the "dungeon" at bottom right; the auditorium is the structure visible at top and behind the school; and the principal's office was front and center on the second floor. The gymnasium, added later, is still there. The school accommodated grades 7 through 12, and for some time, the band director was Mr. Lynn Clyde Pryor. South Pittsburg's black school (McReynolds) burned in 1965, and black students were sent to high schools in South Pittsburg, Jasper, and Whitwell.

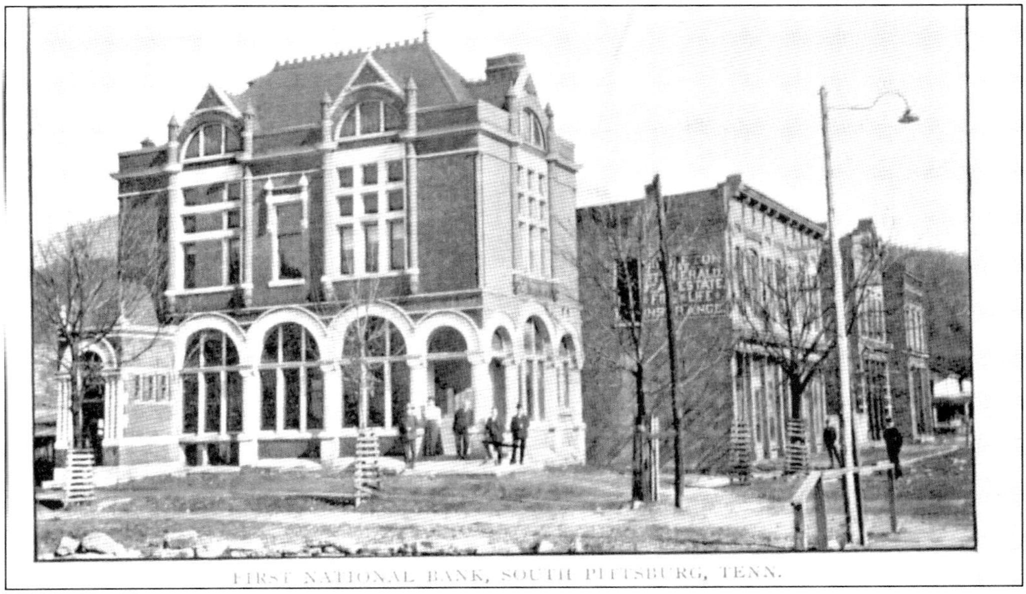

This is one of several cards from a postcard folder. It shows what South Pittsburg's First National Bank looked like in 1906. The people, from left to right, are Tom Mix, company officer for the old Dixie Portland Cement Company; Miss Irene McRae, assistant cashier; T. G. Garrett, president; A. A. Cook, cashier; and Richard Hardy, at the time, president of the cement company. One of the gentlemen on the far right is R. H. Fitz-Gerald. Miss MacRea was the last of these locals to pass away.

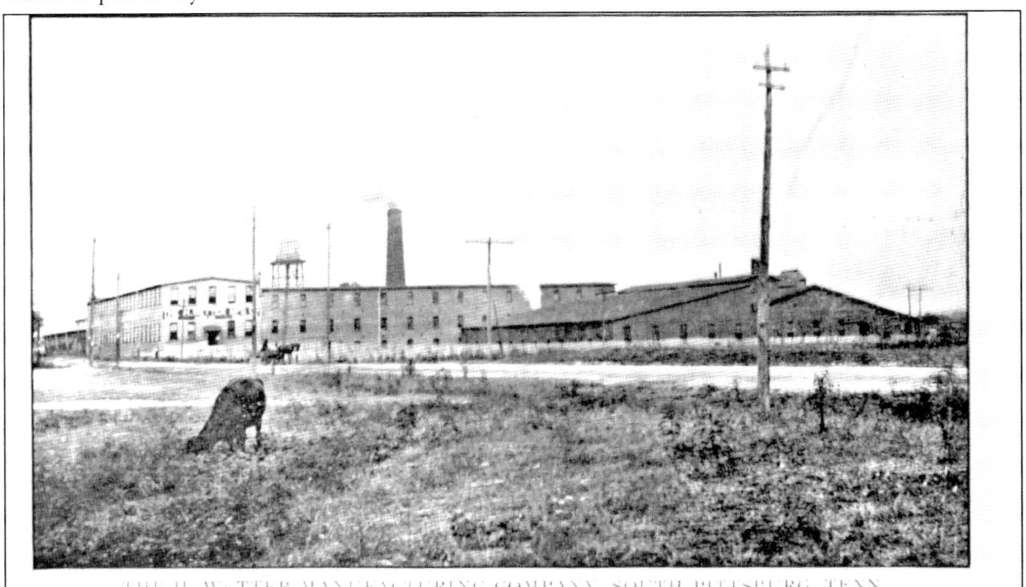

Another card from the folder shows the H. Wetter Manufacturing Company of South Pittsburg. There were two foundries (Wetter owned both), and the smaller one is in the foreground. There is also a cow in the open field in the foreground and a horse and buggy on the road. Note the primitive old water tower to the left of the chimney. There is also a postcard that presents an artist's rendition of this plant.

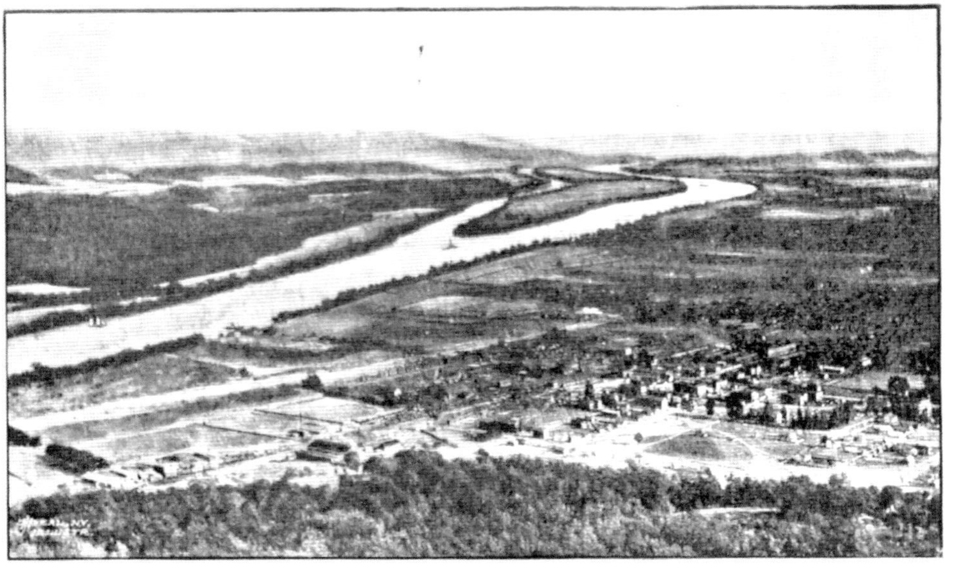

BIRDS' EYE VIEW, SHOWING TENNESSEE RIVER, SOUTH PITTSBURG, TENN.

This is a view taken from Lodge's Point, as there were few planes taking aerial photographs in 1906. It provides a good view of the early town and Tennessee River. You can see Burns Island and a number of boats on the river.

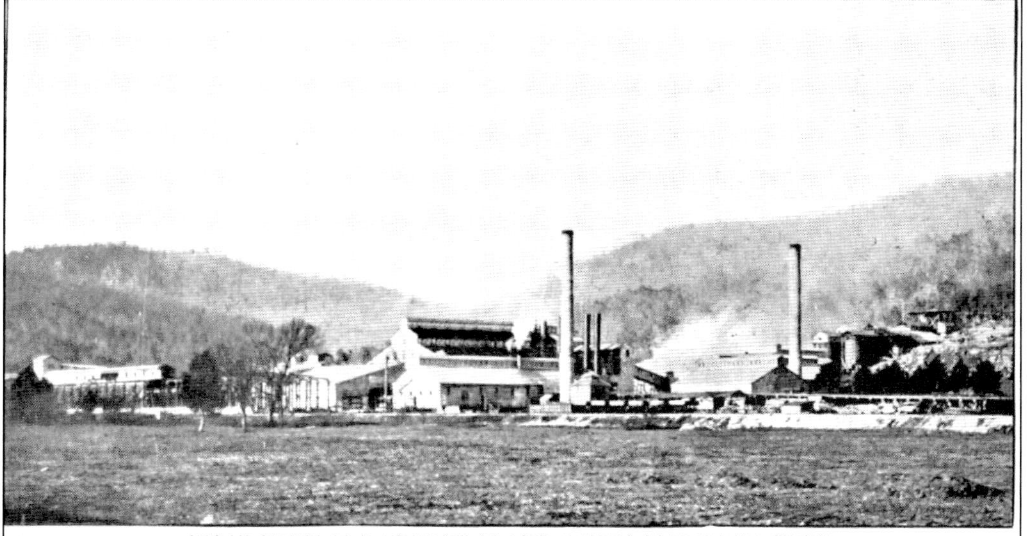

DIXIE PORTLAND CEMENT PLANT, SOUTH PITTSBURG, TENN.

The Dixie Portland Cement Plant of Richard City started in 1906. There were four other Portland Cement Plants. Richard City was on the NC & St L Railroad, a mere mile from the Tennessee River. There was a mountain at the right, but it was ground into millions of tons of cement used throughout the Southeast. The plant was responsible for the birth of Richard City.

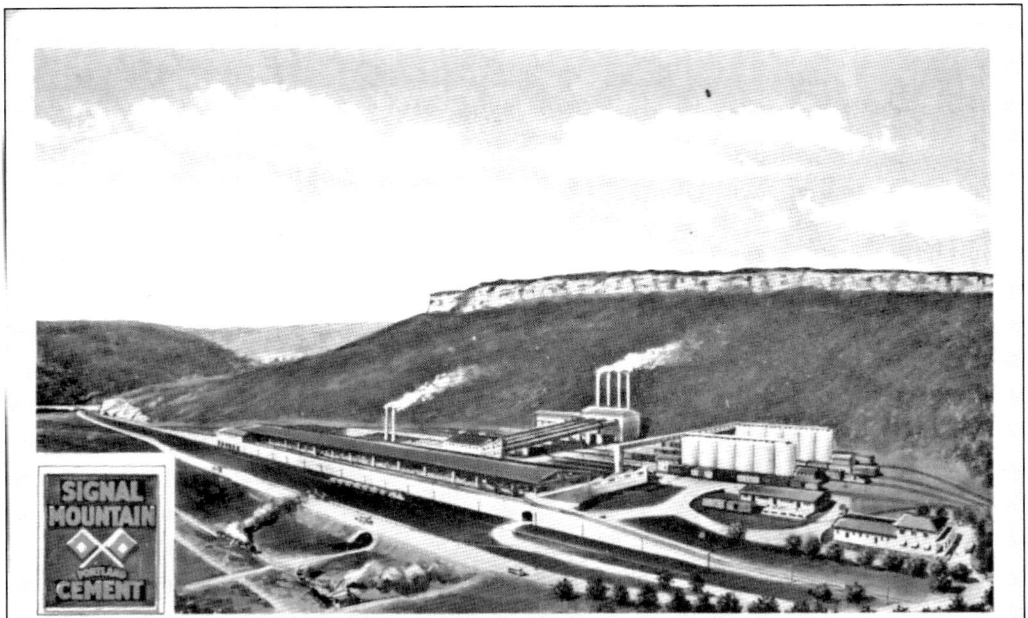

PERSPECTIVE SIGNAL MOUNTAIN PORTLAND CEMENT COMPANY PLANT, CHATTANOOGA, TENN.

The Signal Mountain Portland Cement Company sales office used this advertisement card to let prospective customers know they were "located in the heart of the South and had rail connections with six trunk lines to ensure the best possible service at all times." Jerry Bryant of Tracy City is employed here.

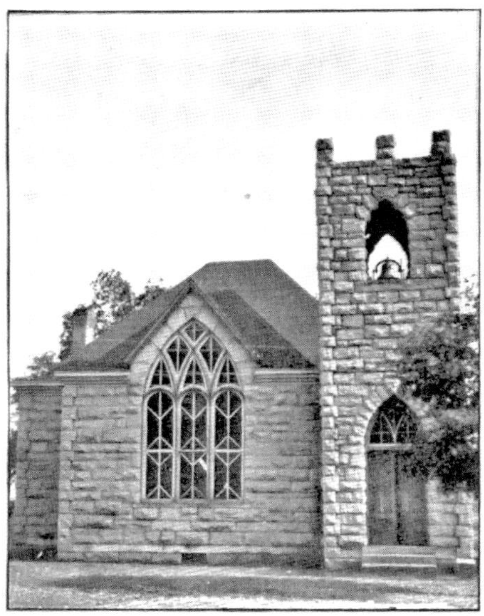
FIRST BAPTIST CHURCH, SOUTH PITTSBURG, TENN.

One of South Pittsburg's architectural treasures, this Baptist church, called the "Old Stone Church" and located at Fifth and Laurel Streets, was torn down and replaced by the current church building.

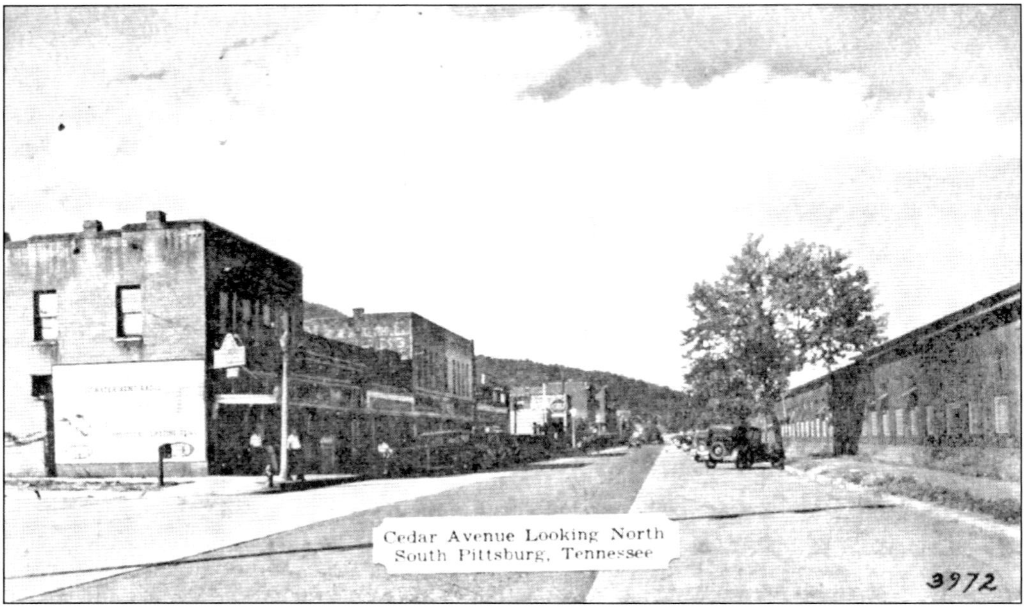

Looking northward on Cedar Avenue, U.S. Stove Foundry is seen on the right; Clepper's Drug Store is the first building on the left. In the 1970s, other businesses along this street burned. Some of those have been replaced with apartments for seniors. The original Perry Stove Works was built in the 1880s. The original opera house was on Cedar Avenue, and on May 5, 1899, *The Hustler* was first printed on the third floor. Lloyd's is the oldest remaining building on the block.

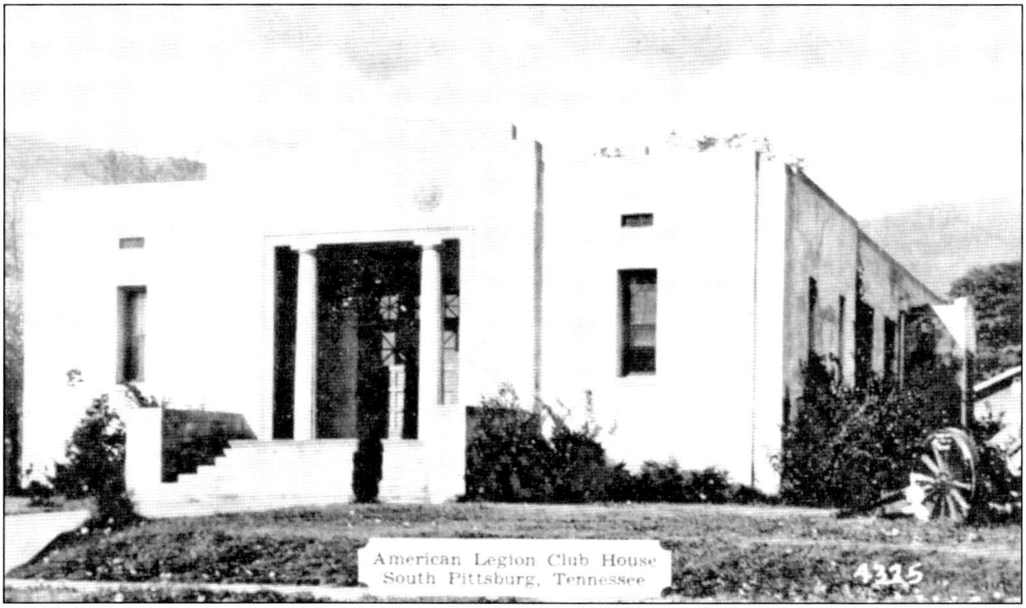

The American Legion Post 62 building was the first meeting place for the area National Guard and looks much the same today. Still owned by the Legion, the front of the building is home to a speech/hearing center, while the back is rented out for parties and other events. It also serves as a polling location, and two small rooms served, for many years, as the library. The 155-mm model of a 1918 artillery piece remains on the front lawn.

Thomas Hezikiah Mix (1880–1940) was born in Pennsylvania but living in Kansas when the cement plant owner, Mr. Ellis Soper, and the plant president, Richard Hardy, recruited him to handle labor disputes. He became the Richard City town marshal. He embellished his resume by saying he fought in the Spanish-American War, when in reality he was an artillery sergeant who deserted in 1901. In spite of that, he was afforded full military burial when he died in a car crash. He had five wives and two daughters, toured with circuses, made 350 films, and was a pallbearer for Wyatt Earp.

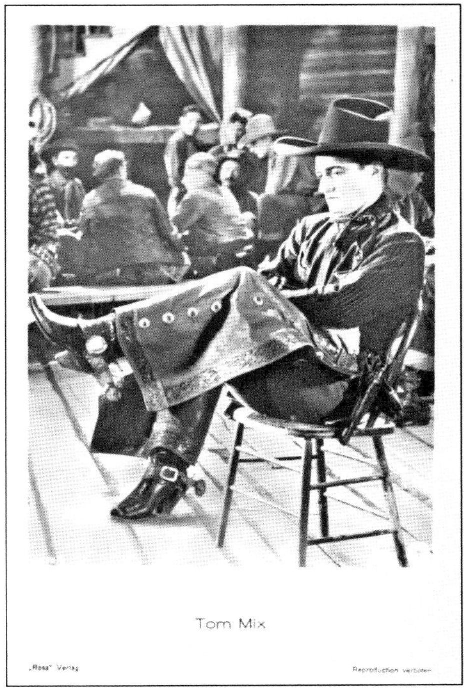

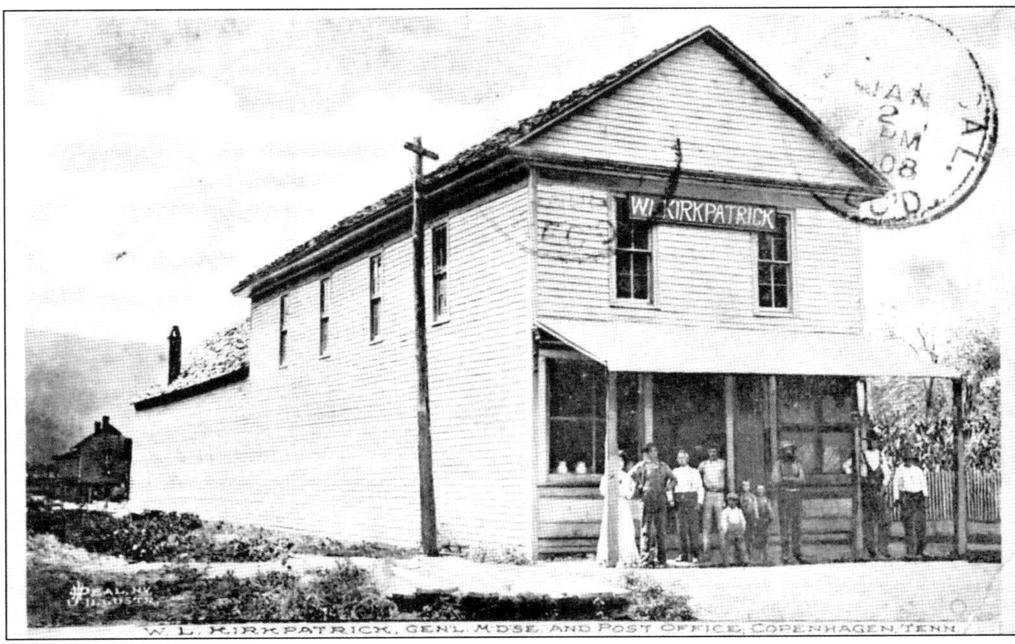

This store was known to carry everything from clotheslines to plow lines. Established July 8, 1878, Copenhagen's name was changed to Deptford in 1890 and back to Copenhagen in 1893. The community was dissolved in 1918. From left to right are Della Loving, Sam Giles, W. L. Kirkpatrick, John I. Cox, Bryan and Bruce Kirkpatrick (sons of W. L.), unidentified, Frank Lawson, and A. M. (Zan) Kirkpatrick. Kirkpatrick's two-story white frame house is still there, and many descendants of the family live in and around South Pittsburg.

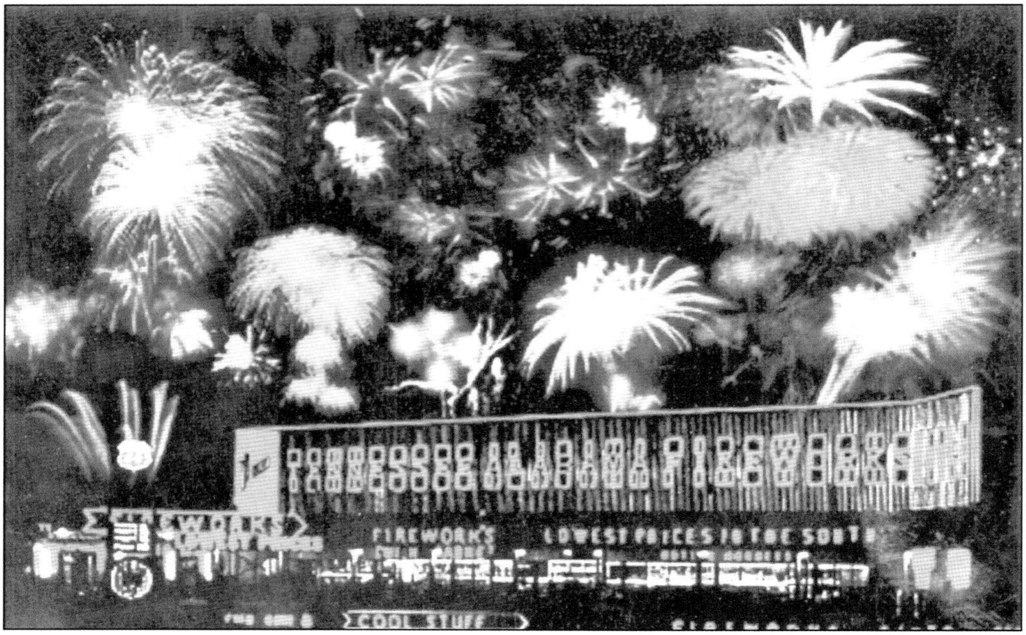

Anyone who has ever traveled past this business remembers it. It is just off I-24 at the Kimball exit and is now owned by Richard Talley. This fireworks display image was "created" by Joey Hookey. Chili Warren has worked here for many years. Lew Lloyd started selling firecrackers out of his hip pocket, and now Lew Wilson Lloyd Jr. has the fireworks business across the street and a fireworks manufacturing plant in Richard City.

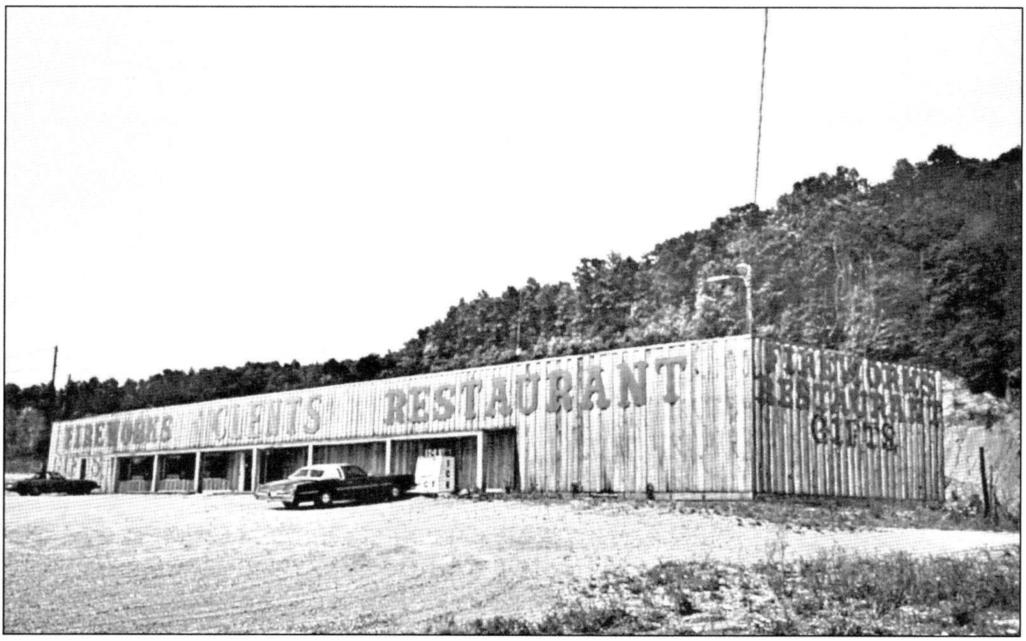

Clent's was owned and operated by a newcomer to the area who has since left. It was a restaurant, gift shop, and fireworks shop. It was at the Martin's Springs exit just south of where Walter McClain's shop is now. This rustic business is where scenes for the movie *Starman* were filmed.

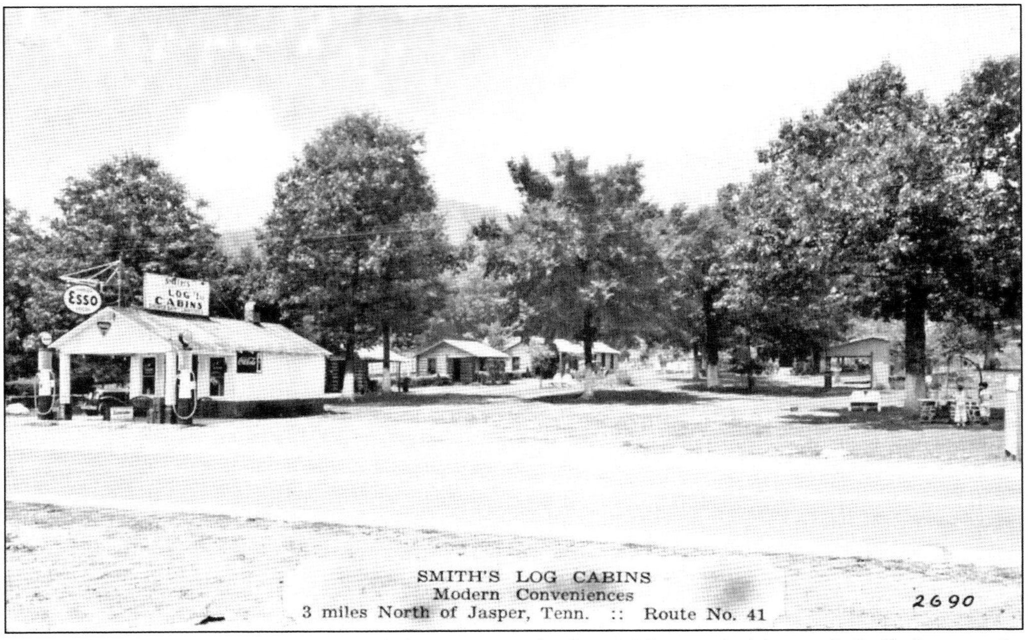

This is an original photograph used for a postcard of Smith's Log Cabins and Café that was in Kimball. The cabins faced Jasper along Kimball Cove Road. Kimball's A. J. Gudger remembers Smith's eight cabins. A. J. traded at George Roberts Grocery nearby. The author has an earlier postcard of these cabins.

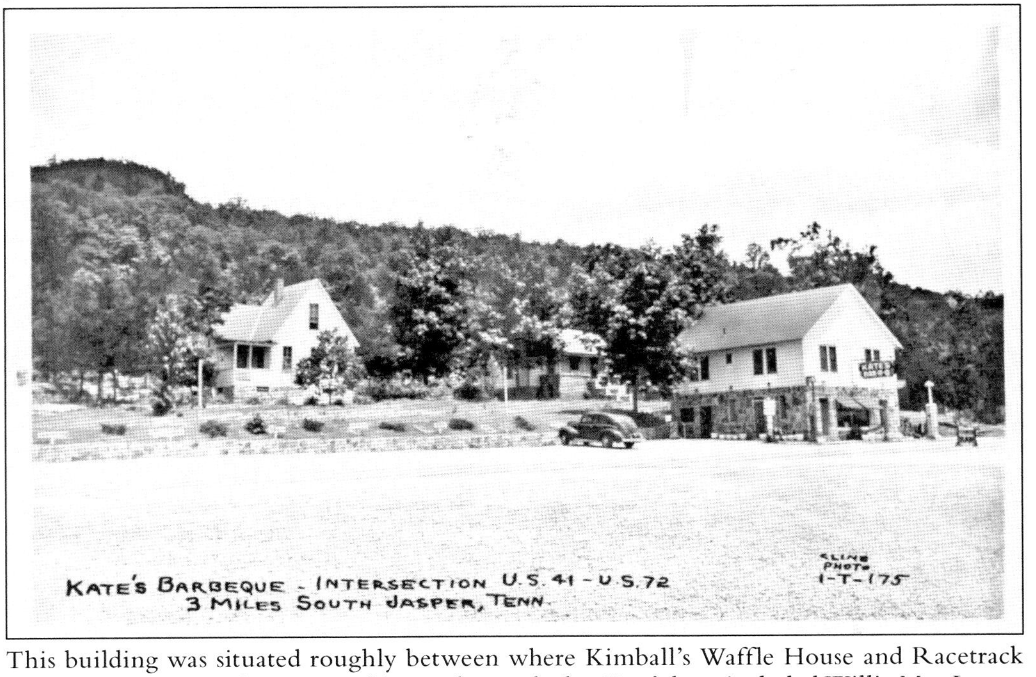

This building was situated roughly between where Kimball's Waffle House and Racetrack Service Station are today. Some of those who worked at Kate's have included Willie Mae Layne, Ruth Gudger, a Miss Harviston (dead now), Audrey Norvell, and Katherine Jones. The knob seen on the mountain today has a cleared area where a home is being built.

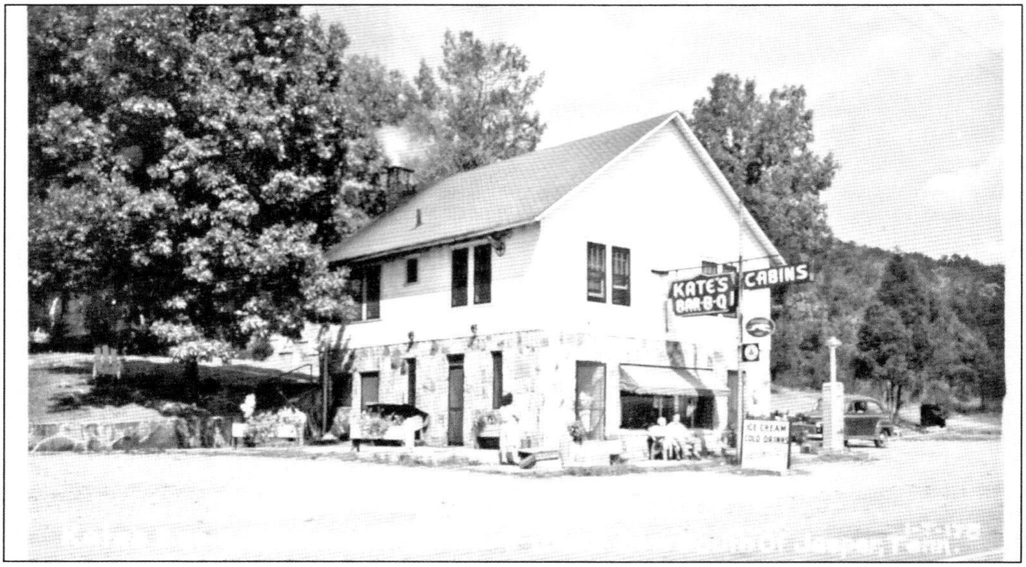

Six people are seen in this card, and the couple sitting directly in front of the building is thought to be the owners, John and Idabel Legg. They had a public telephone (which almost everyone used in the 1940s and 1950s), served food, sold gas, and were the Greyhound bus stop. John Hewgley's father, Bill, married Johnnie Legg and had a "whittle and piddle" furniture shop here. Legg's car, seen in the picture, is a 1939 or 1940 Ford. The family later had Pete's Place on U.S. 41 near the Hamilton County line.

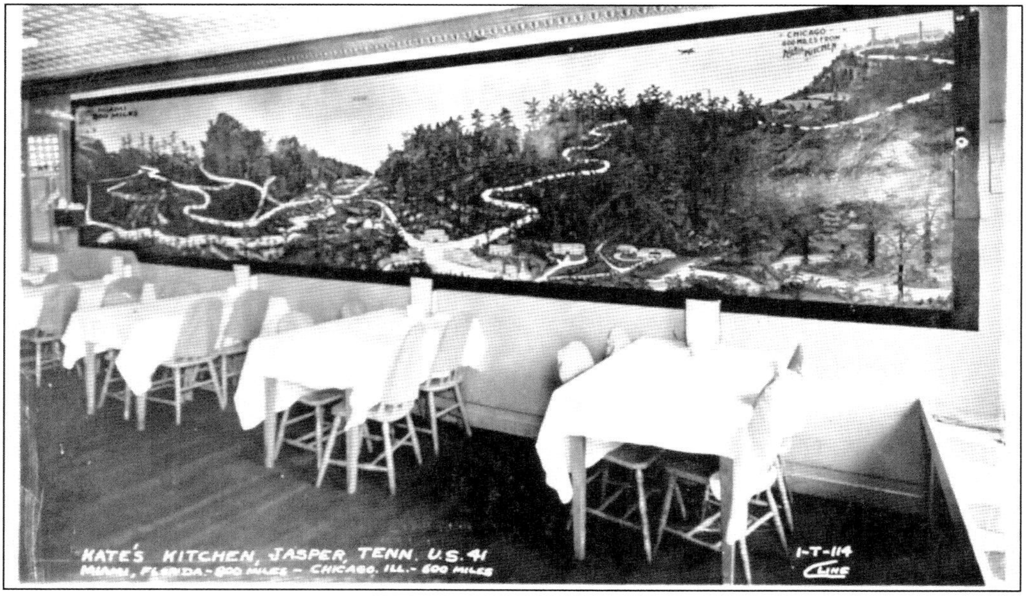

Started by John Authur Legg and Jerry Walker, Kate's Kitchen in Jasper was open from 1926 until World War II began. In 1938, Legg established Kate's BBQ at Dixie Lee Junction. The place was named for his daughter, Katherine Pearl Legg. Richard Gault was the cook, employees were paid \$1 a day plus meals, and the cash register was a cigar box. In 1930, a hitchhiker named Dixon passed through and painted the mural on the wall. Legg died in 1954, and two years later, the place was sold to Dave Martin, Lew Lloyd, and Paul Graham. It was later destroyed by fire.

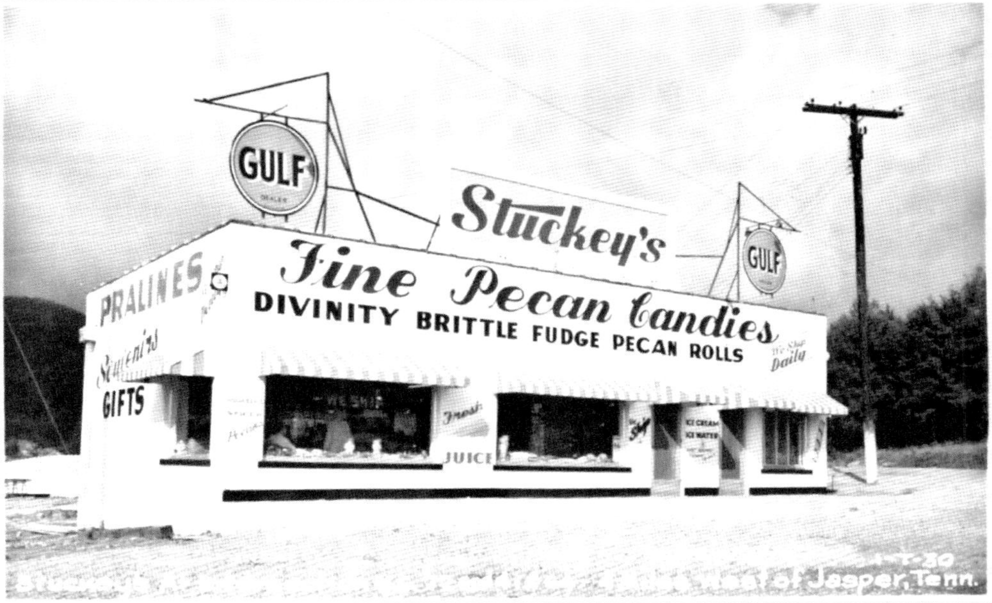

In the 1940s and 1950s, Stuckey's at Kimball was located where the Krystal is today. The back of the card says, "On our honeymoon Nov 13th, 1949 stopped to get some lunch." This is the first Stuckey's at this location. The later one was a more sprawling business. There are later colorful linen postcards of the business.

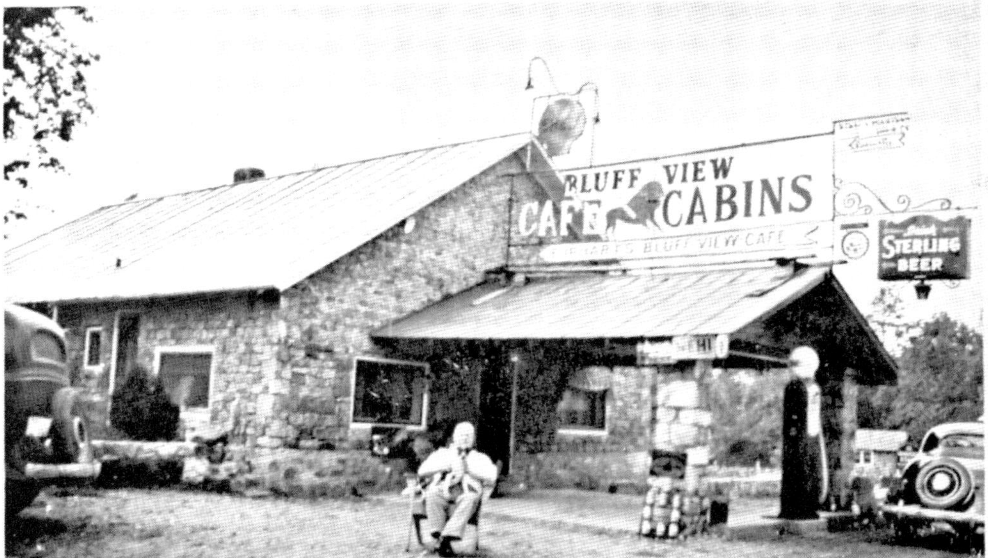

"SHORTY" EHRHART'S CAFE. STATE AND MADISON. KIMBALL. TENN. B-757

This is Shorty Ehrhart in front of his café that also served as his residence. During World War II, Shorty was accused of being a German spy and was harassed relentlessly. The stone used to build Shorty's came from the creek bed at the foot of the mountain just across U.S. 41. In 2005, this building is rental property. The rock columns out front were replaced with block when Joe Hill drove a telephone truck through them.

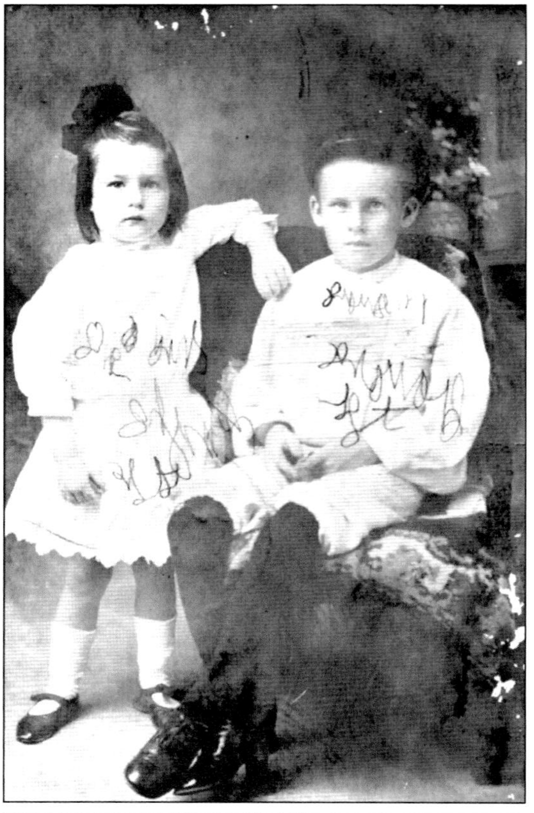

Members of Fred Smith's family lived in Jasper, Kimball, and South Pittsburg. This card was sent from L. Smith of South Pittsburg to Fred Smith of Jasper in 1909. In part the message says, "our younguns," leading one to believe these children are members of L. Smith's family. This card was among a group of cards to and from Fred Smith, all of which placed him in Jasper or South Pittsburg. This is most likely not the Fred Smith who was later in charge of the cement plant.

Dixie Freeze is still one of South Pittsburg's and Kimball's favorite places to eat and meet with friends.

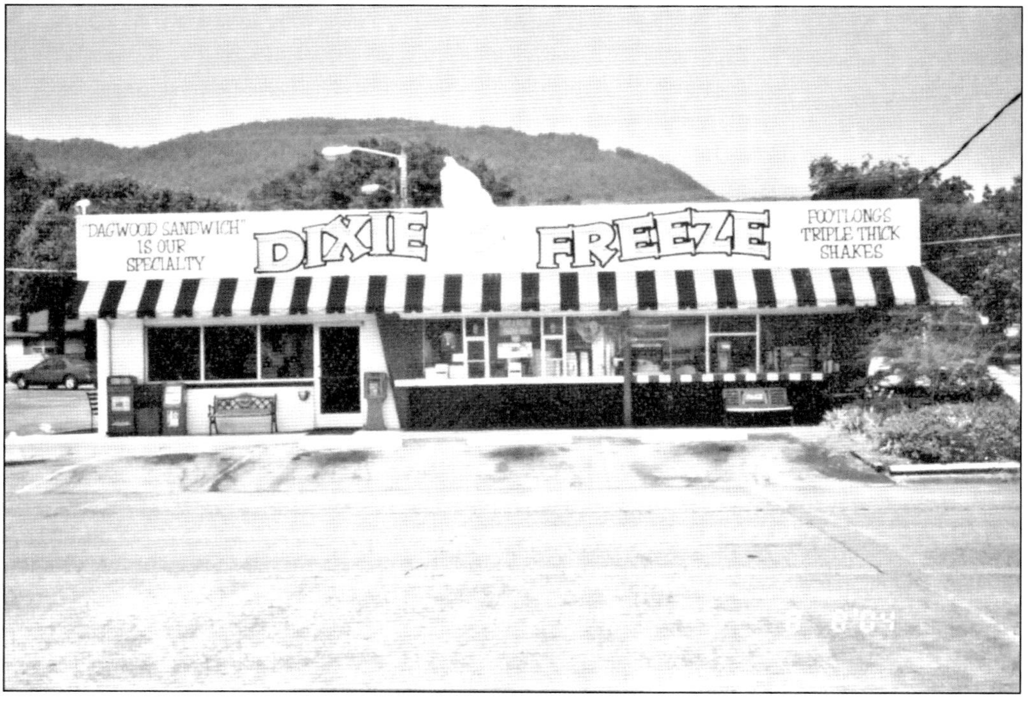

Four

Monteagle and Martin Springs

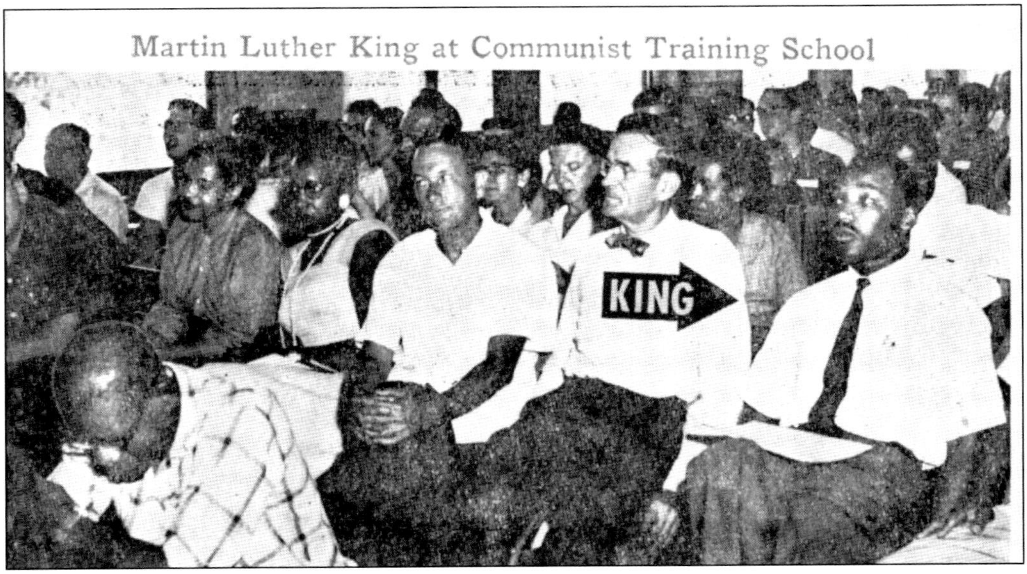

Lower left, arms folded, is Abner W. Berry of the Central Committee of the Communist Party. The arrow points to Martin Luther King, and to his right is Aubrey Williams, president of the Communist Front SCEF, and Myles Horton, director of Highlander Folk School for the Communist training at Monteagle. A secret counteragent took the photograph on this postcard during a Communist workshop in race agitation. For additional copies, at 50 for $1, you could write to the following address: Councilor, Oil & Gas Bldg., Shreveport, Louisiana.

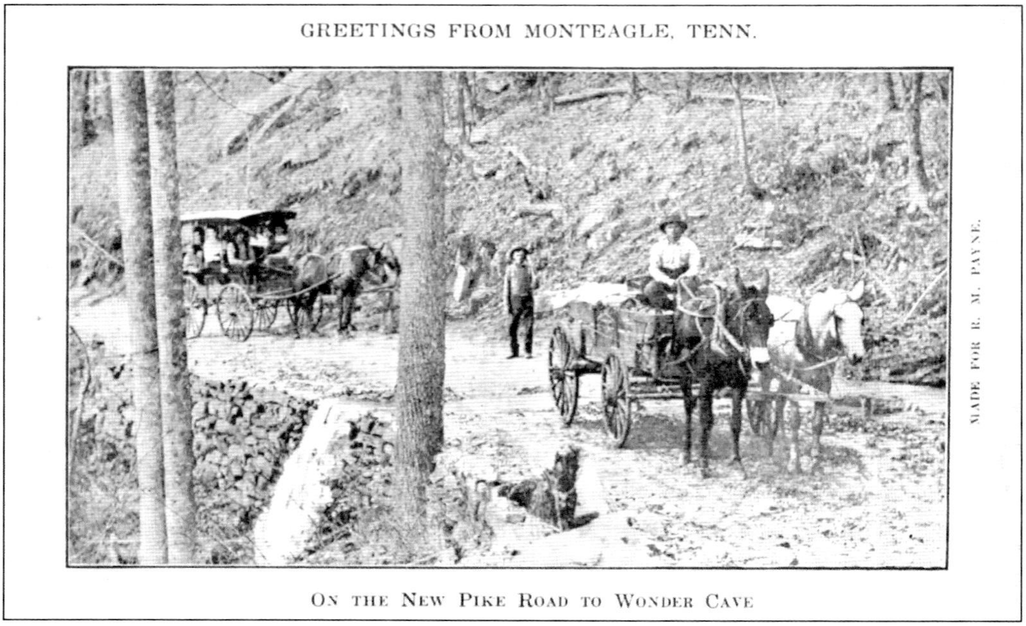

This is what appears to be two or more families going on a picnic. "New Pike Road" refers to the toll road from Monteagle to Wonder Cave. No one is certain of the origin of the name "Monteagle." It may have come from Lord Monteagle of Brandon, Ireland, who had an interest in the area. While the preponderance of Monteagle is in Marion County, Grundy County can lay claim to a part of it, and some would argue it flows across the Franklin County line as well.

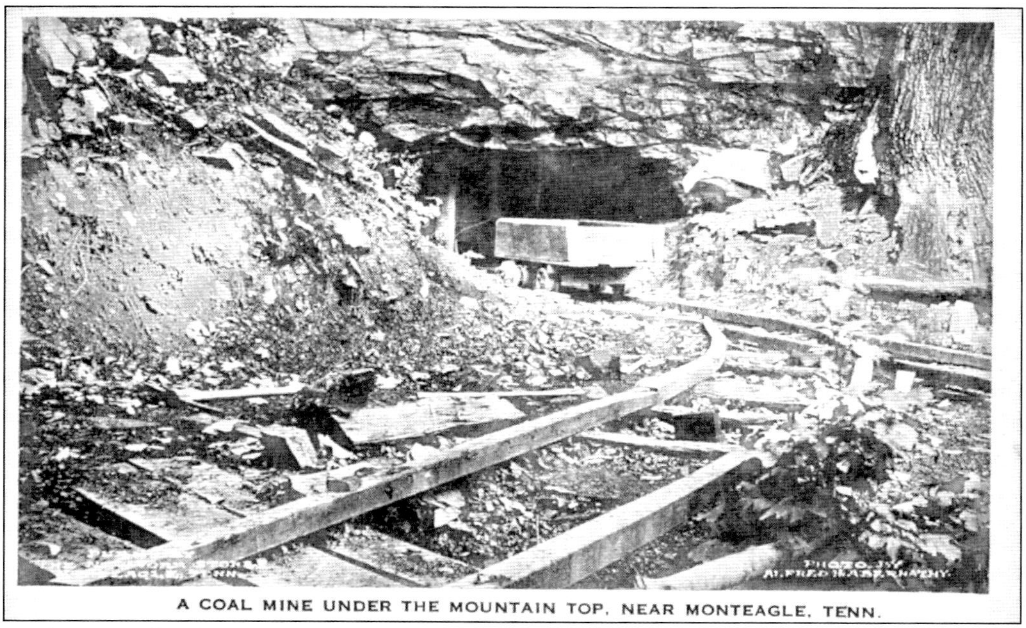

Coal mine–related postcards are scarce. This one shows a coal car that is being returned from the tipple. The track is all wood, and the car is one-half ton. Wooden tracks were used in new or small mines. In spite of what the card says, it is more likely this is Tracy City. In family mines, digging coal was done by hand (picks and shovels).

This is a companion card to the previous one. New York Store of Monteagle, Tennessee, published both. The photographer was Alfred H. Abernathy.

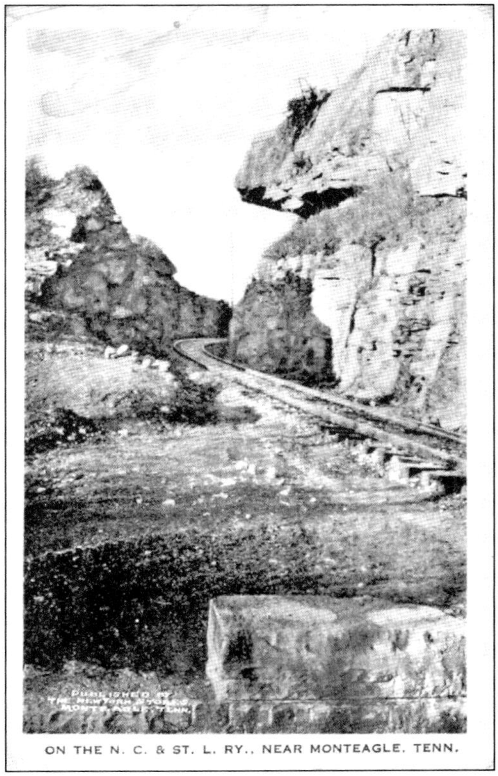

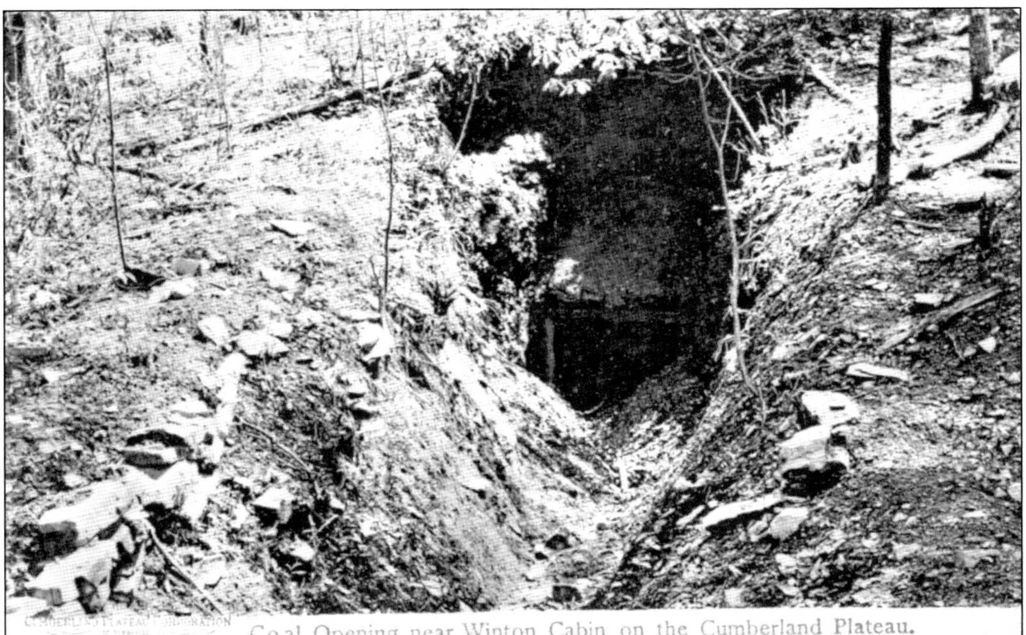

This is the opening to a small, privately owned coal mine on the mountain.

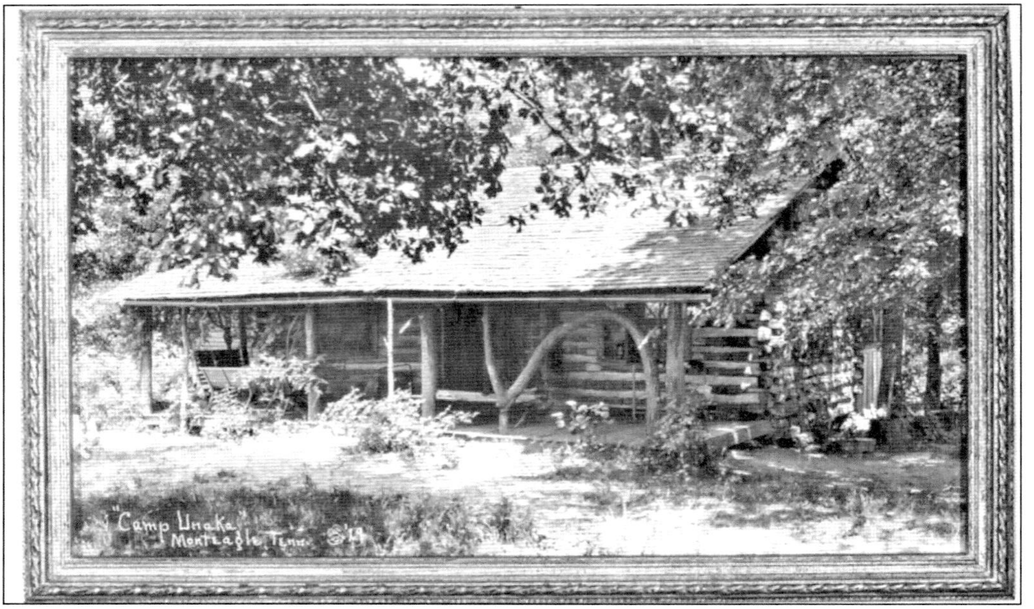

In 1921, Mrs. Bertha Taylor, originally of Friendship, Tennessee, and Mrs. John P. Keiser (who would leave in 1929) of Osceola, Arkansas, opened Camp Unaka on Fairmount Falls property. Attendees were daughters of the South's affluent. When their natural pool (the creek) was dry, the girls were taken to the Assembly to swim. Bertha lived here until her death in 1968, and members of her family still live on the property. The closing of the camp was precipitated by a polio epidemic.

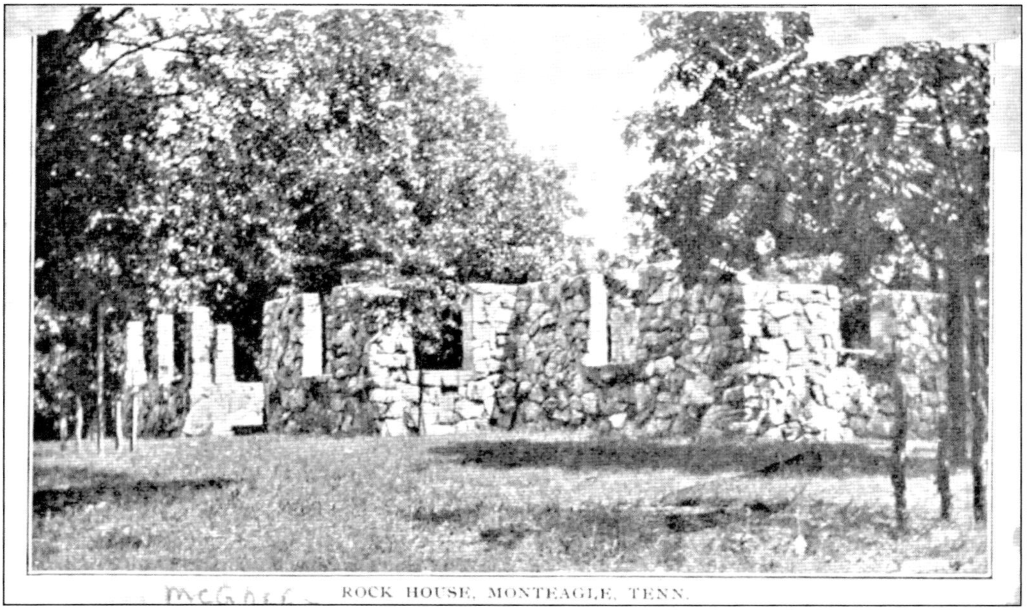

Lida McGhee, who willed the property to Miss Rena Cox Reeves, started the old rock house before 1911. It was never finished. One would turn directly behind the Assembly grounds toward Sunset Rock and bear left to reach this old structure, which still stands and is easily recognizable from the image in this postcard. Glenn and Betty King live near the site.

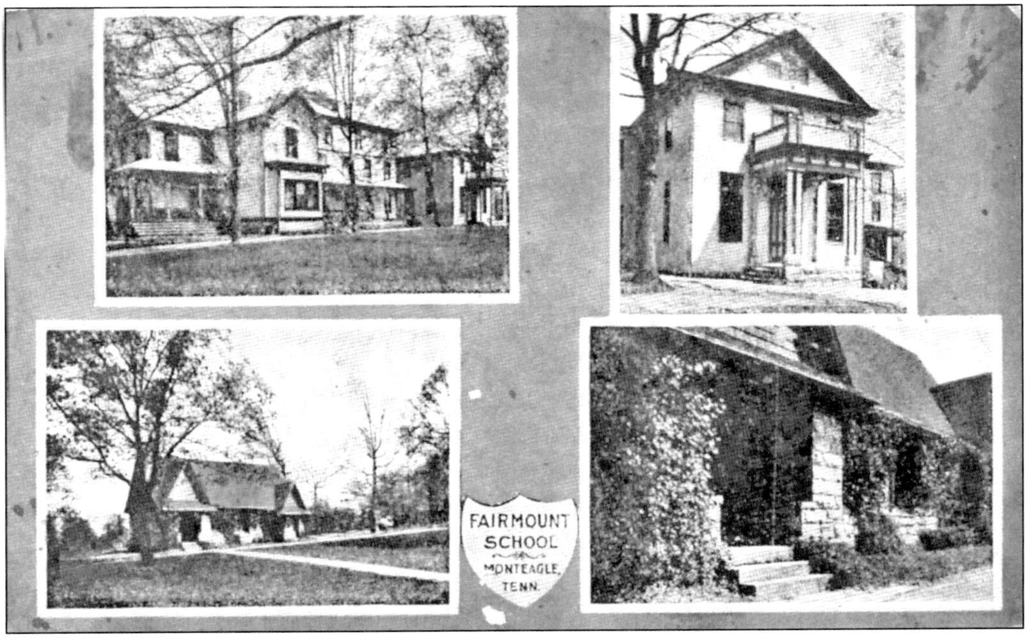

Fairmount College began in 1872 at the isolated village of Maffat's Station (the early name for Monteagle). Fairmount's most noted student was Soong Mei-ling, later Madame Chaiang Kai-Shek, wife of the general and president of both mainland China and Taiwan.

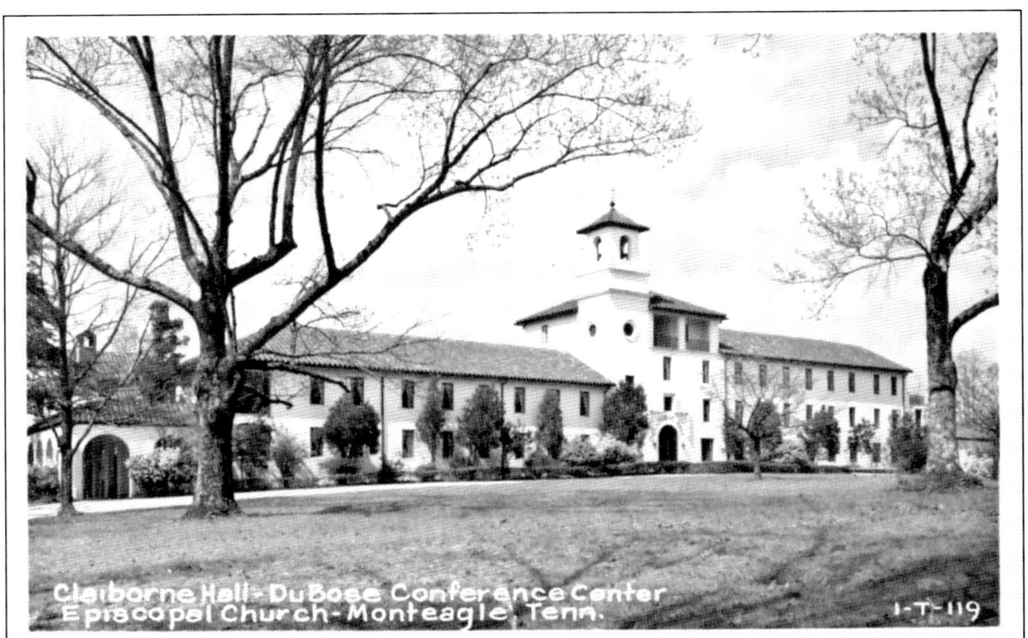

Operated by the Episcopal Diocese of Tennessee, Dubose has a long and illustrious history. The ashes of a man were once spread under a tree on the front lawn.

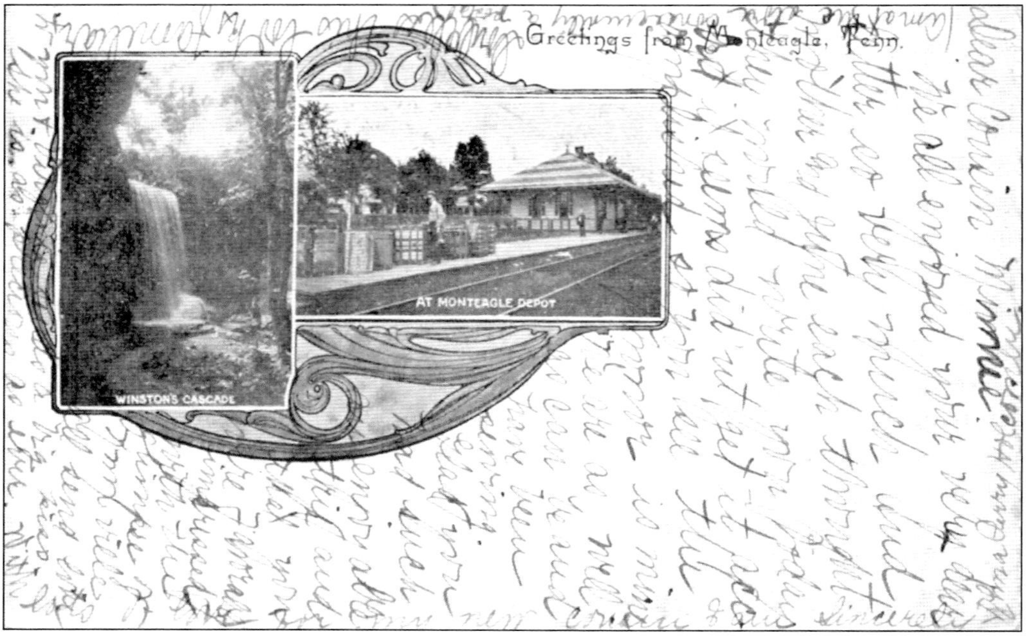

This is a beautiful old undivided-back card printed around 1900. The back includes a patriotic eagle and flag. It is a "Mrs. Grundy Print" mailed from Cowan, Tennessee. The insets are of Winston's Cascade and the Monteagle Depot. Passengers and a freight handler stand along the railroad by the depot. There were section houses behind the depot with dogtrots connecting them. The Marion/Grundy County line ran down the middle of the track until it was moved 25 feet from center toward Marion County.

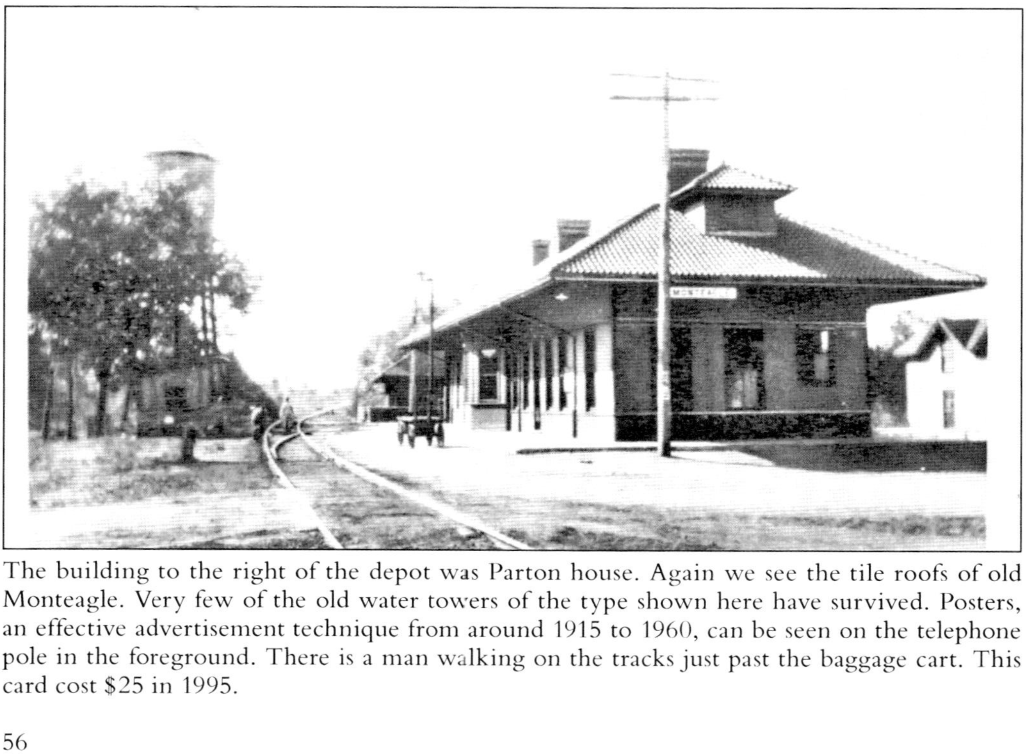

The building to the right of the depot was Parton house. Again we see the tile roofs of old Monteagle. Very few of the old water towers of the type shown here have survived. Posters, an effective advertisement technique from around 1915 to 1960, can be seen on the telephone pole in the foreground. There is a man walking on the tracks just past the baggage cart. This card cost $25 in 1995.

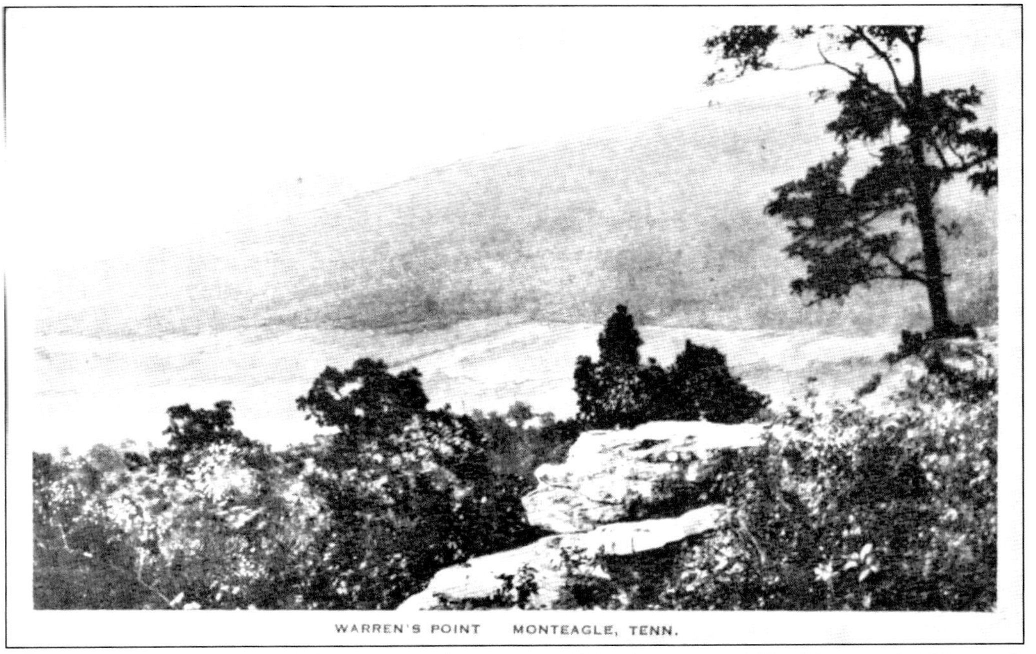

Warren's Point was named for Reverend Warren of Murfreesboro. The Monteagle Woman's Association published the card. This area abounds with these panoramic bluffs, valley views, and rugged rocky cliffs. Bluff scenes are significant because they are at risk of being destroyed by developers, the Department of Transportation, and Mother Nature.

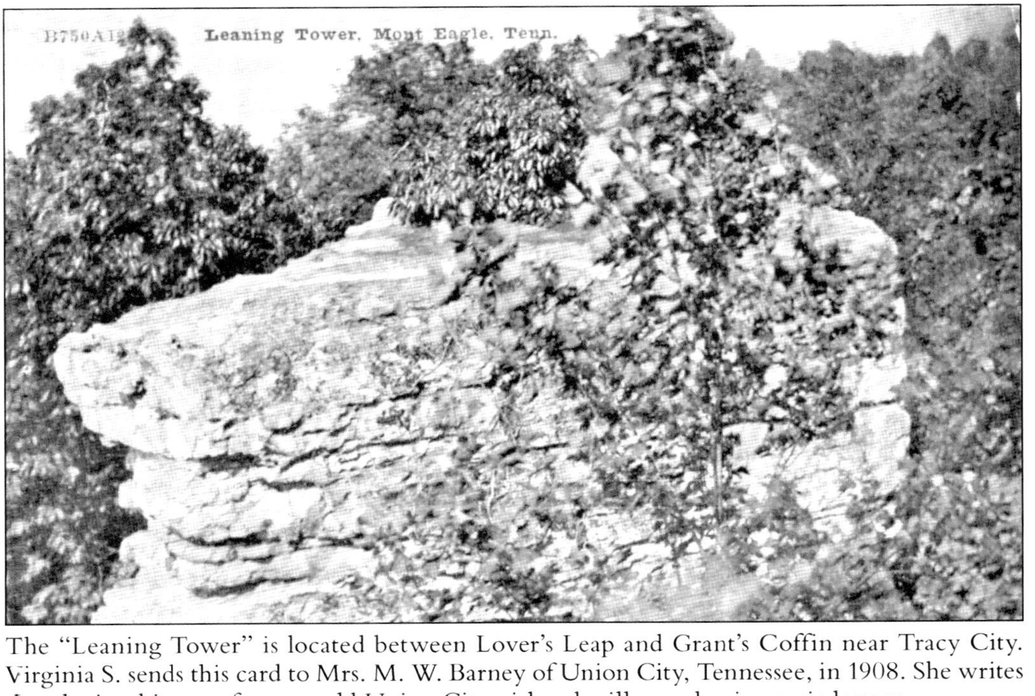

The "Leaning Tower" is located between Lover's Leap and Grant's Coffin near Tracy City. Virginia S. sends this card to Mrs. M. W. Barney of Union City, Tennessee, in 1908. She writes that she is taking art from an old Union City girl and will soon begin music lessons.

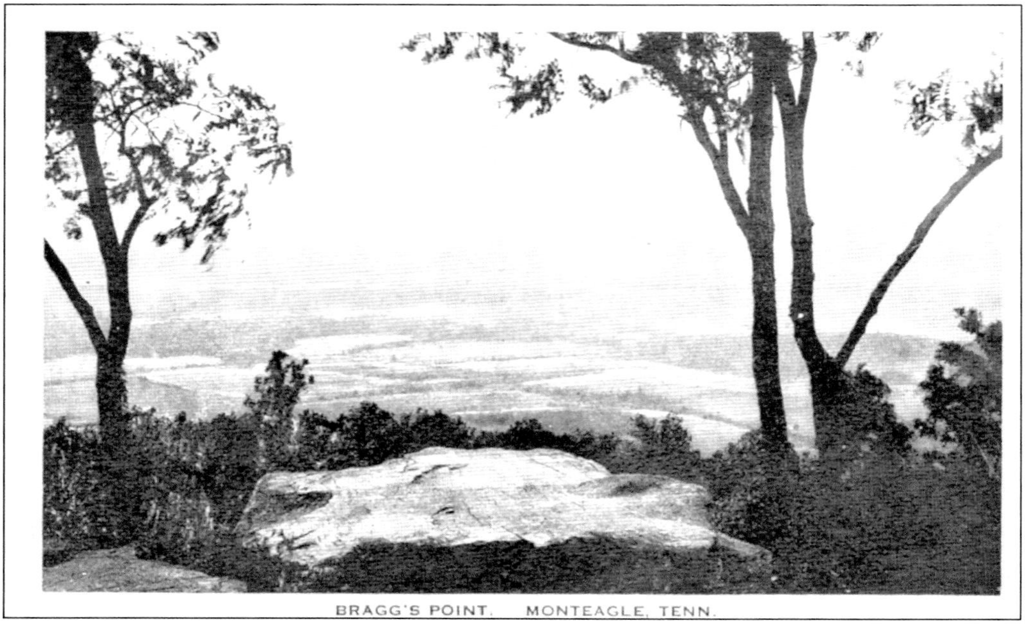

Bragg's Point (now Sunset Rock) is approximately two miles northeast of the Assembly. Yankee soldiers once trapped the great military leader Nathan Bedford Forrest at the bottom of this rock formation. A 16-year-old mountain girl who was intimate with the area led Forrest and his troops to safety.

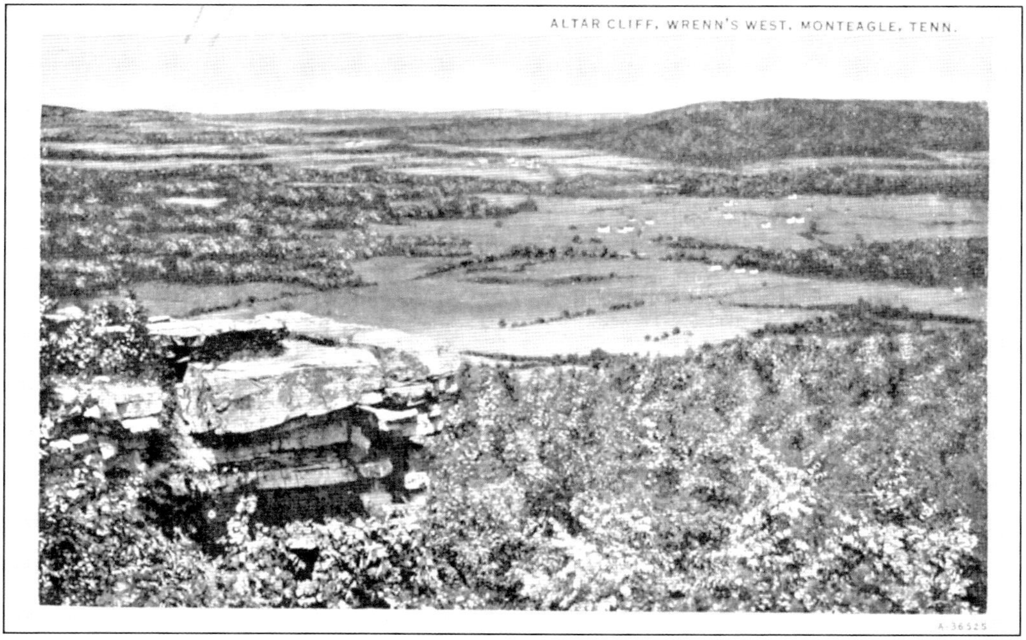

Altar (or Alter) Cliff is located at Wrenn's West (*sic*—it should be Wren's Nest) near the home of Ridley Wills II. Ridley's Cabin was brought from Nashville and is next to Eagle Cliff. This view is perpetuated in postcards.

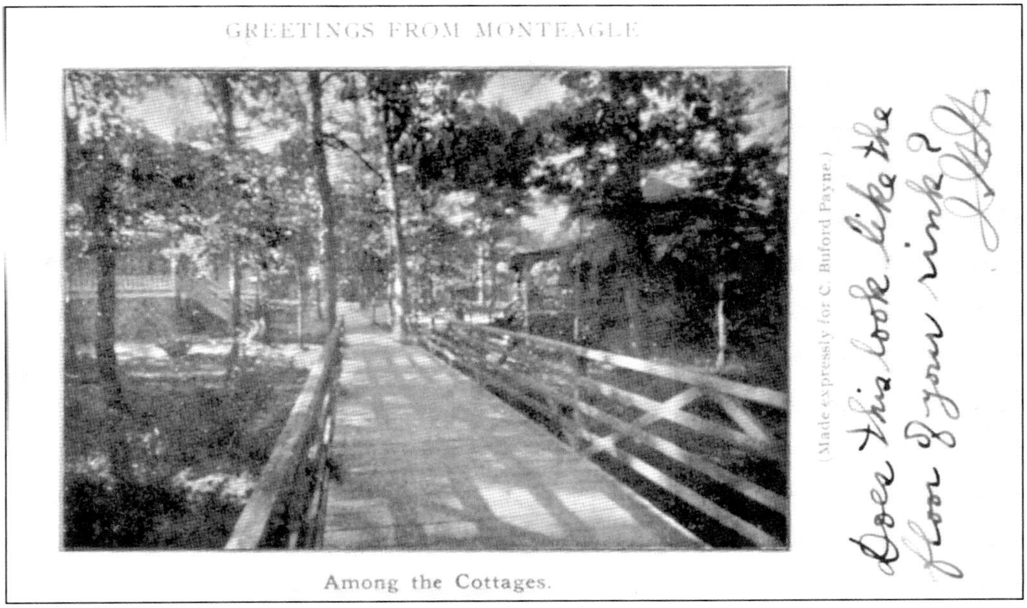

Local residents have viewed the 96-acre Assembly, comprised of summer homes for the affluent, as an intrusive enclave. It is located in Grundy County, but there have been disputes about property lines and road access over the years. There were six long wooden pedestrian bridges erected in the 1890s. This card, one of a set of six or more, is from Mrs. Woodcock, who resided here in 1907.

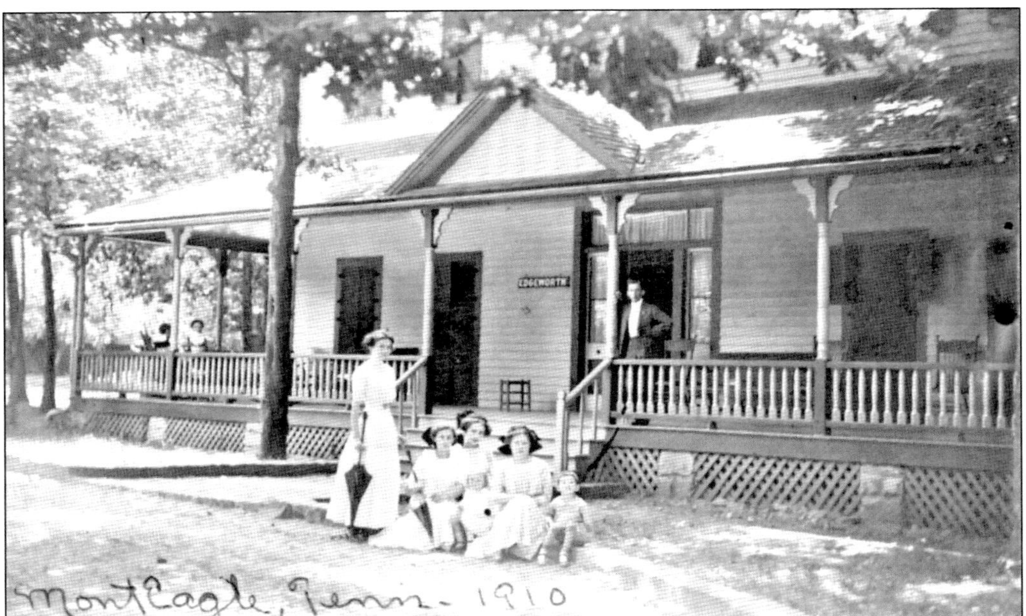

Life was good in the Assembly in the early 1900s in considerable contrast to how "others" on the mountain lived. This is Edgeworth in 1910. Mitch Kinder of Cleveland, Tennessee, provided this card.

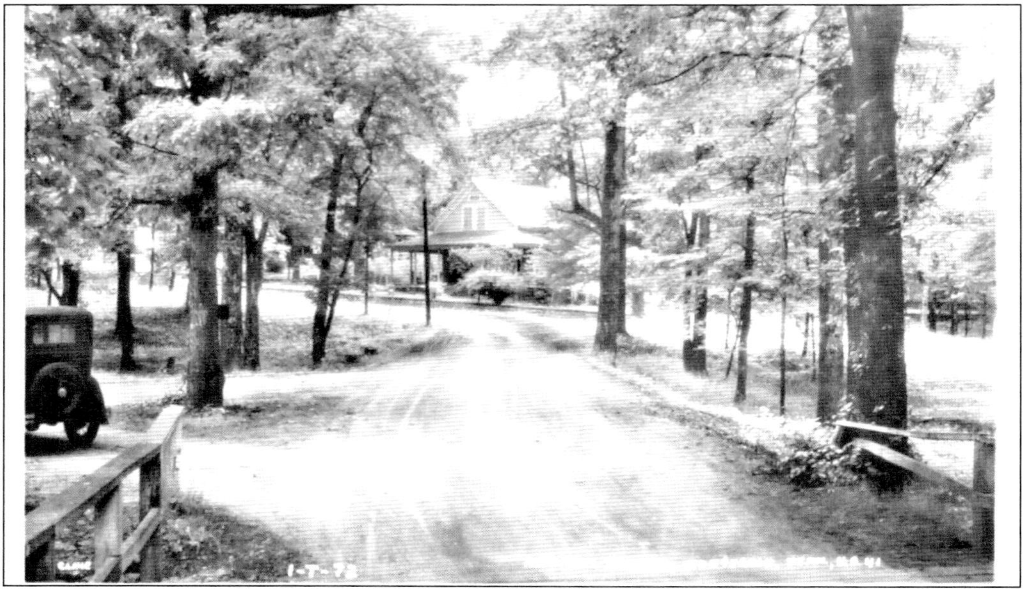

Cline did very few cards of the Assembly. The first building on the right is the home of an Assembly women's suffrage leader, Josephine Pearson. Ridley and Irene Wills own Glen Haven #130 on the Assembly. John Harton of Tullahoma bought the Assembly Inn in 1926. Its four stories, attic, and basement were consumed in less than one hour in a 1961 fire. Harton also owned Monteagle Hotel (the first one), and the family still owns Million Dollar View.

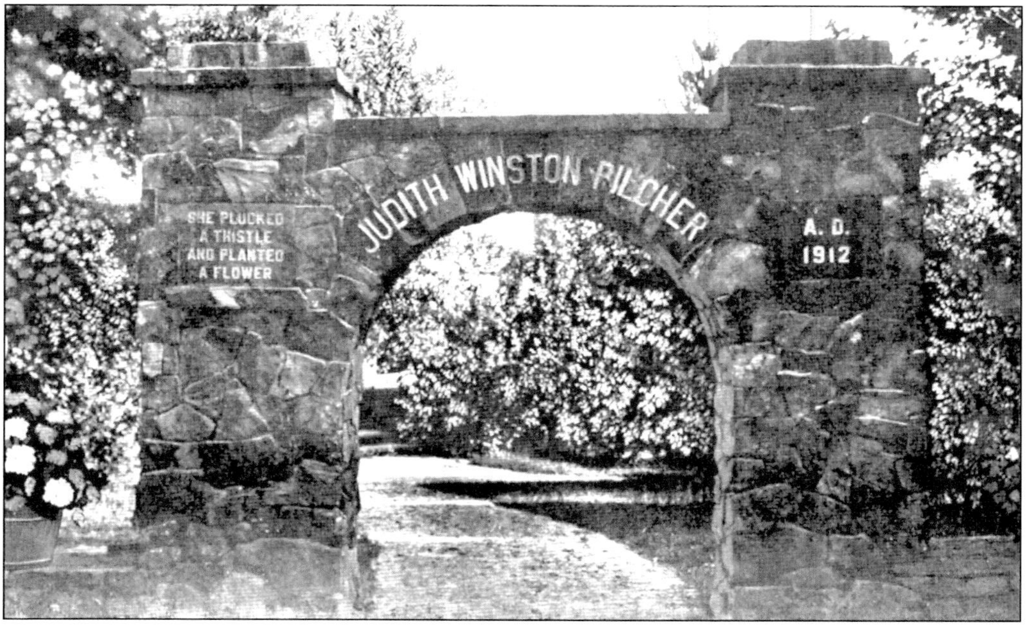

Judith Pilcher, the Assembly ladies association president, beautified the grounds, and in 1912, the Woman's Association erected this monument to her. The arch led to the auditorium gardens until they were transformed into a child's playground. This archway is not to be confused with the main entrance with its "Gate House." Referred to as "the Ritz," the gatehouse was built in the 1890s and provided lodging for boys who manned the gates until early 1920s.

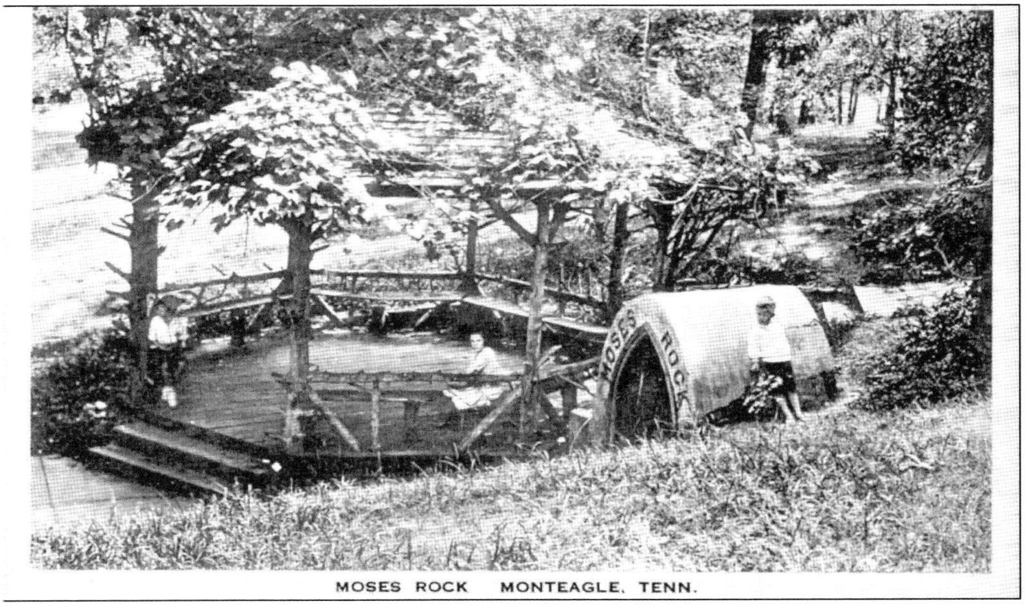

An open way lead from the amphitheater up to the spring at Moses Rock, which provided one source of water in the Assembly before the NC & St L Railroad piped water up the mountain. Many came here to try and avoid consumption (later determined to be tuberculosis) and other diseases. The rustic springhouse, pavilion, and sanitary drinking fountain were still here in the 1930s but are gone today.

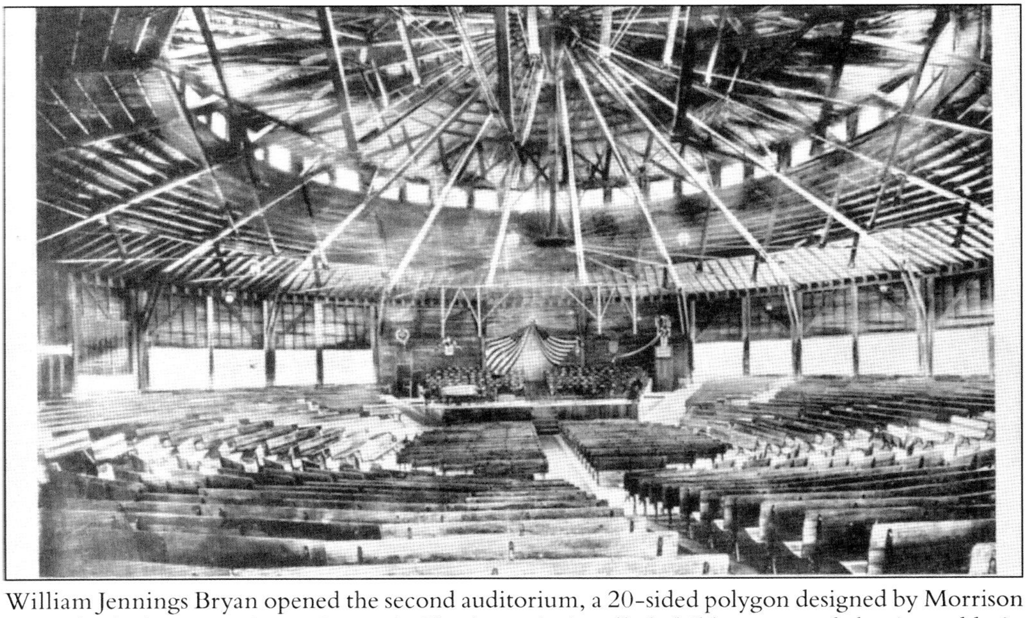

William Jennings Bryan opened the second auditorium, a 20-sided polygon designed by Morrison H. Vail of Chicago. Nigger Porgy (a Charlestonian) pulled children around the Assembly in his goat-drawn red wagon. In the Assembly theater, the audiences stood and cheered when "Dixie" was played. Like most structures in Monteagle, it was the victim of an arsonist on September 11, 1926. Monteagle had more fires than could have been coincidental, and a local man known to be an arsonist was suspected of setting a number of the fires.

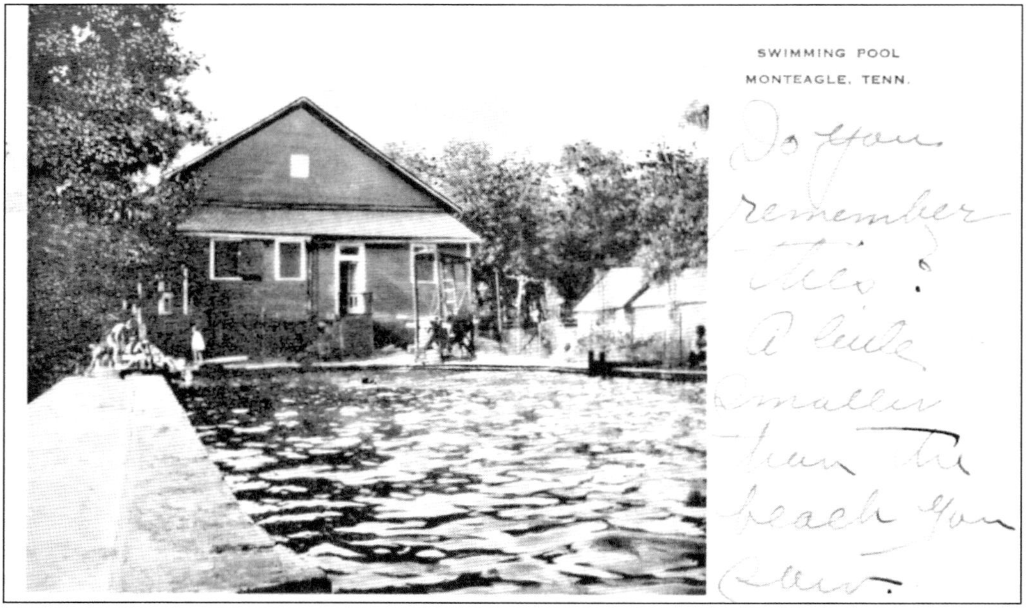

This is an early 1930s view of the Monteagle Swimming Pool that was part of the Assembly. There is a group of children in the left corner of the pool and one child swimming. In front of and at the right corner of the building is a crude wooden diving tower that appears to be about three meters high. This is reputed to be the first in-ground pool in Tennessee. In 1894, Assembly regulations required that bathing suits provided coverage from neck to knees.

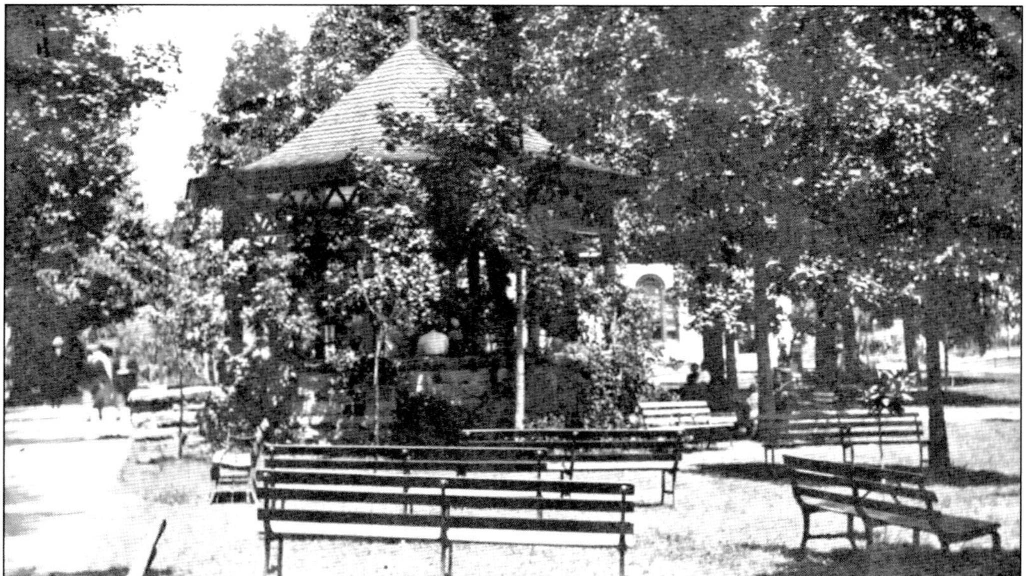

While there were other pavilions in the Assembly, this one is the music pavilion, better known as the Bandstand. The Ladies Association, at a cost of $400, built it from 1897 to 1899. C. Ferguson created several black-and-white, five-by-seven-inch postcards of the "mountain," including one of this bandstand. Another pavilion is rendered in a drawing by architect James Franklin, which is shown in the book *Mountain Voices*.

The postcards of "the Million Dollar View" came from Lacy's Drug Store (the old New York Store) or the Diner. This view is from U.S. 41 looking west toward Nashville. Once you see this view, you understand the name. On the mountain, it is said that, due to inflation, it is now the "Two Million Dollar View."

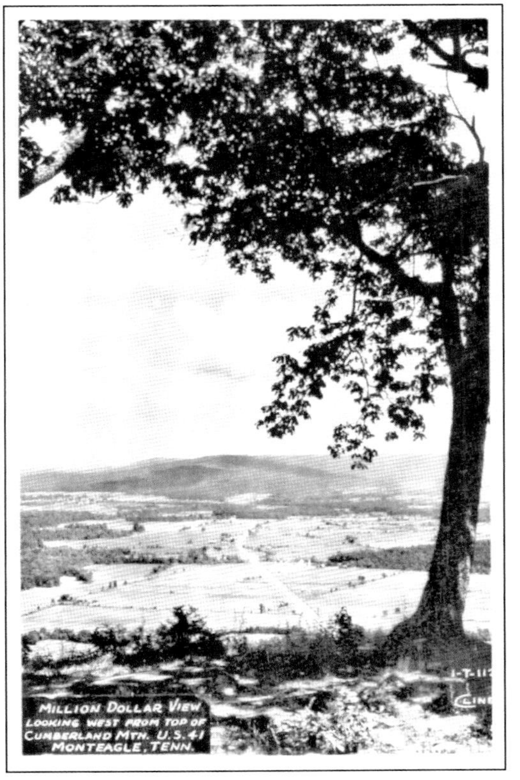

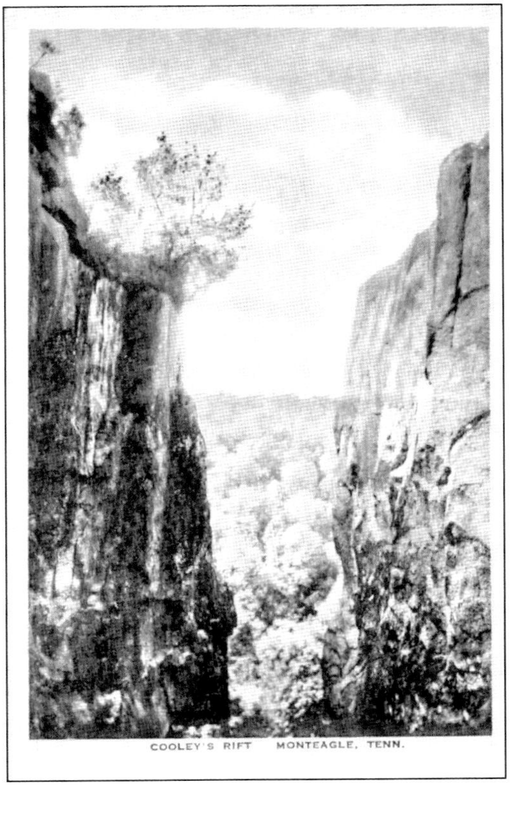

This is Cooley's Rift in the early 1930s. It was named for the secretary of Old Monteagle Hotel Company. The rift was two miles southwest of Monteagle (in Marion County) and intentionally destroyed during the construction of I-24. Winston's Cascade and Ravine are nearby. Lacy & Company of Monteagle, Tennessee, published the card. In 2005, lots here are available for as much as $200,000.

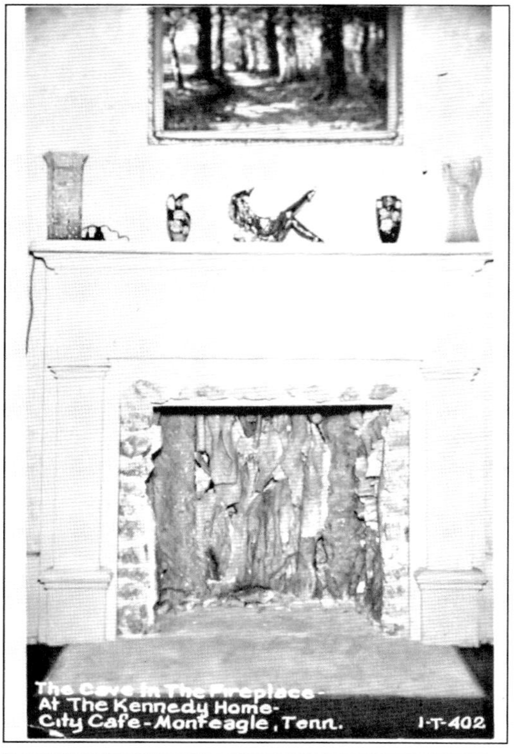

Stalactites or drapery-like cave formations are in the home fireplace of Fred and Ruby Kennedy, owners of the City Café. They had an only child, Fredrick Jr., who died in Monteagle. When Fred died, Ruby married Nathan Hammons and sold the business to Lem Wallace in 1960.

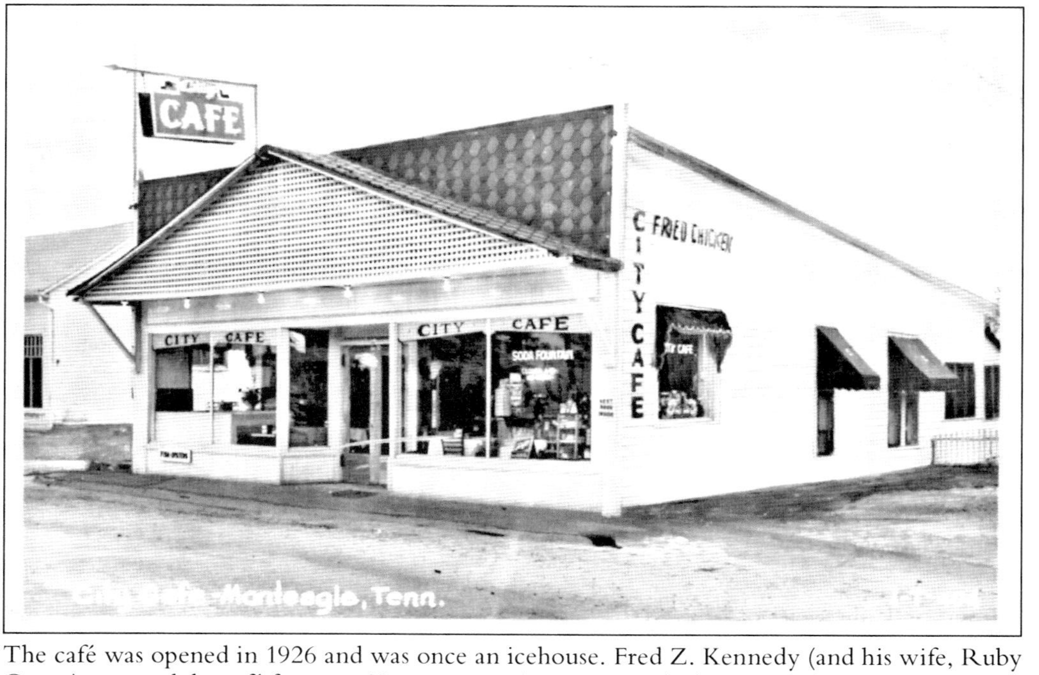

The café was opened in 1926 and was once an icehouse. Fred Z. Kennedy (and his wife, Ruby Coons) operated the café for some 30 years. Margie Guest was the head cook for 30 years. Located near the site of the Dairy Queen and the Clock Doc, it was later torn down. Six stark-naked light bulbs are on across the front porch.

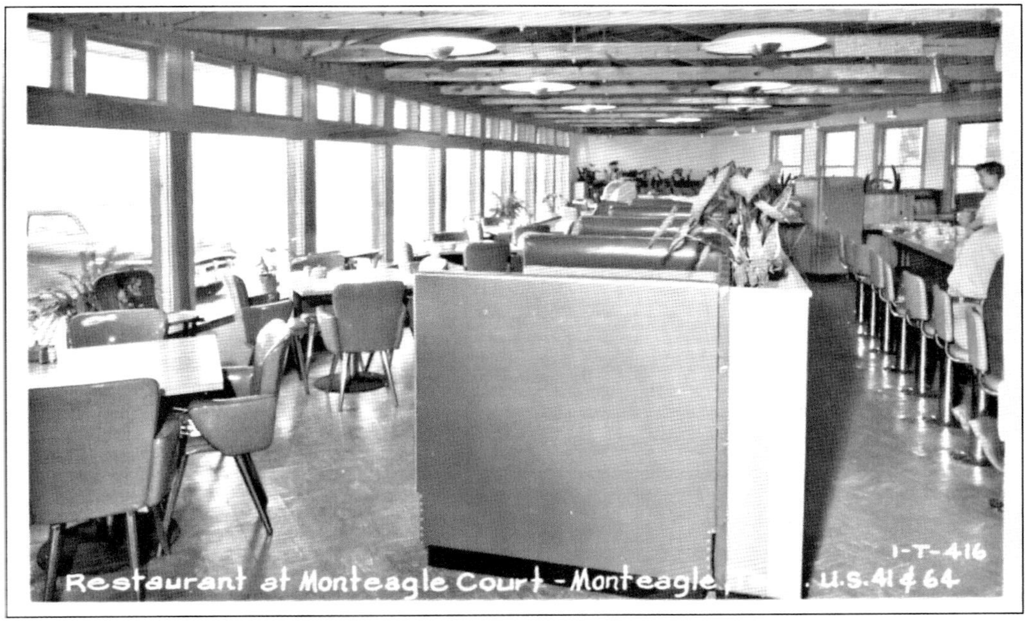

In August 1951, Mr. and Mrs. J. M. Colston opened a new restaurant at their Motor Court. Notice how squeaky clean the place is. Cline photographed this around November 1955—the same time *Life* magazine photographers toured the Moffitt home.

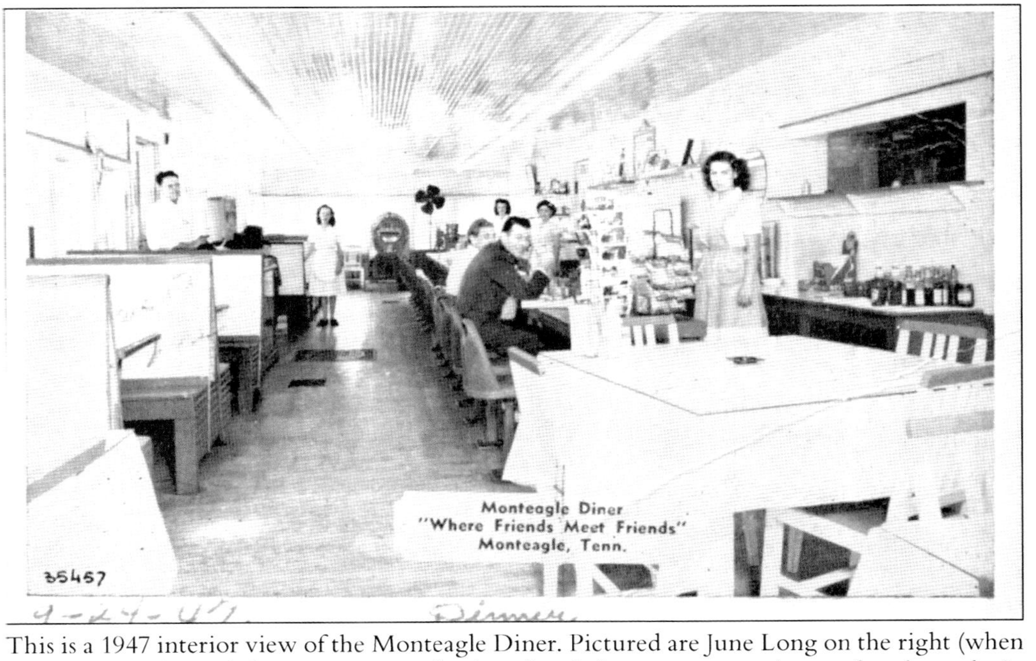

This is a 1947 interior view of the Monteagle Diner. Pictured are June Long on the right (when interviewed, she said the aprons were checkered and she was pregnant); two female cooks in the back; Thelma Thomas (who was a twin to Alma), standing in the aisle; and owner Norman Corn, behind the cash register at left. The man at the counter is thought to be John French. June recalled the night Ernest Tubb and Hank Williams Sr. came in for dinner and sang along with the jukebox.

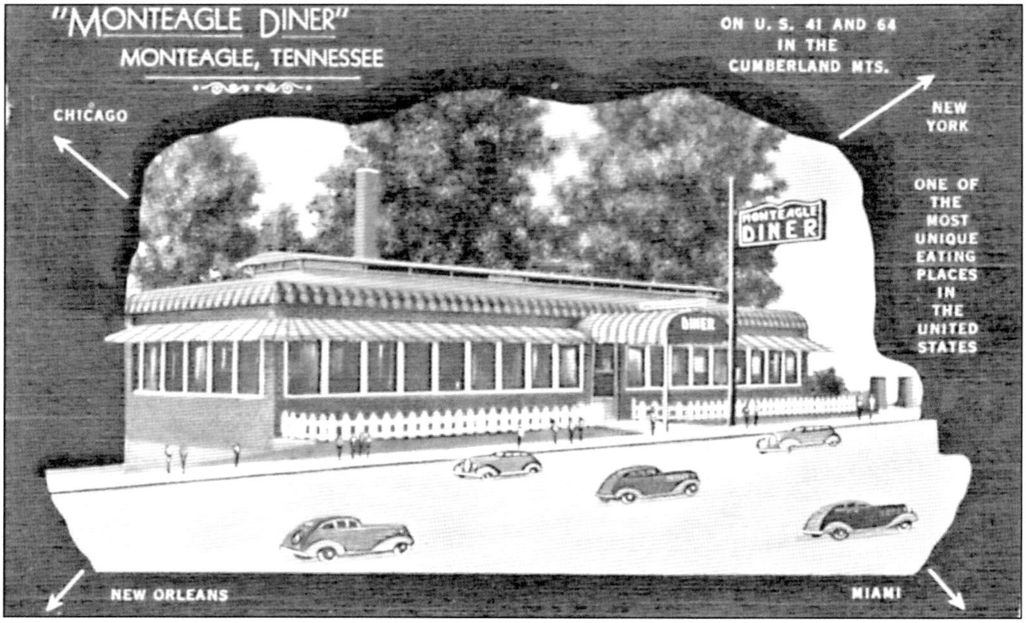

It is thought J. T. Brannon moved this old railroad diner car, one of the more unique eateries in Monteagle, to this Main Street location. Owners included Mr. Clarity, who lived in Maplehurst, Mrs. Lassiter, and Norman H. Corn, all of whom left the Monteagle area. Clara Shoemate had it from the late 1940s until 1953. Harvey and Clarine Thomas and then the Oliver brothers operated it. Bill Lockhart, who owns/operates the "new" Monteagle Diner, sold this one just before it burned in 1984.

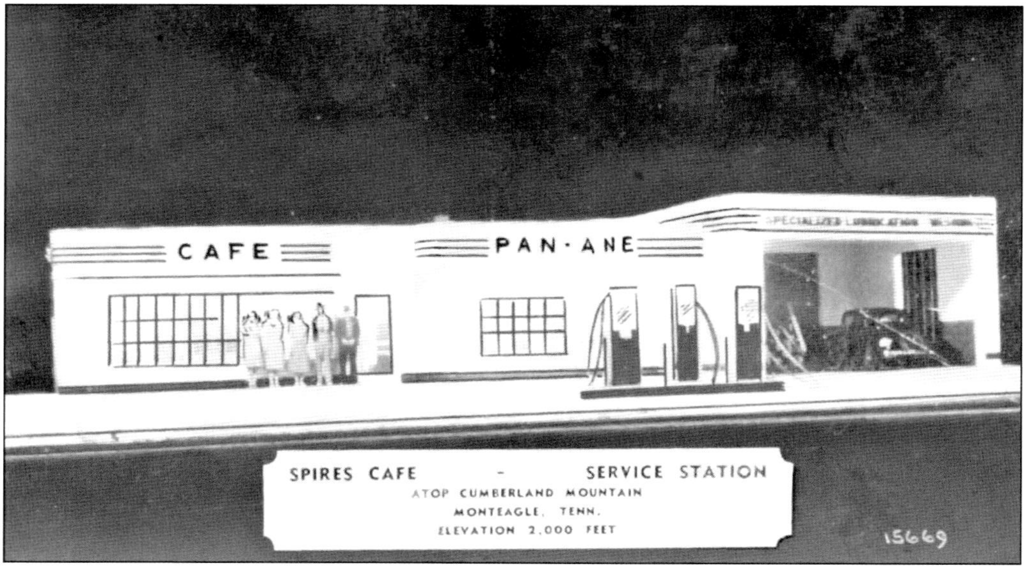

Known as the Pan Am Restaurant or Spires Café, this business was located across the street from where Papa Ron's is today. Bill Meeks found employment here in the 1940s. Preacher Speegle and then Glenn and Evelyn Hassler owned it. In 1951, there were three other filling stations in Monteagle. They were J. R. Gosset Pure Oil, Monteagle Shell Station, and Speegle Brothers Esso.

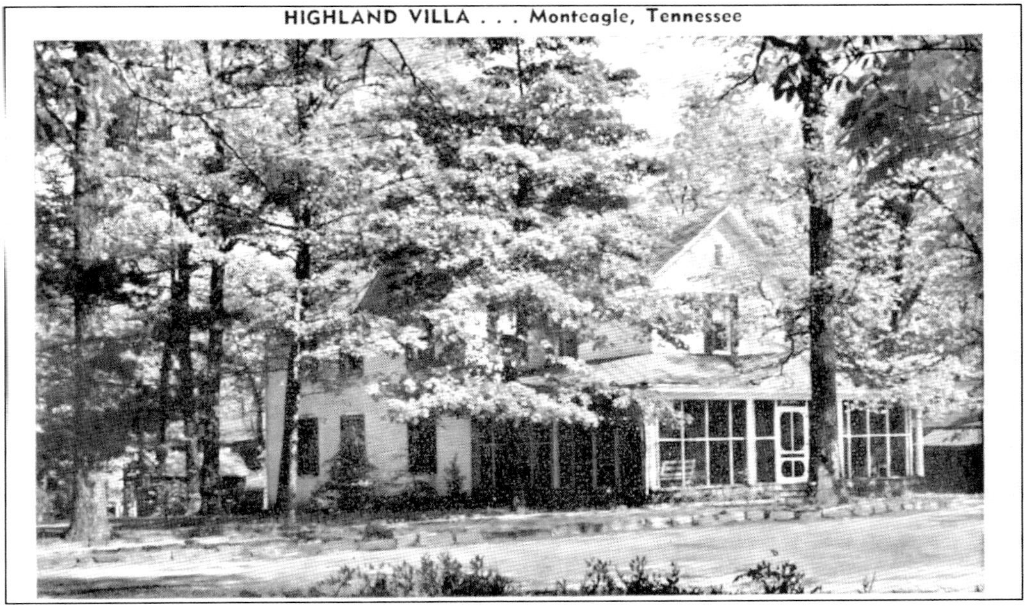

Highland Villa #104 is on the Assembly grounds fronting Tulip Avenue. It was the year-round home of Mrs. Wayne Jervis, built *c.* 1892 by W. B. Ward. Passed on to Kate Eastman in 1900, it was acquired by Mrs. W. W. Carre in 1905 and christened Villa Carre. In 1920, it became the property of Beulah Ward McCloud, who made it a boardinghouse. Mrs. M. B. Lake (soon to become Mrs. Fitzgerald Hall) purchased it in 1940.

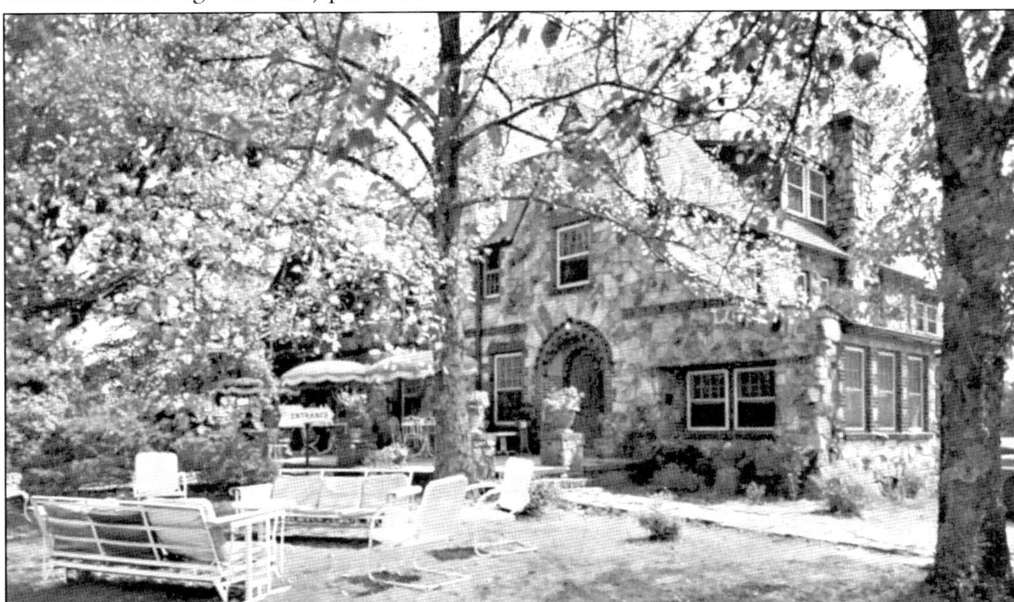

Around 1912, the Claramont was home to Irene Maybe (brother Carl had a home out back) and later home to Hugh Barnes, a furniture maker. It then became the Claramont Restaurant, and today it is High Point. Rumors abound of escape hatches, underground tunnels, and floors complete with a lining of sand between each to prevent the penetration of bullets. High Point is reputed to have been financed by Al Capone for his mountain girlfriend, who was also his bookkeeper.

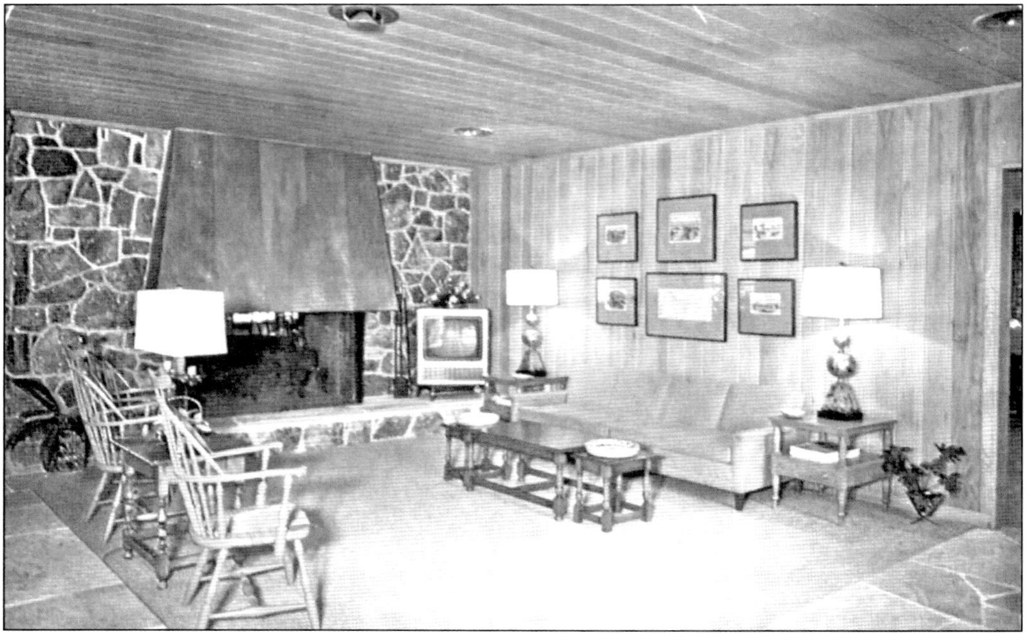

William Turner, noted historian and museum curator of Tracy City, helped build the Claramont Restaurant and Sewanee Inn.

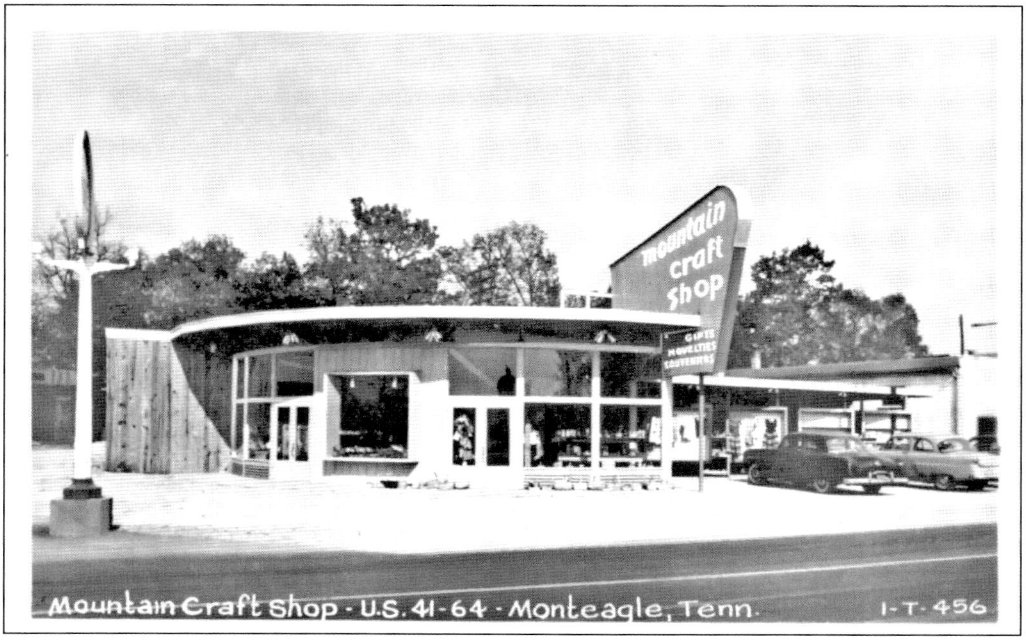

Located where Iva Michelle Russell has opened the "new Tubby's," this was built and owned by Grady Crownover. The original Tubby's was Tubby's in name only. His wife, Iva Overtuf Wallace, a former member of the Women's Army Corps, ran it. When her niece Ruby was shot in the face with a shotgun, Iva took her in, cared for her, and employed her.

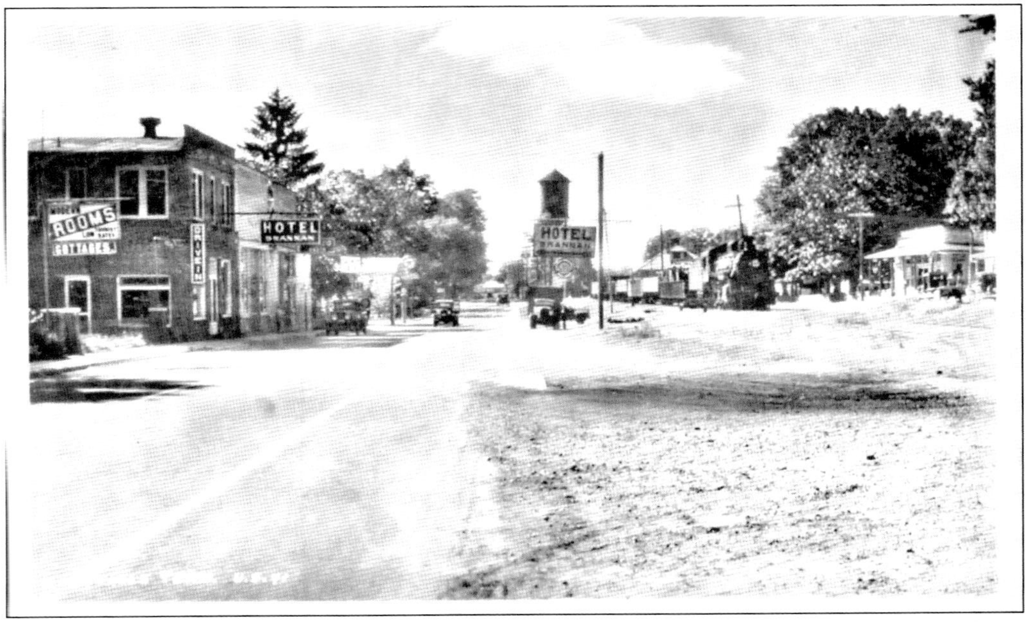

On the left is the Brannan Hotel. Just beyond it is the barbershop. The water tower by the depot is on the left, and there is a train waiting to leave.

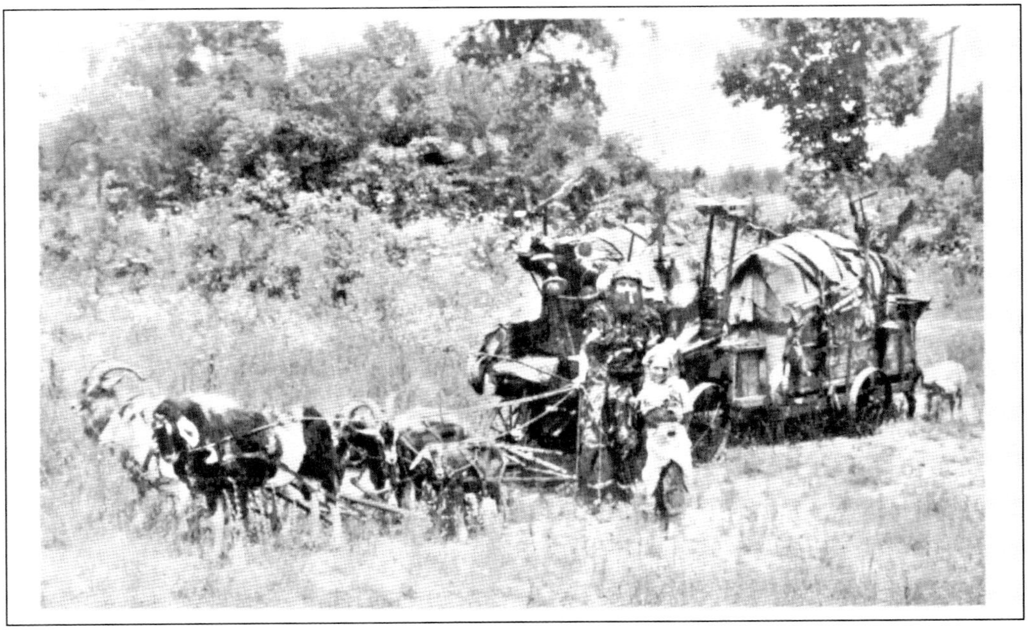

This is Charles "Chess" McCartney and his goat caravan. His son accompanied him as he meandered all over the country, beginning in 1936. This was taken, as it says on the back, in "Mt. Eagle [*sic*]" in 1949. Based on the size of the child, the date is likely incorrect also. In his 80s, he became infatuated with soap star Morgan Fairchild and went to Los Angeles to woo her but was beaten and robbed before he could meet her. Returning to Tennessee, he was beaten savagely by someone who cut the throats of his goats, and he ended up in a Georgia nursing home. He was in his 90s when he died in 1998.

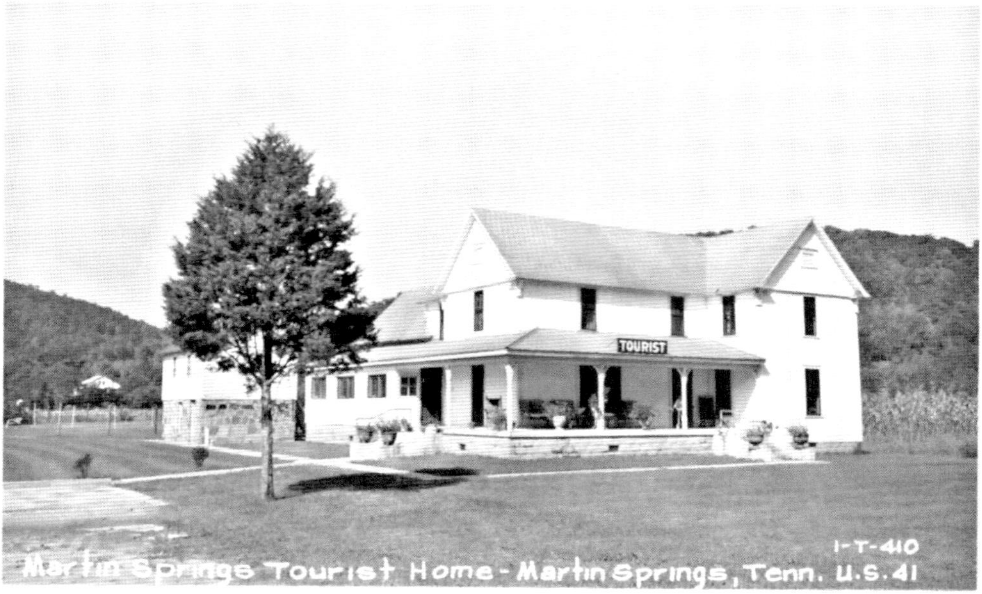

Martin Springs, once known as Dove, Tennessee, was a popular vacation/picnic spot. This is where Battle Creek originates. This tourist home, owned by Miss Ann Martin and shared with her widowed sister, was located near Martin Springs (there were actually three Martin Springs) and Cave. Blind cave trout once lived in the cave.

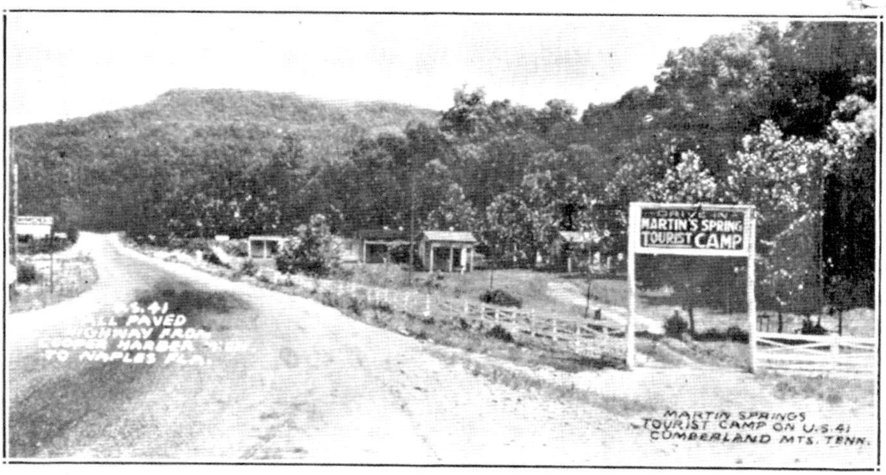

MARTIN SPRING TOURIST CAMP
In the Heart of the Cumberland Mountains, Martin Springs, Tenn.

This card may date to the 1920s. It says, "U.S. 41 all paved highway from Cooper Harber [*sic*] Mich. to Naples Fla." The sign down the road on the left says, "Rooms Meals Post Office." There is an Esso gasoline sign across the road from the tourist camp where a store/service station once stood. Bathing in and drinking the spring water had medicinal value, and for years, the spring was a magnet for those seeking "rest cures."

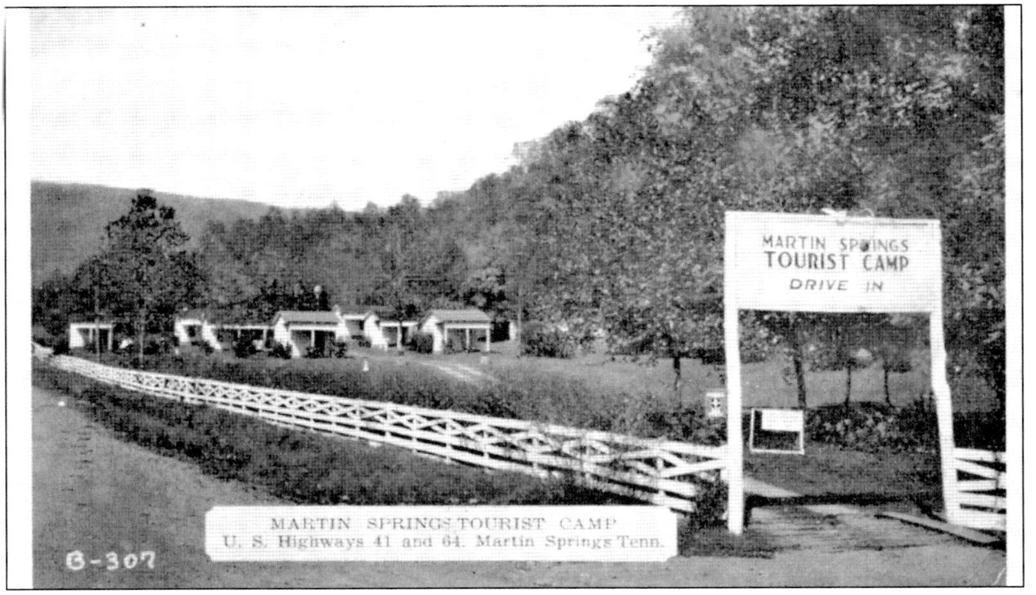

Big Bill Martin and his son Tom held influential positions with the highway department but could not influence the path of I-24 that would divide their property. The Martins were never compensated fairly for the loss/division of their land. Most of this land was transferred/sold to the Tate clan and reacquired by the Martins. This is the scene of Civil War battles, and it is a part of the Cherokee Trail of Tears.

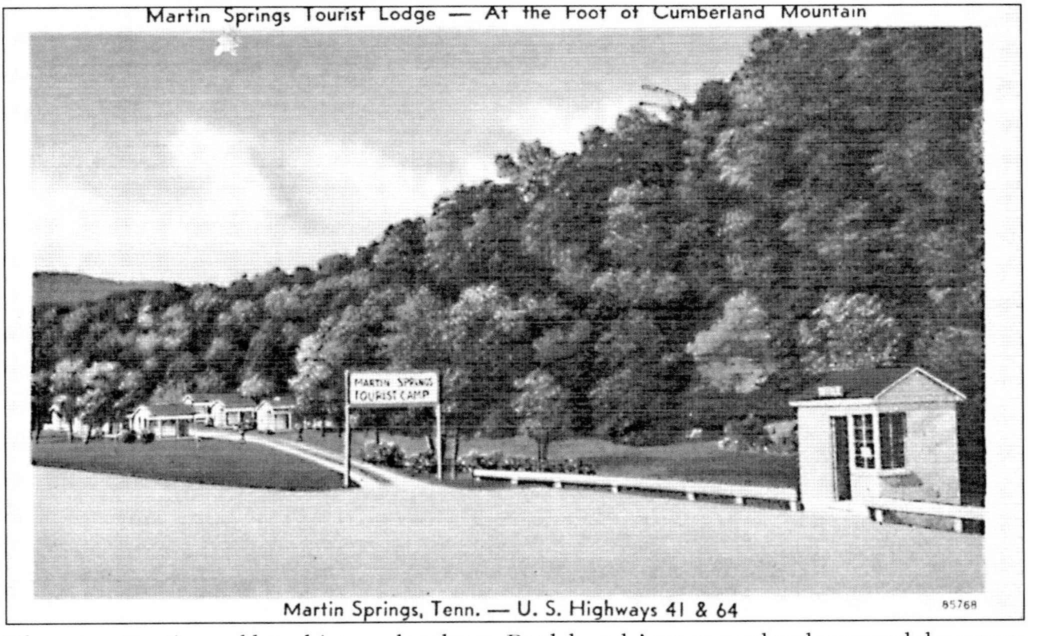

Thornton Martin, and later his two daughters, Beulah and Ann, owned and operated the resort. It was in this area in the 1930s when the Kelly family (who still reside there) hid Al Capone out for a week. Capone's car had broken down with a load of whiskey bound for Miami. This card was created by Walter M. Cline Jr., who, with his mother, took over his father's photography business in 1941, shortly after his father accidentally shot and killed himself.

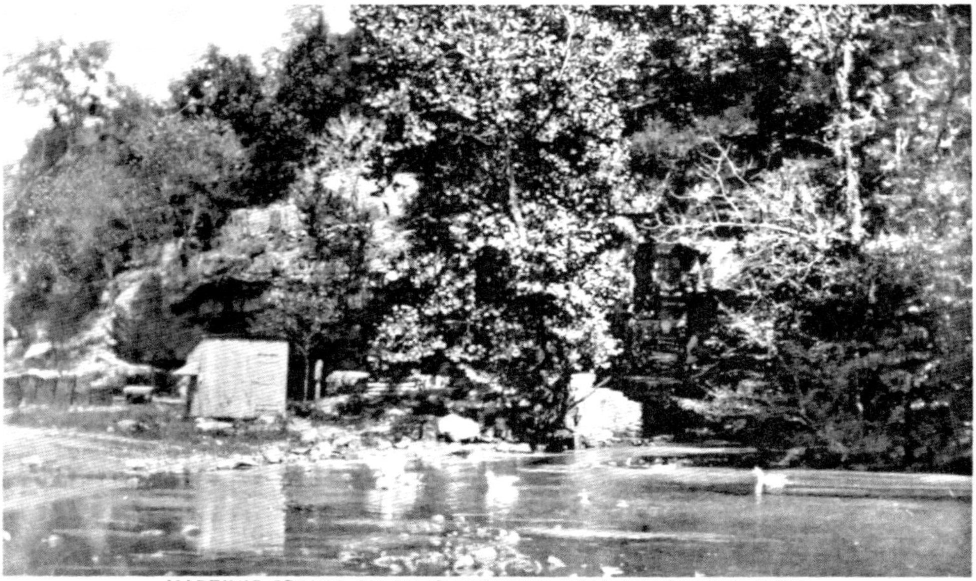

MARTIN'S SPRING ON DIXIE HIGHWAY NEAR MONTEAGLE, TENN.

This card, published by New York Stores, of Monteagle, Tennessee, is different for two reasons. It identifies the spring as being near Monteagle and as being on the Dixie Highway (which is what most locals called U.S. 41 into the 1950s). There are wooden structures in this image not seen in the others. There are also swans on the creek.

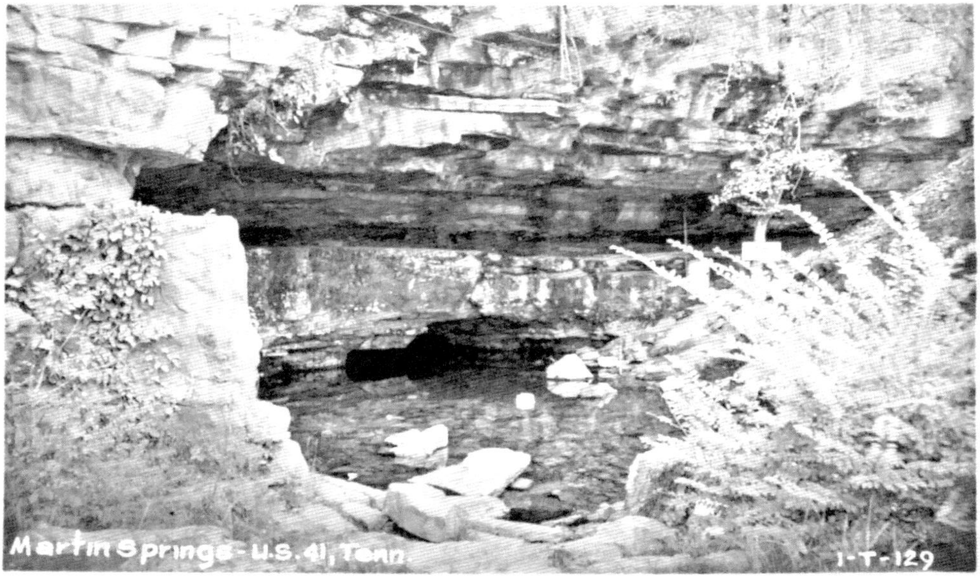

This is the only close-up view of the cave's mouth the author found on a postcard. Signs say, "Help us keep the spring clean" and "No wading in the spring." Wires strung overhead suggest the cave was electrified. There is a pump positioned in back of the sign on the right. One card's message says, "This is where the fan belt broke—got to Hopkinsville 10:30 PM no place to sleep. What a day."

Five

Whitwell and Sequatchie

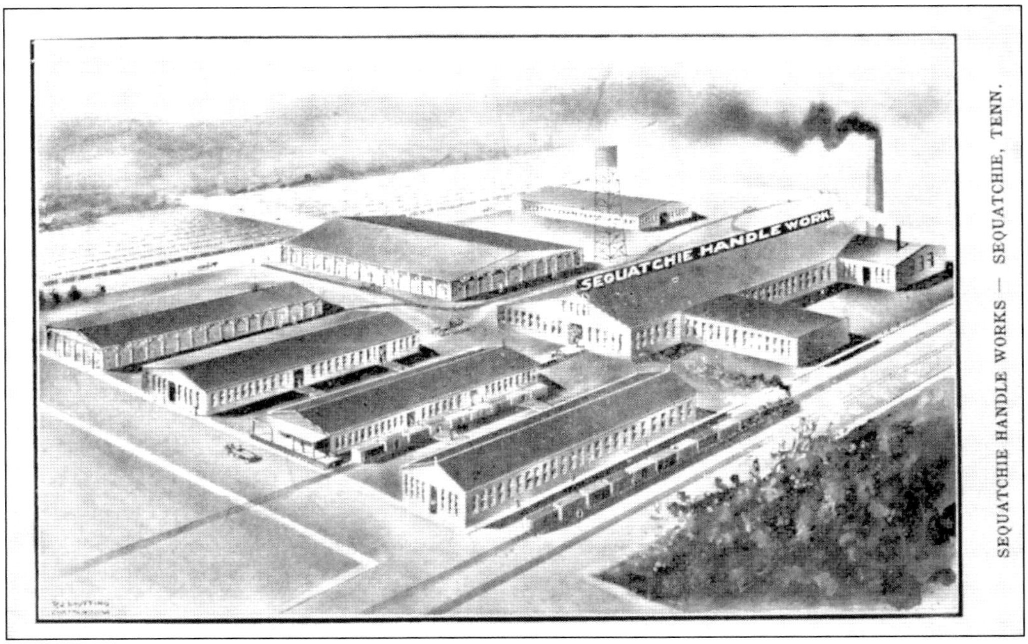

Steve Grimes, Melissa Condra, Jack Womack, and approximately 27 others (8 of whom are females) are employed here today. Several years ago, Sonny Rogers and Clara Levan worked here. The volunteer fire department's location immediately outside the factory gates was more than coincidental. In 2005, the factory was sold to Seymour Manufacturing.

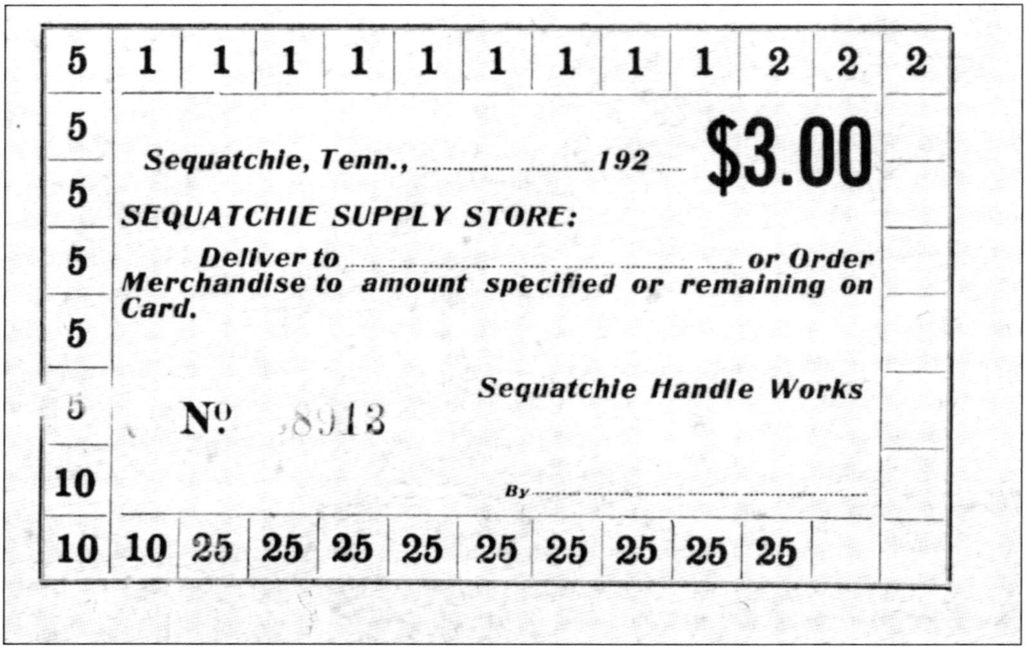
5 1 1 1 1 1 1 1 1 1 2 2 2

5 5 5 5 5 5 10

Sequatchie, Tenn., ... 192 ....

$3.00

SEQUATCHIE SUPPLY STORE:

Deliver to .... or Order Merchandise to amount specified or remaining on Card.

Sequatchie Handle Works

No. 8913

By ....

10 10 25 25 25 25 25 25 25 25 25

Glancy Sherman arrived in Sequatchie in 1889, built a company store in 1890, and followed with the plant in 1899. The Sherman family ran the factory until 1939, when they sold it to O. P. Link. The factory flooded in 1963. The Sherman mansion is now the home of Clifford Layne. Tru-Serve and Ace are the factory's big customers today.

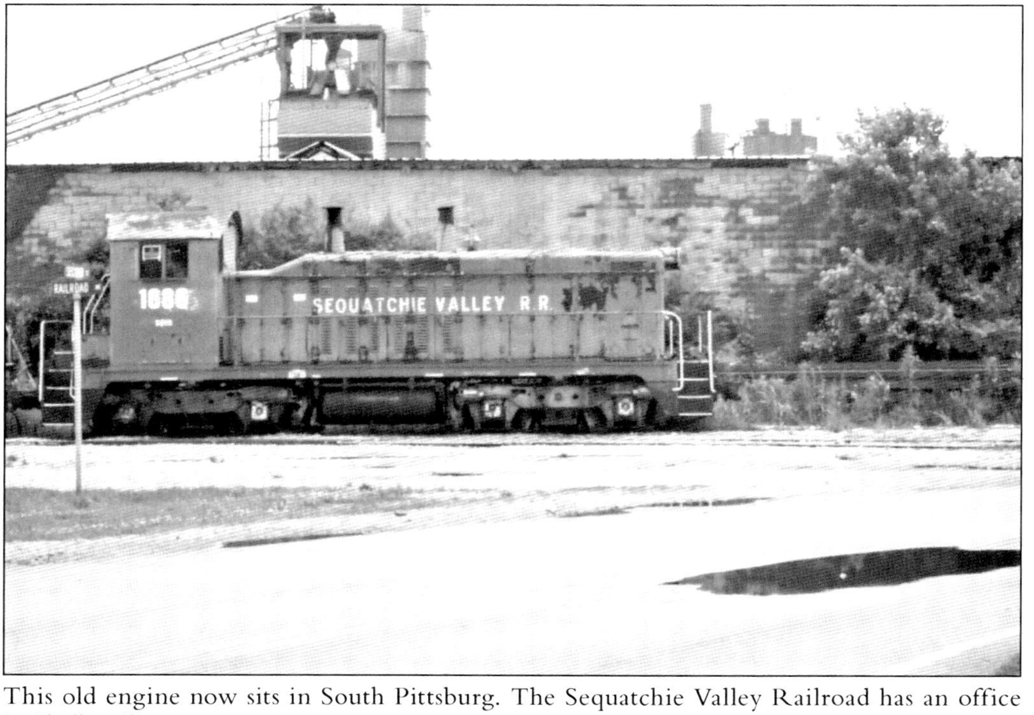

This old engine now sits in South Pittsburg. The Sequatchie Valley Railroad has an office in Shelbyville.

Sequachee Valley Coal and Iron Company.

49 Shares.

I hereby constitute and appoint THOMAS H. HILL my proxy (with power of substitution) for me, and in my name, to vote at the annual meeting of the Stockholders of the Sequachee Valley Coal and Iron Company, to be held on Monday, March 4th, 1895, at the Marion House in Sequachee, Tenn., (or any adjournment thereof,) for Directors, and on all other business which may properly and legally come before said meeting.

Eugene A. Stowell

Note the spelling of Sequatchie. Eugene A. Stowell is a stockholder in the Sequatchie Valley Coal and Iron Company and owns 49 shares.

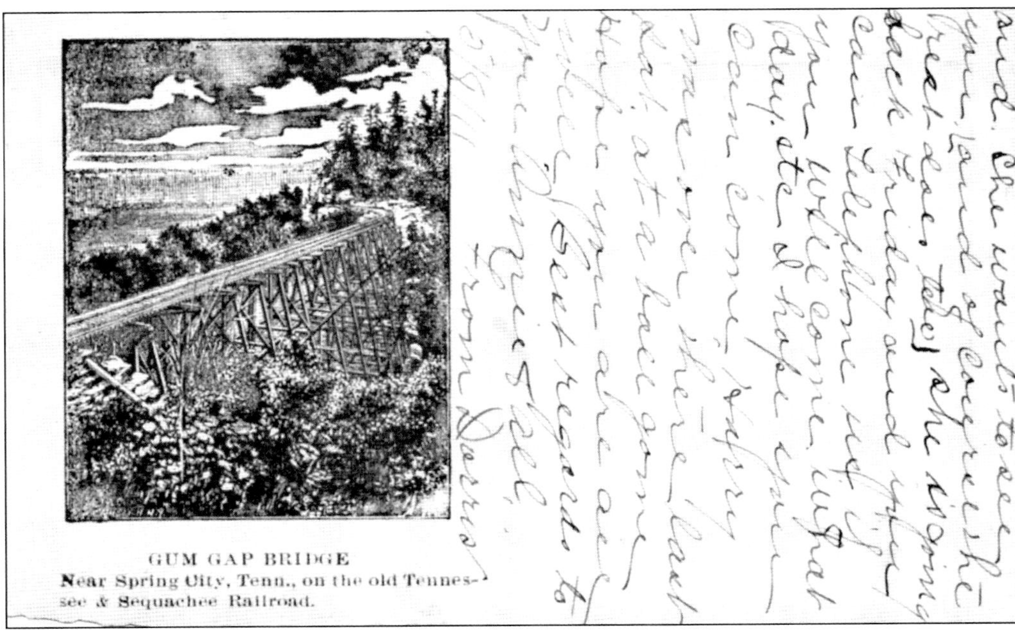

This is a rare old Private Mailing Card (PMC) of Gum Gap Bridge near Spring City, Tennessee. PMCs were authorized by Congress on May 19, 1898. In the early 1900s, this was referred to as the "old" Tennessee & Sequatchie Railroad. Today, for the most part, the trains are gone from the valley, as are the American Indians, the bears, and the panthers—and soon, I suppose, we will all be gone, too.

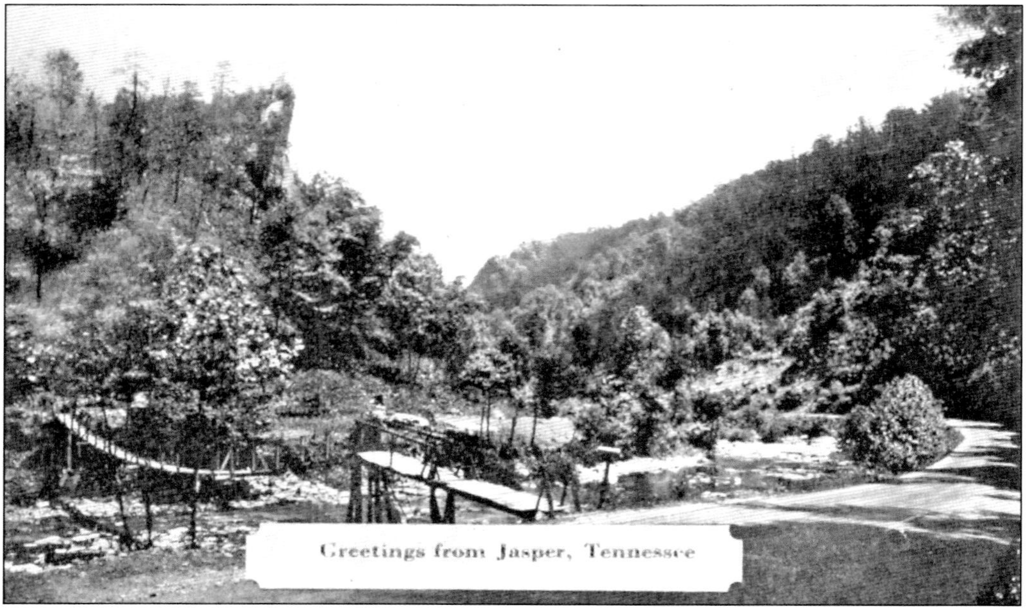

This view is believed to be of the Girl Scout camp at Camp Glancy. If it is, the water was unusually low. Glancy Sherman, who owned Sequatchie Handle Factory, donated the 50 acres for Camp Glancy, build the Glancy Sherman "mansion," and married Bertha Tower of Chattanooga. He died in 1967 in Sequatchie at age 73. Bertha lived until she was 94. They never had children, and she left a considerable fortune to her lifelong maid, who was a dwarf.

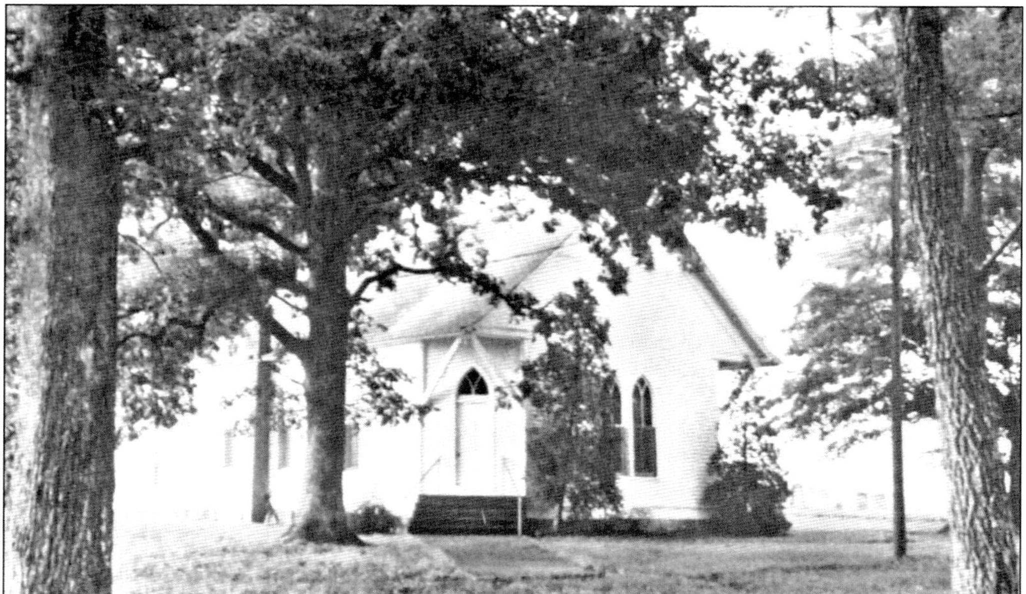

Originally built from 1888 to 1890, Oak Grove Church has a hallowed burial ground nearby. The small white clapboard sanctuary had two unique corner entrances and a worshipful interior. It was known by its congregation as the "Little Church in the Wildwood." This Cumberland Presbyterian Church burned on October 21, 1986, but was rebuilt. Go to Crossroads and turn south on East Valley Road to find this beautiful church.

One of the older cards of this area, this card was provided by Mitch Kinder of Cleveland, Tennessee.

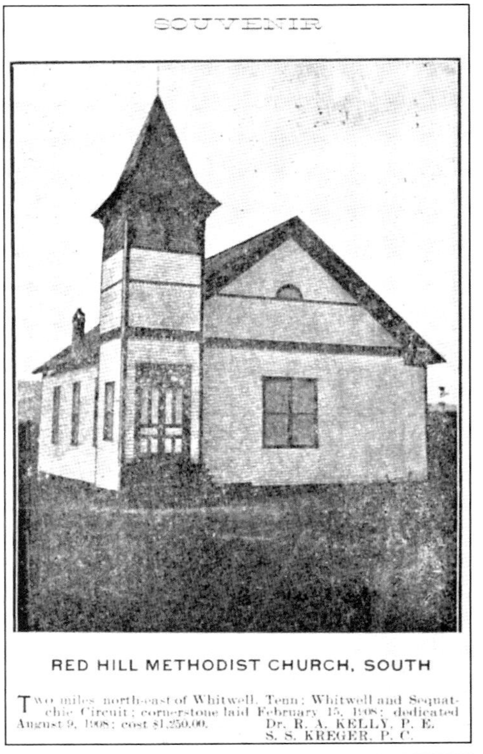

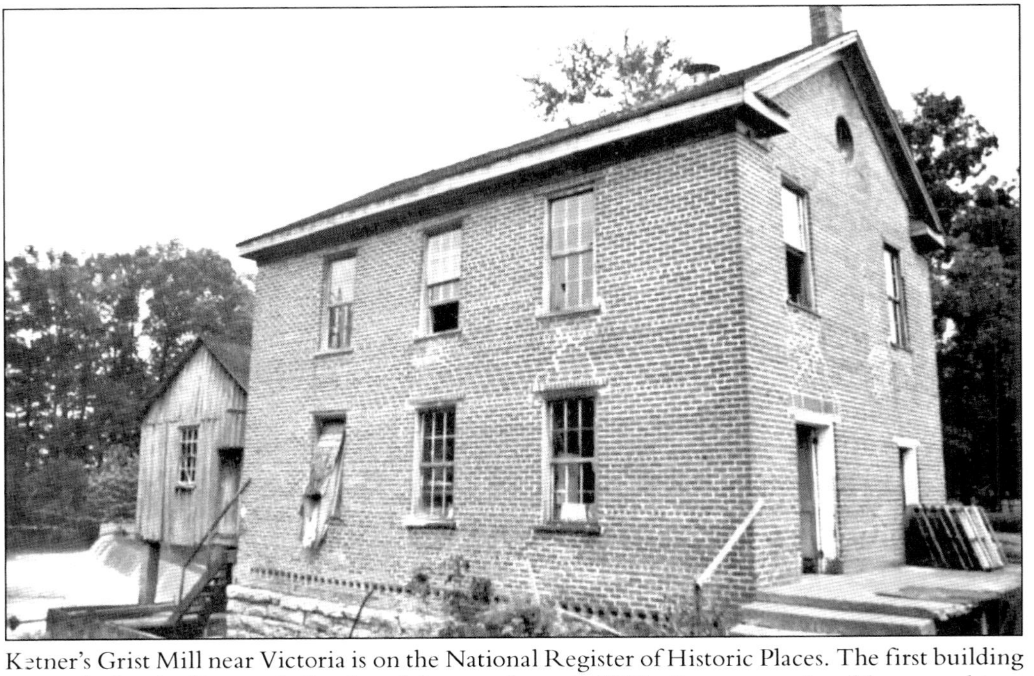

Ketner's Grist Mill near Victoria is on the National Register of Historic Places. The first building was at the head of Looney's Creek and dates to the early 1800s. Its construction, like everything, was interrupted by the Civil War. The brick for the building was handmade one at a time. It has been featured in *Southern Living* magazine. In 1976, they constructed a new dam.

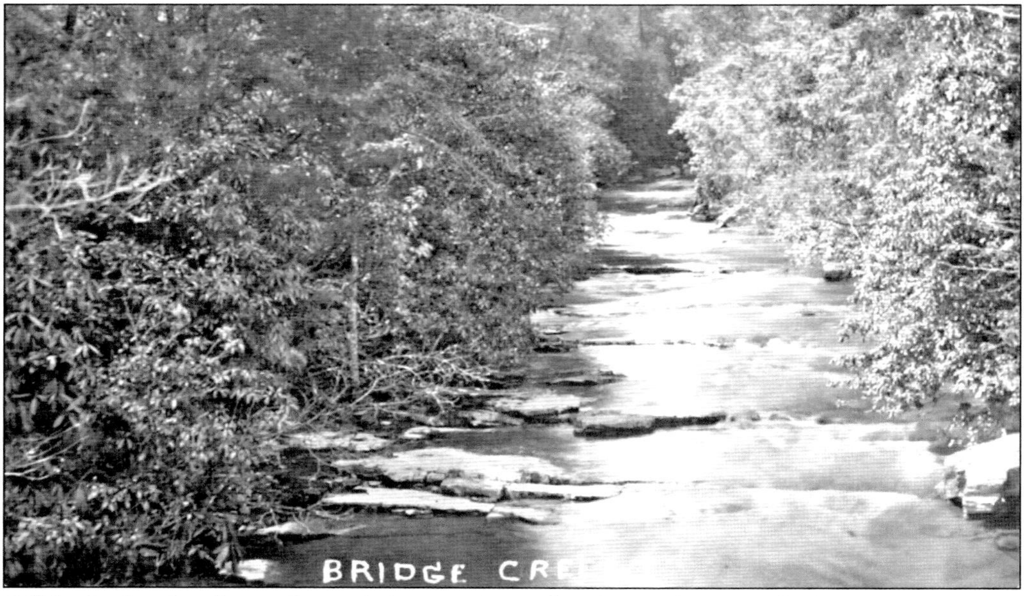

Off the Pocket Road, near Bryant's Grocery (now closed), is Kilgore-Goforth Road. Down that road you will find this pristine creek, a dam, and the remnants of a mill. This is one of several early RPPC created by Bottomlee, a Whitwell photographer. In 1873, Thomas Whitwell came from Wales to establish a coal/iron industry here. In 1878, Victoria mines opened and brought in new families. Tennessee Products closed those mines in 1962, bringing an end to the coal-mining era.

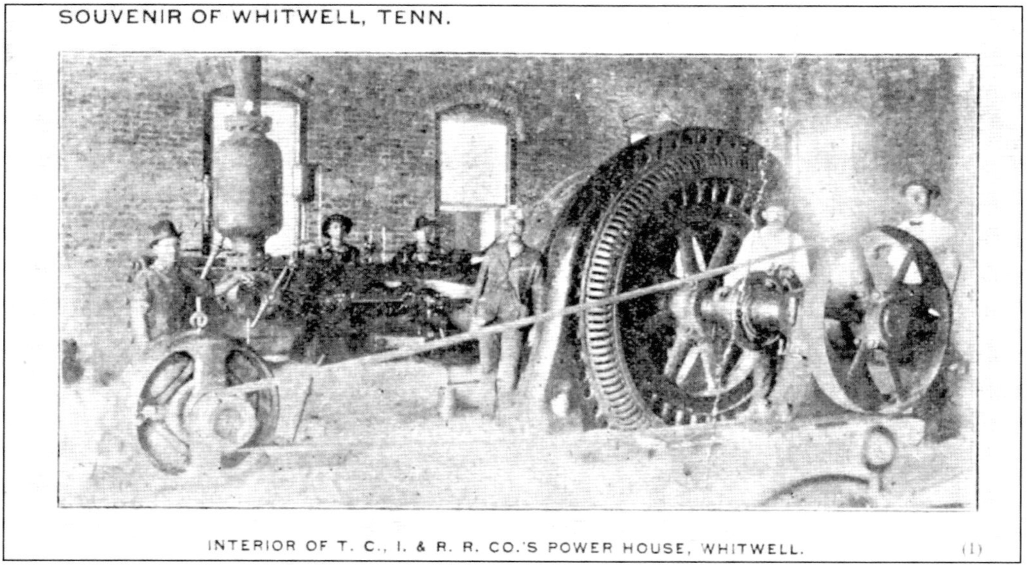

This is a view inside the Tennessee Coal, Iron and Railroad (TCI & RR) Company's powerhouse. Whitwell's story is the story of coal—and mine operators exercised absolute dominion over the towns they built. They had company stores, coal camp schools, and homes owned by the company. This card was postmarked in Whitwell in 1911 and was from Tassie Kelly to Ida Barker in care of Earlie Kelly, all of Whitwell. The men, from left to right, are thought to be Oscar Algood, Jimmie Dixon, Russell Duncan, unidentified, J. D. Morrison, and unidentified.

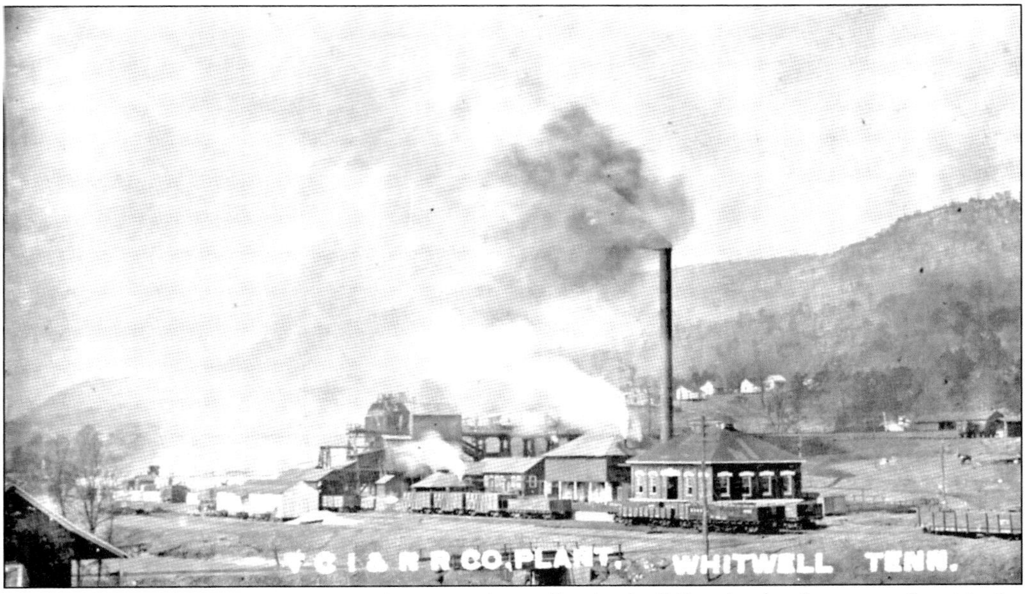

This is the TCI & RR Company plant in Whitwell. The building in the foreground, with the tall chimney, is the same building shown in the previous image. On the left is a chute and tipple. In 1928, a new steel tipple was brought in from Bay View, Alabama (also on the TCI & RR), at the cost of $30,000. It had the capability of screening to four grades of coal. The predecessor of TCI was the Sewanee Mining Company. Eventually TCI built a bathhouse, ran lighting into the mines, and provided drinking water for miners.

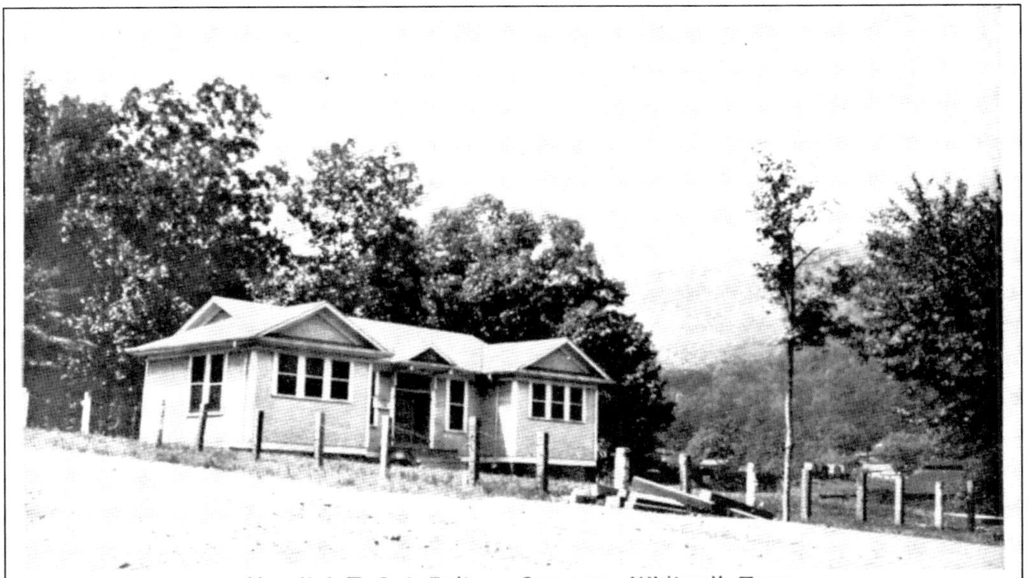

Hospital, T. C. I. Railway Company, Whitwell, Tenn.

TCI once had an office in Jasper. All that is left of that empire now is an office in Kentucky dedicated to helping victims of black lung. TCI turned properties over to Black Diamond Company in 1929 and announced the change of command by lengthy blasts on the company's whistle. Over the years, there were numerous deaths from mining accidents in the area. Accidents and fatalities were accepted as the cost of doing business.

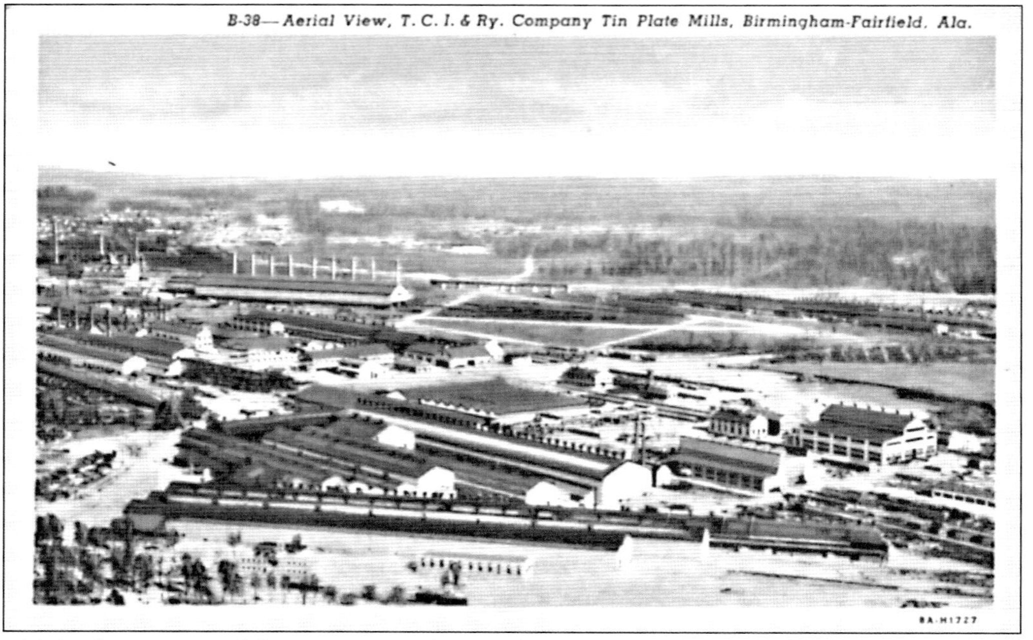

This is a linen postcard showing an aerial view of TCI & RR Company's Birmingham/Fairfield tin plate mill. This huge cluster of 11 buildings includes the cold reduction, tinning, inspection, and warehousing departments. When Whitwell got a cold, this place sneezed.

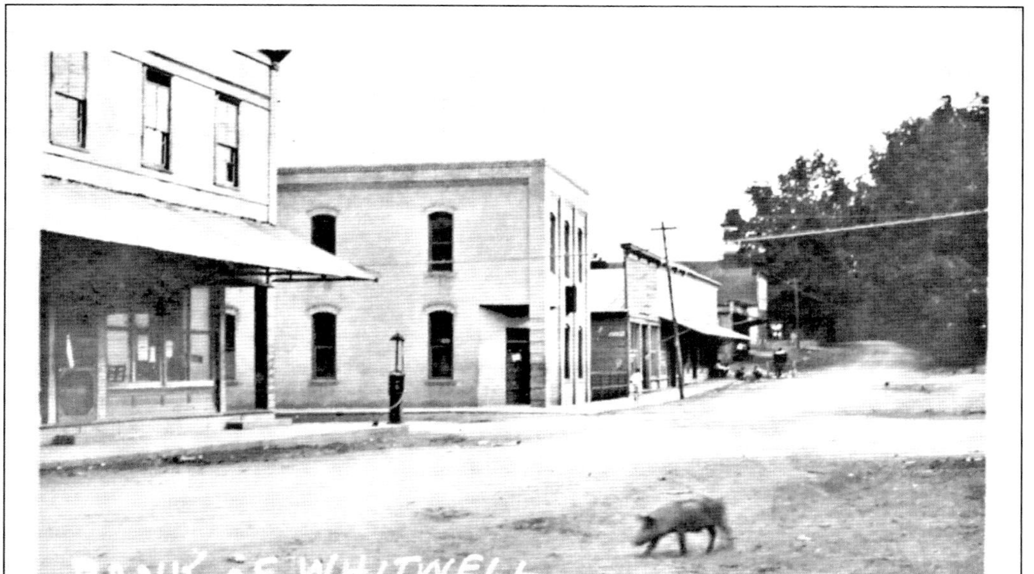

There is a group of black men sitting/squatting at the far end of the street by a horseless buggy. A close examination of the card also shows chickens down the street to the right and, of course, the pig in the foreground. The bank, constructed in 1906, is the two-story building at center. The apparatus on the sidewalk is a kerosene pump. Formerly known as Cheekville (changed to Whitwell in 1887), it, like Tracy City, had numerous mines and coke ovens.

Six

Surrounding Communities

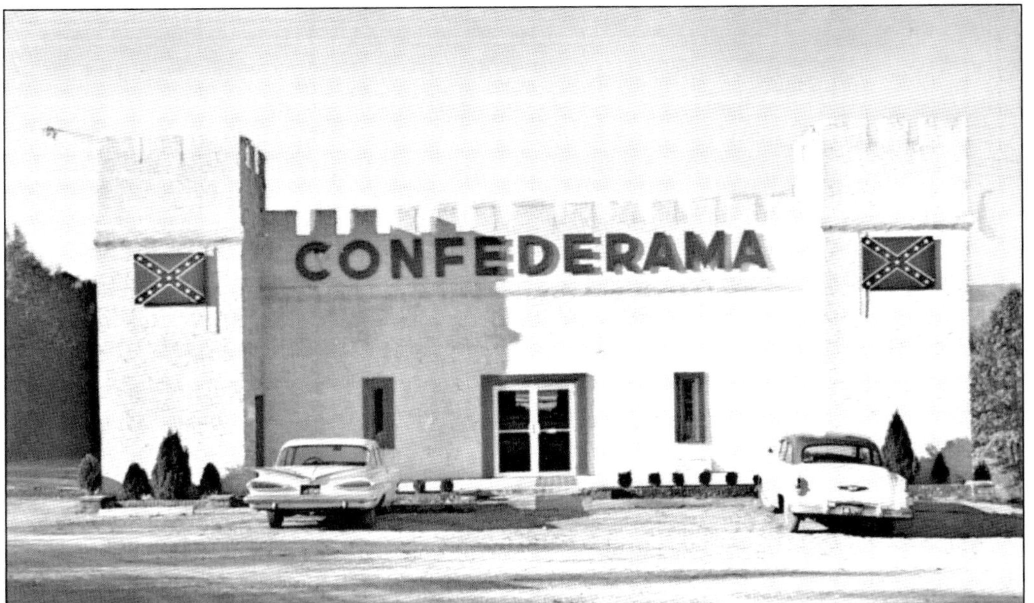

Chattanooga is, of course, the largest neighbor to Marion County, and most folks living in Marion County visit the city frequently. The Confederama included 650 flashing lights, 5,000 soldiers, cannons puffing real smoke, and a step-by-step explanation of local Civil War battles.

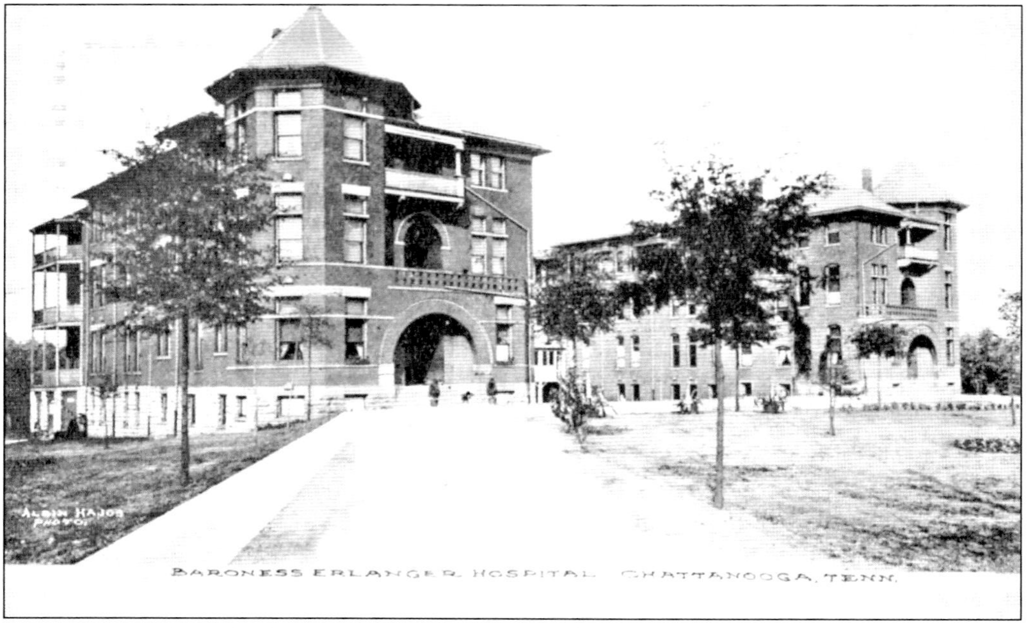

In September 1957, Mrs. Martha Thorpe Amonette of Tracy City completed her nurse's training here. It is doubtful that there is a family in Marion County who has not had a relationship of some sort with Erlanger Hospital.

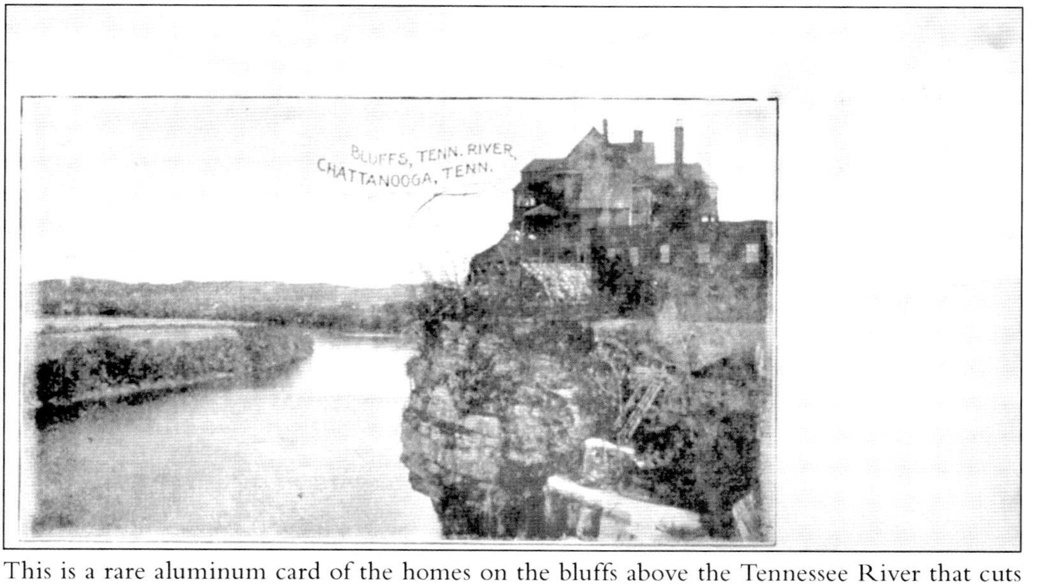

This is a rare aluminum card of the homes on the bluffs above the Tennessee River that cuts through Chattanooga.

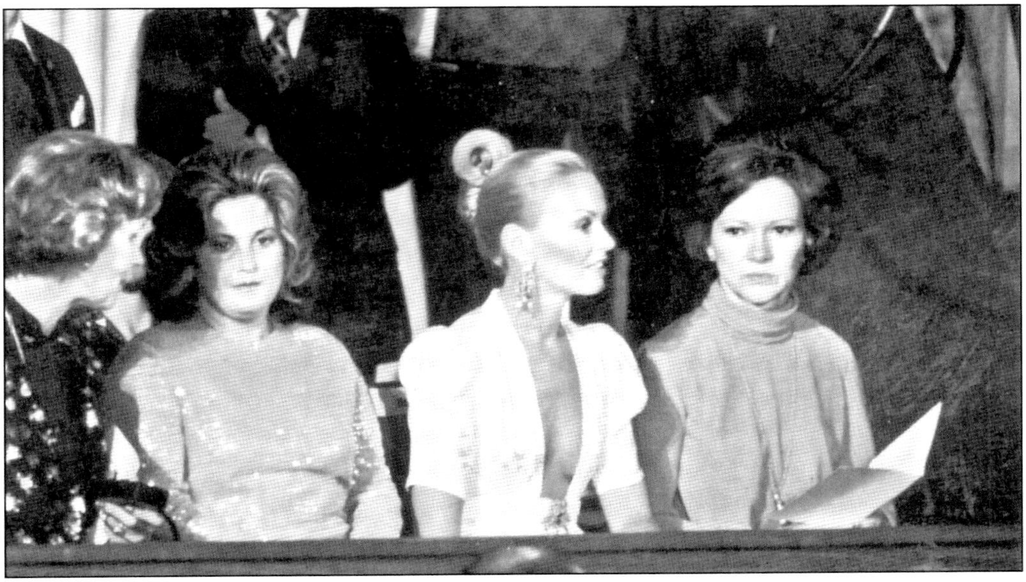

Tennessee claims three presidents: Jackson, Andrew Johnson, and Polk. Of these only one, Jackson, is known to have visited Marion County. Many do not think of Marion County as being bordered by the state of Georgia, but it is. That neighbor claims a single president, Jimmy Carter. In this card, Mrs. Carter is noticeably bothered by the dress Mrs. Omar Torrijos is wearing. Torrijos and Carter signed a treaty returning the Panama Canal to Panama.

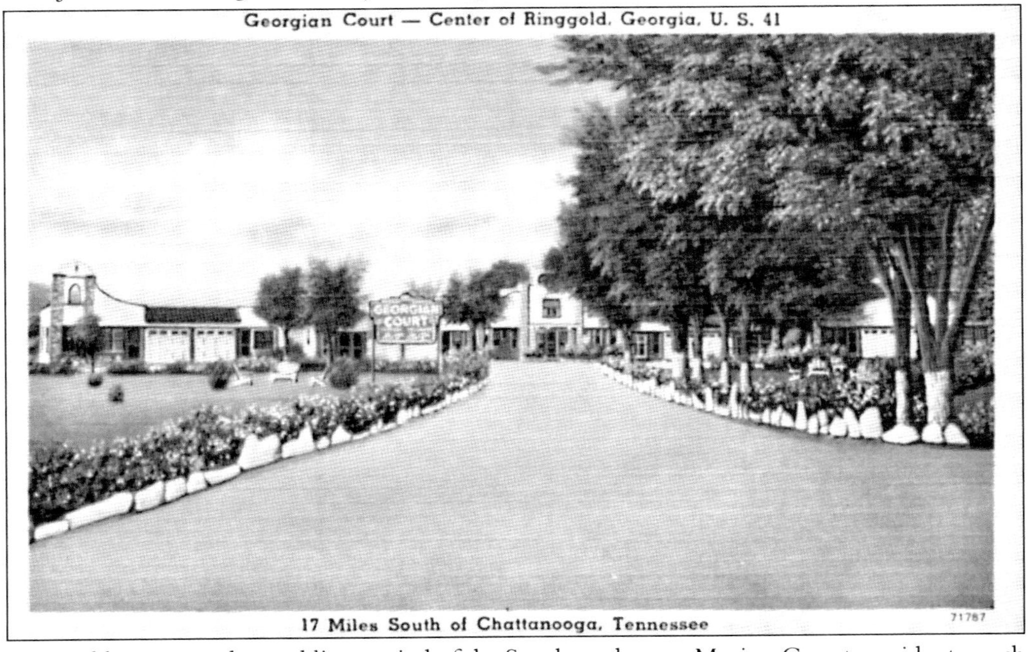

Ringgold was once the wedding capital of the South, and many Marion County residents, such as Junior Lewis and Peggy Morrison, were married there. Large numbers of GIs were married there before the soldiers rushed off to World War II duties. Dolly Parton was married there, and Mayor Billy Simpson's mother was born in the Ringgold Jail (his grandfather was sheriff of Catoosa County).

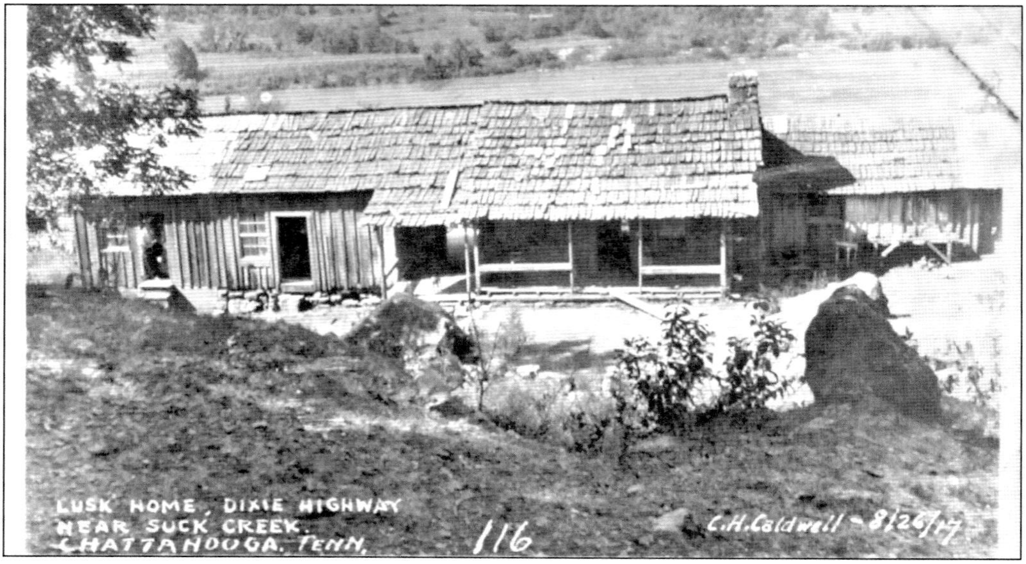

Horace Burnette's mother was a Lusk from Suck Creek. U.S. 41 was referred to as the Dixie Highway for decades. Suck Creek Mountain is inside the boundaries of Prentice Cooper State Park in Marion County. There is also a Lusk Cemetery there. C. H. Caldwell took this photograph of this beautiful old home on August, 26, 1917, and Photographic Appliances Corporation of Minneapolis, Minnesota, printed it. John Lusk provided the large cut stones that lined the highway up Suck Creek Mountain.

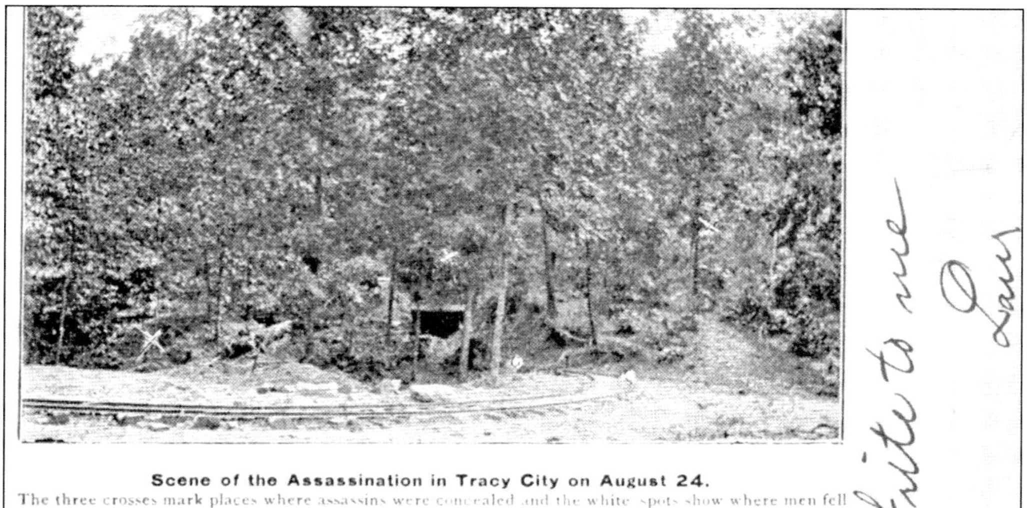

Tracy City is just across the Grundy County line, but most people in Marion County don't think of it that way. Many locals drop the "City" and just say, "Tracy." In 1905, the federal government sent prisoners from Nashville to man the Tracy City (Reed Hill) mines. The miners lay in wait, killed two marshals, put the prisoners back on the train, and sent the train and prisoners back to Nashville. The Xs show where the armed miners were and the white spots where the marshals were killed. Dr. William Carol Barnes of Tracy City treated many of those shot or injured during the incident.

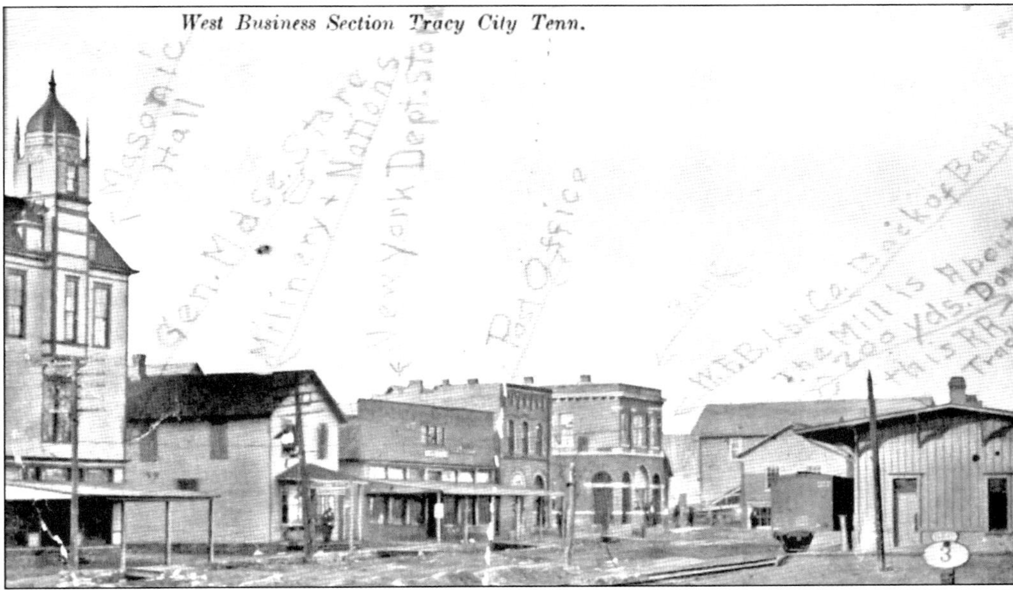

The sender of this 1911 Tracy City card was thoughtful enough to identify the business along the western section of town. People are standing all along the storefronts. The oval railroad sign on the right says, "SEC 3," which should indicate the mileage to the next depot, but three miles would be near Sander's Crossing. In 1850, the Wootens and Bobos were some of the first miners in the Heading. In 1890, the Grundy County Census reported 436 blacks living in Happy Bottom. Today Flury's General Store is more than 100 years old and thriving. Until a few years ago, the store sold dynamite.

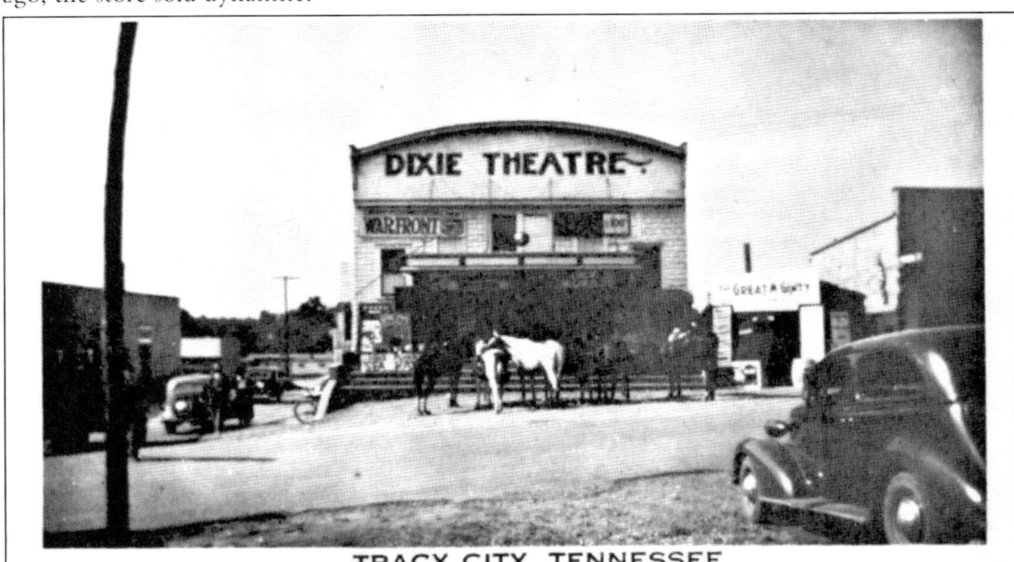

You can see a hitching post out front, and those who rode their horses to the theater got free admission. Elgin Ramsey, from Rome, Georgia, managed the theater, which was built in 1926 by Samuel Werner, renovated in 1950, closed in 1960, and burned in the late 1970s. "Dixie" was a popular name in the South. In addition to the theater, there was the Dixie Telephone Company, Dixie Savings Store, and a ball team in the Mountain Softball League named Dixie Home.

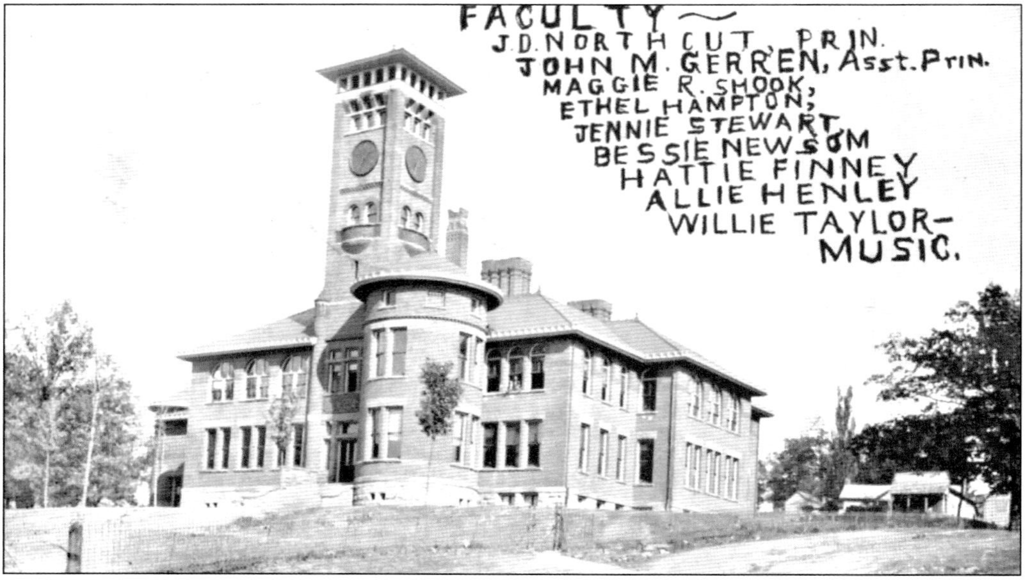

Col. (honorary) A. M. Shook, of TCI, opened this school in 1890. He advanced the miners the money to build the school in 1889. Shook School burned May 26, 1976, and was then taken over by Grundy County. According to Mrs. Grundy "News" (so named because Mrs. Grundy knew everything), there were nine cases of polio in the county in 1949. The census showed in 1950 that the Grundy County population was 12,541. The school was located at the intersection of Clouse Hill and Highway 108.

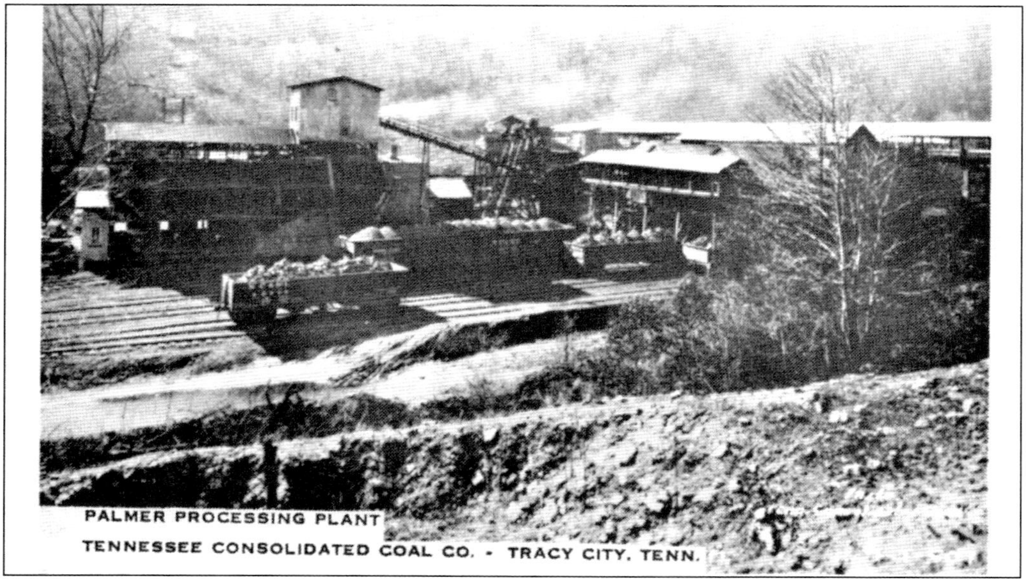

No town in Marion County can ignore the impact coal has had on its history. Tracy City and Palmer are certainly not exceptions. This is Tennessee Consolidated Coal Company's (TCC) Palmer processing plant near the "Big Mines." TCC began to mechanize these mines in 1954 and had a mule barn on the Mill Creek side of Ducktown Road. There is a relationship between timber and mining, and Grundy County's 34 sawmills turned out half a million board feet of lumber in 1947.

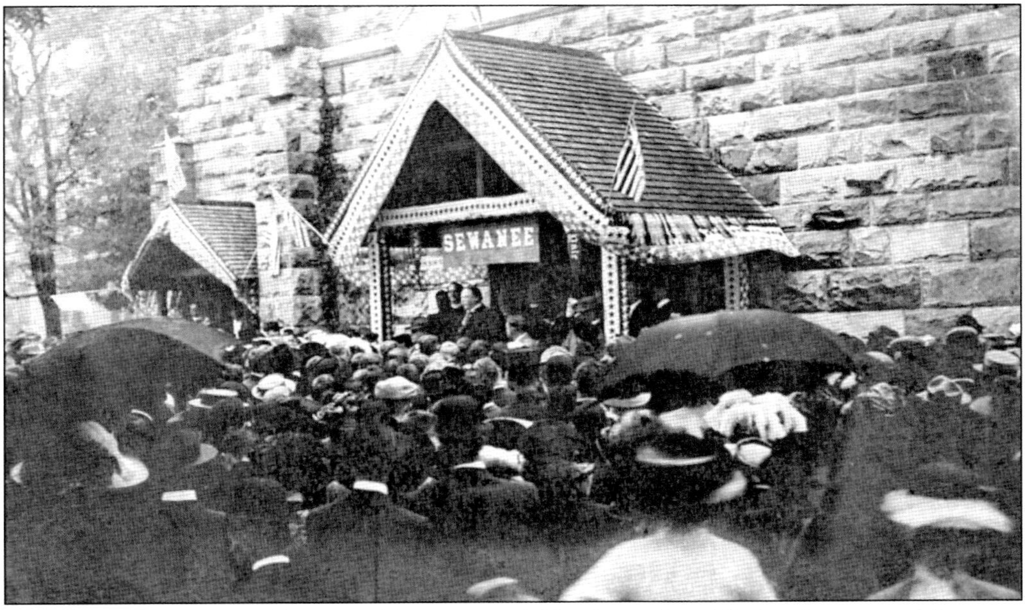

While Sewanee is physically in Franklin County, it bleeds over into Marion County and the town of Monteagle in every way. This is a 1907 scene of President Taft visiting the University of the South. Founded in 1857 by Episcopals, this is a stately university with her 10,000-acre domain. Tennessee Williams left part of his estate to the university. St. Andrews school for boys is also in Sewanee. In February 1960, the school was blanketed with a record snowfall of 18 inches.

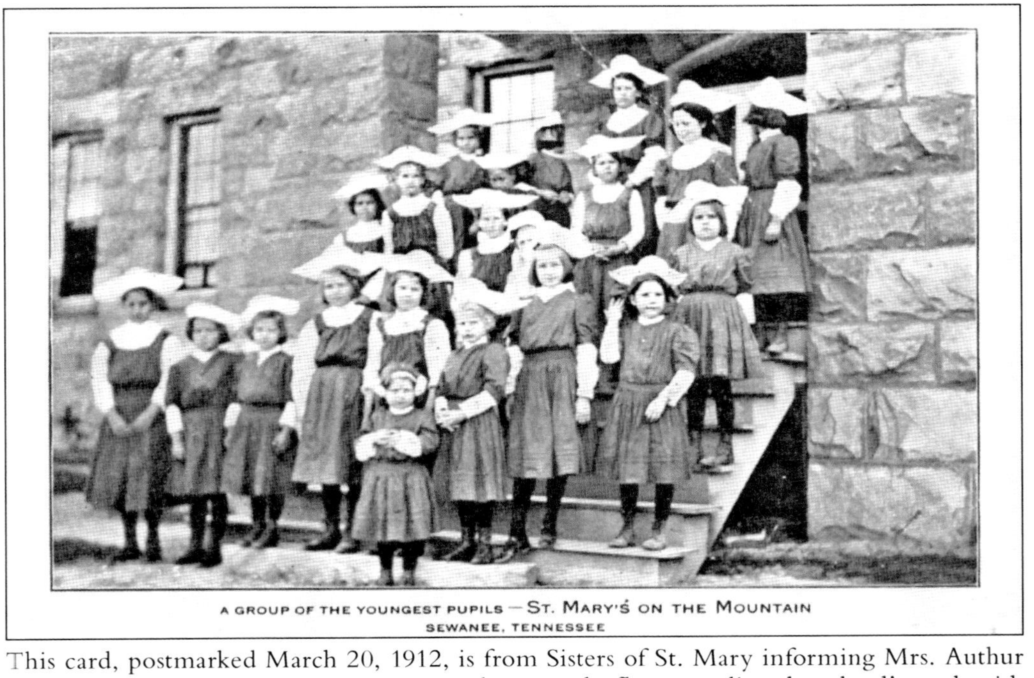

This card, postmarked March 20, 1912, is from Sisters of St. Mary informing Mrs. Authur Norton of Middletown Springs, Vermont, that some leaflets regarding the school's work with girls have been sent. St. Mary's closed long ago.

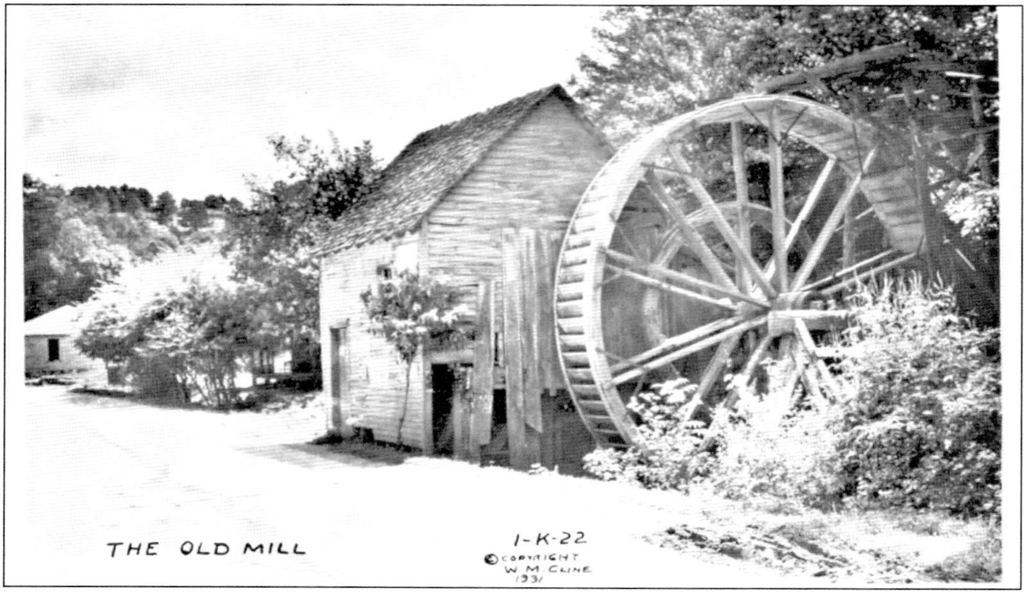

Bell's Mill is gone now but once stood proudly on the Elk River in Pelham Valley (mountain folks have never referred to the valley by its official name—Pelham). It was built by Sumner Bell. There was no mill on the mountain. It was a longstanding tradition to send grain there and bring it back to the mountain by wagon. Examine the image and determine the water source.

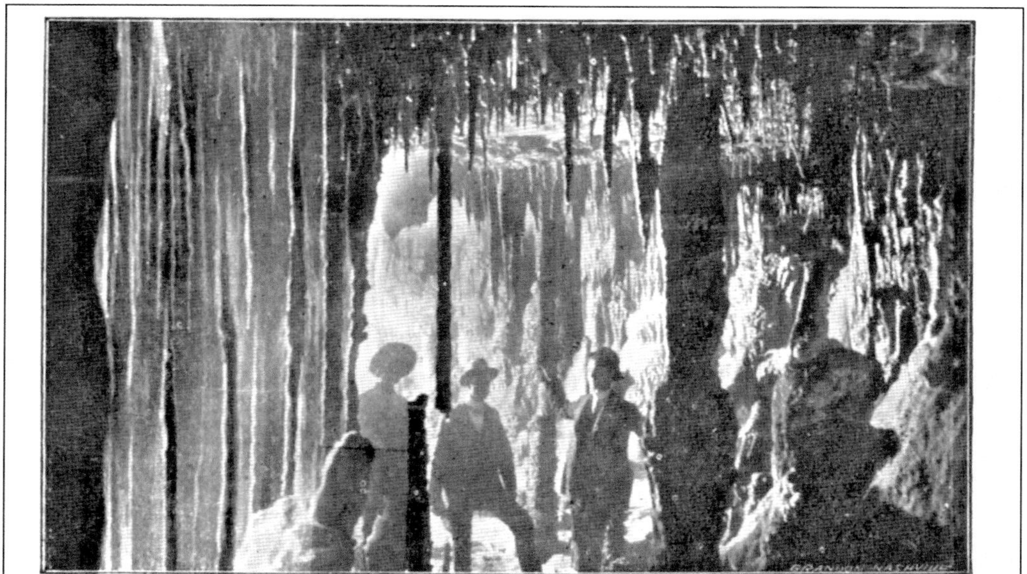

There are more than 150 postcards of Wonder Cave. Records indicate the cave was discovered in 1897. In 1900, R. M. Payne of Monteagle bought the land around the cave and commercialized it. He lighted the cave with acetylene gas. Marion Greer "Fod" Raulston (whose family later owned the cave) had a lifelong attraction tc the cave. After leaving the mountain (in 1963) to teach in Georgia, he would bring boys from his school here to dig for artifacts. Fod, who was eccentric, served as Monteagle postmaster in 1961. He was known to keep large sums of money in feed sacks or buried on his property.

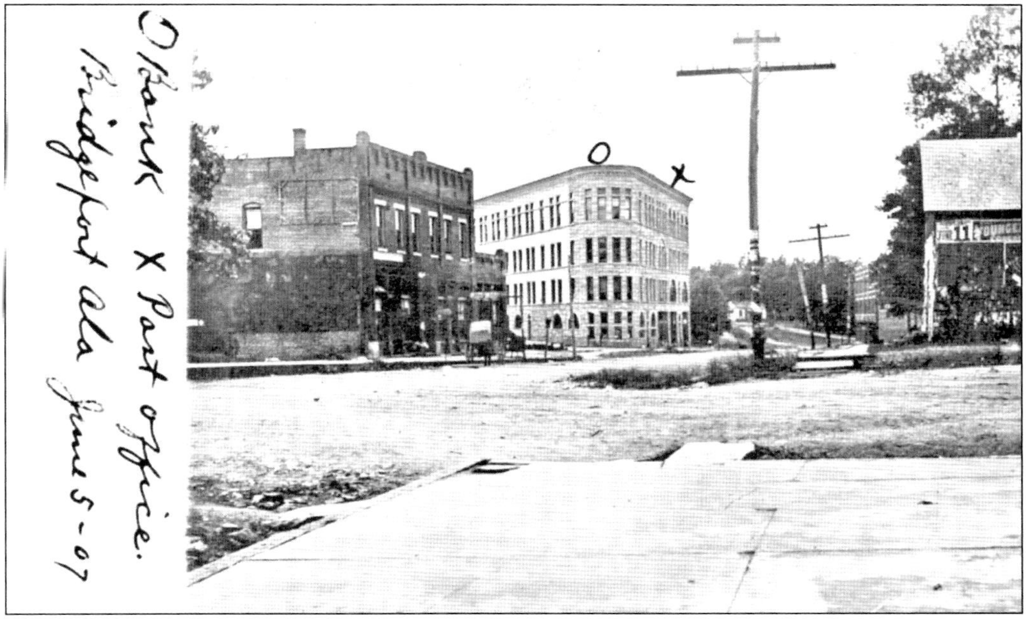

Bridgeport is in Alabama, but people in Marion County view it as just another bordering community. This is a 1907 view of downtown. One of the signs on the building at the right advertises a "Cole Dunger Concert." There is a horse and buggy in the center of the card and a man sitting on the sidewalk just to the left of it. "O" is the bank and "X" the post office. The four-story sandstone building at Alabama and Brummell Avenues was built in 1891. Dorothy Toliver died when she jumped from the building as it burned January 23, 1937. The glow of the fire could be seen as far away as Jasper.

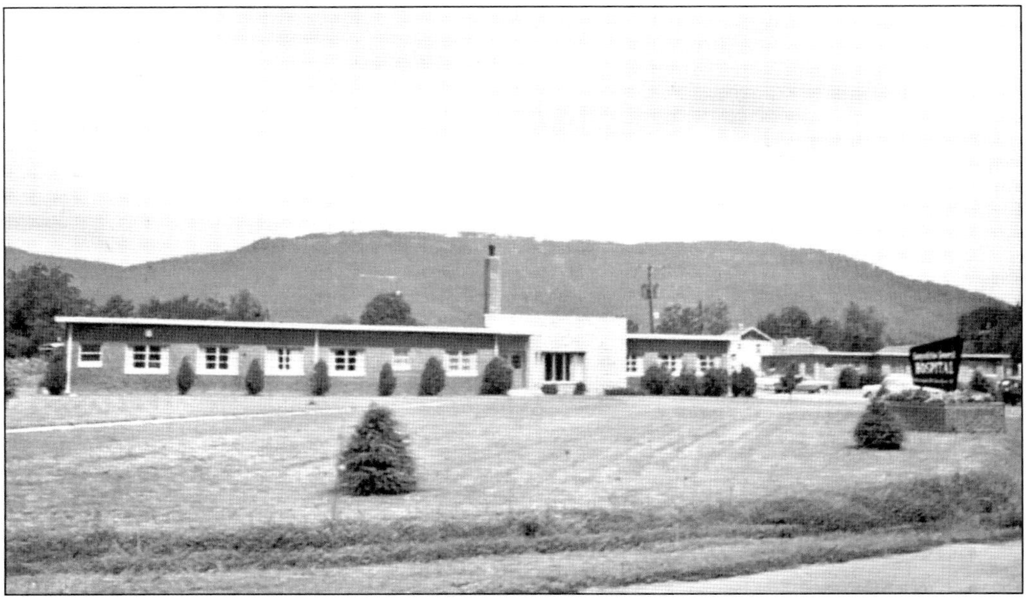

This is Sequatchie General Hospital in Dunlap, Tennessee. The photographer was Frank Shannon, and Cline printed the card. On May 23, 1956, Dunlap physician Dr. Rufus Eddie Standefer died in this hospital.

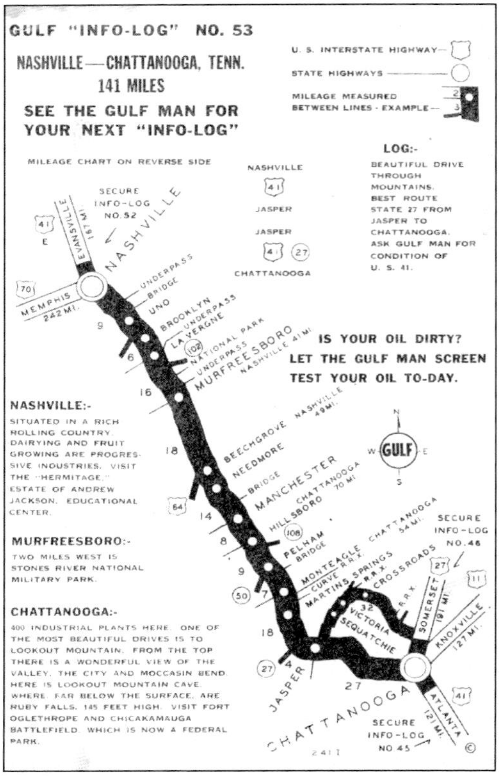

The other half of this postcard has been removed, as evidenced by the perforated edges. The map includes Crossroads and Victoria. Gulf (and other companies) produced these mileage charts as early as the 1930s. Victoria is neglected in postcards and maps. It is believed the Glass Slipper was previously the medical clinic of Dr. Johnson, who, it turns out, was not a doctor at all.

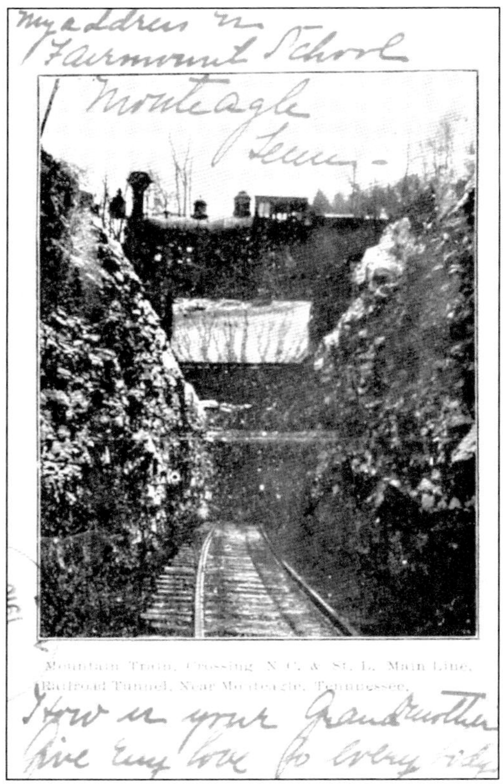

This is a primitive card showing the Sewanee and Monteagle mountain train (affectionately known as the Mountain Goat for its ability to go up and down the steep Cowan side of the mountain) crossing NC & St L Main Line Railroad Tunnel in 1885. In 1985, Monty Wanamaker Studio in Monteagle released a print of this scene. The girl mailing this in 1910 was attending Fairmount School, which only operated during the summer. The cool mountain climate during the dog days of summer was believed to prevent typhoid and other illnesses.

Seven

Hotels and Motels

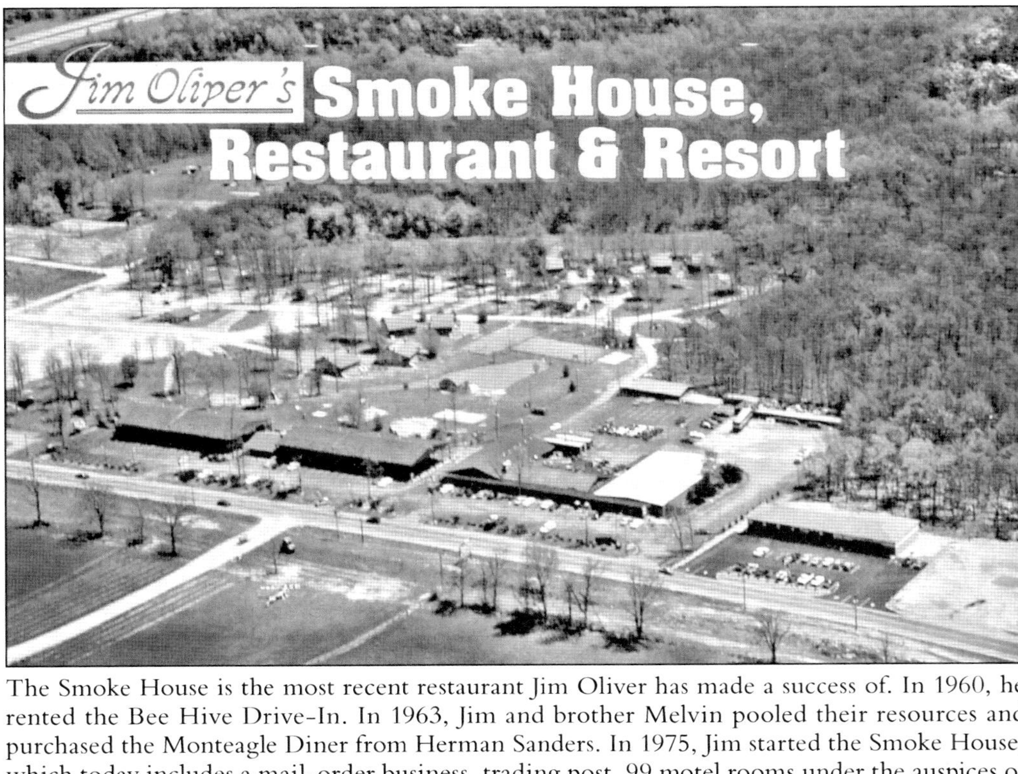

The Smoke House is the most recent restaurant Jim Oliver has made a success of. In 1960, he rented the Bee Hive Drive-In. In 1963, Jim and brother Melvin pooled their resources and purchased the Monteagle Diner from Herman Sanders. In 1975, Jim started the Smoke House, which today includes a mail-order business, trading post, 99 motel rooms under the auspices of Best Western Corporation, 14 rustic log cabins, and a wedding chapel, and there is no end in sight. Not bad for a boy from Payne's Cove in Pelham, Tennessee.

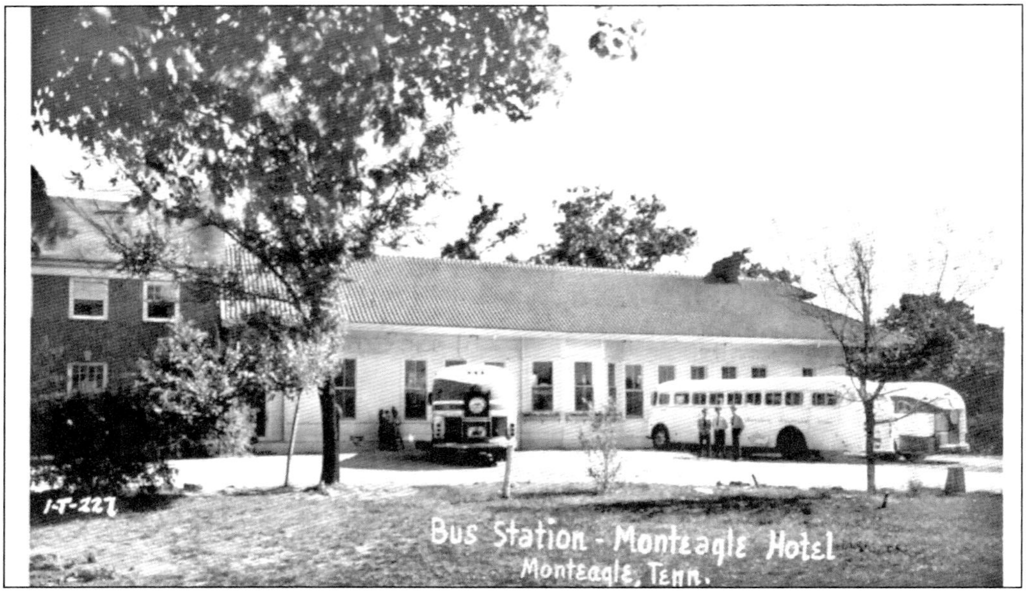

In 1947, John Harton relocated the depot to this site, and it became the Greyhound Bus Station, where many young wives could be seen making their way to army camps to see their husbands. Shown here are drivers and their Southeastern Greyhound buses beside the Monteagle Hotel. A group of passengers is standing to the left of the bus. The card was mailed in 1942. In 1950, while it rained, the hotel burned after a fire started in the bus station.

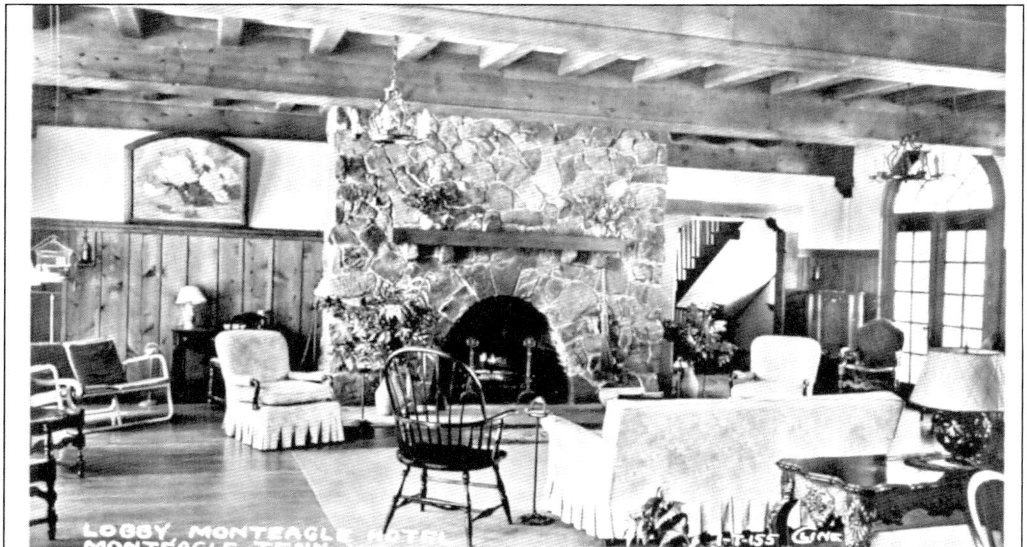

For a brief period around 1884, the Assembly owned the Monteagle Hotel. Re-designated Hotel de Corzelius in 1888, it was renamed Monteagle Hotel by Mr. R. M. Payne two years later. There was a bad fire in 1914, and it burned to ashes in 1929. John Harton built a new one in 1930. Fort Campbell Medal of Honor recipient and Cleveland, Tennessee, native Paul Huff spent his honeymoon here. The Monteagle Hotel's large eagle was often vandalized, was dynamited twice, and was stolen and returned before finally being given to Tennessee Tech (the Golden Eagles). Today it sits atop the school's administration building.

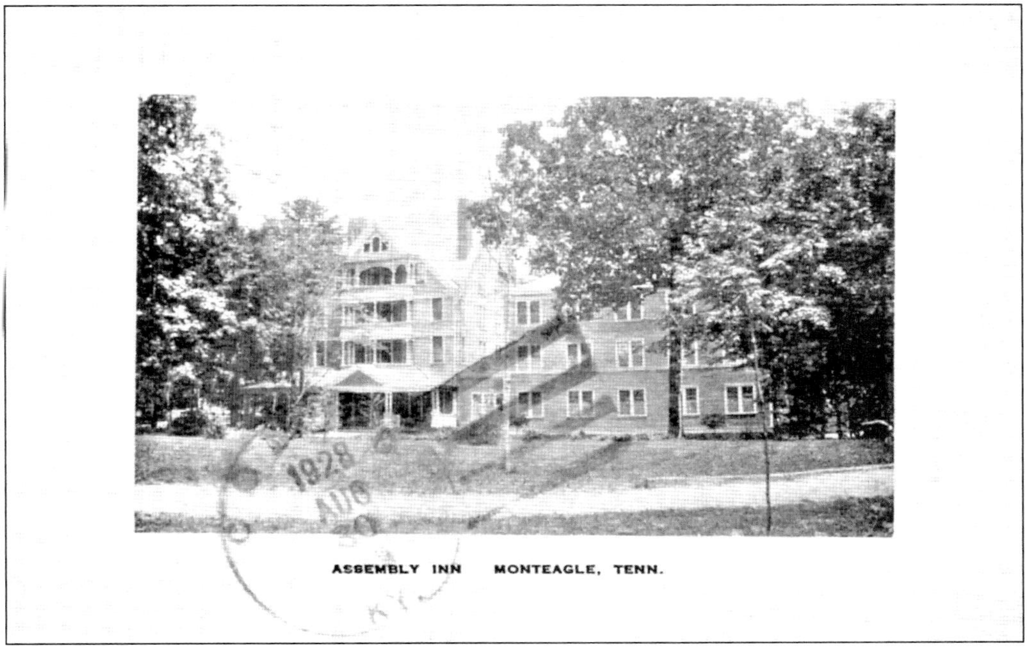

Another New York Stores postcard, this one is postmarked 1928. The Assembly Inn burned November 3, 1961. This structure was designed by Chattanooga architect R. H. Hunt.

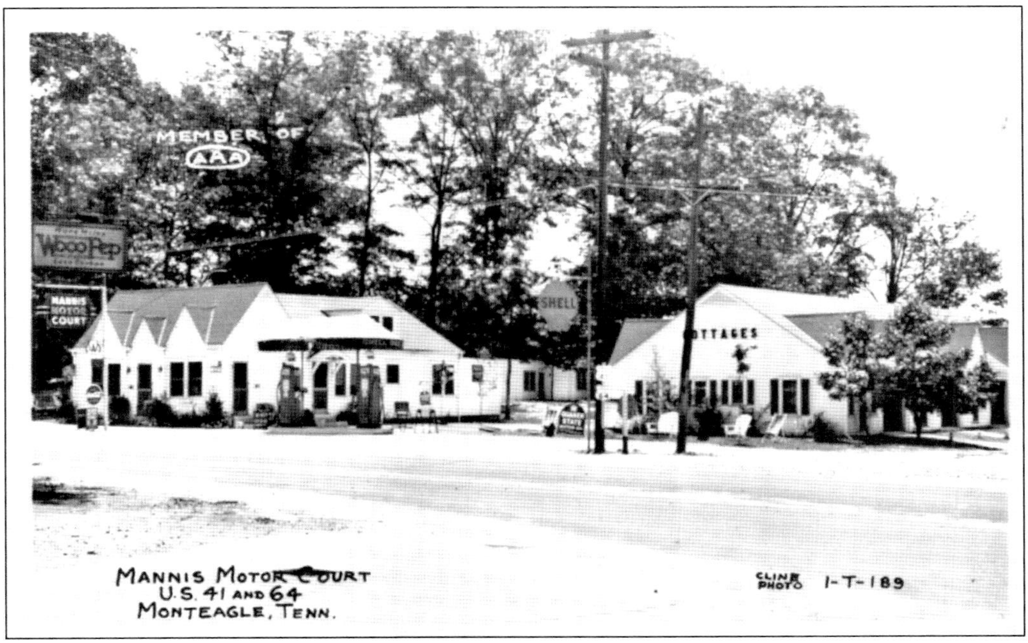

This Cline RPPC is of the Mannis Motor Court and Cottages. The card was mailed February 19, 1941, and the writer states it is 10 degrees at Monteagle. This was a time when advertisement by signs was of paramount importance. In this postcard, there are signs for AAA, Dr. Pepper, Quaker State Oil, restrooms, Coca-Cola, WocoPep (the king of motor fuel), and Shell Gasoline. The Colstons, who were both high school teachers, owned this business.

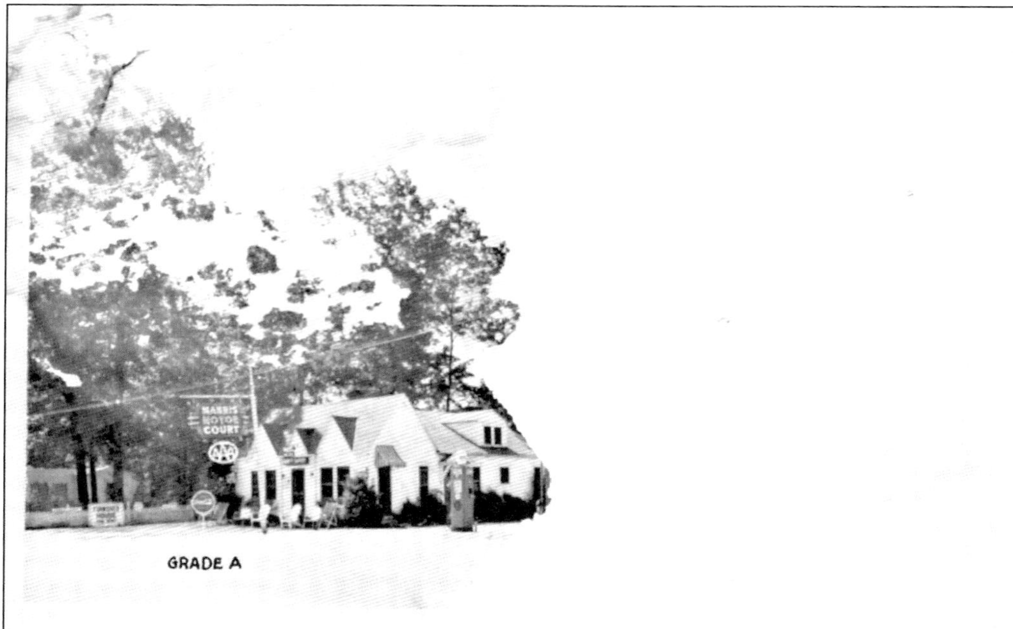

This battered card provides a different view of Mannis Motor Court. It also shows the results of exposure to light, moisture, and insects—the three reasons postcards do not have as good a survival rate in the South as they do in many parts of the country.

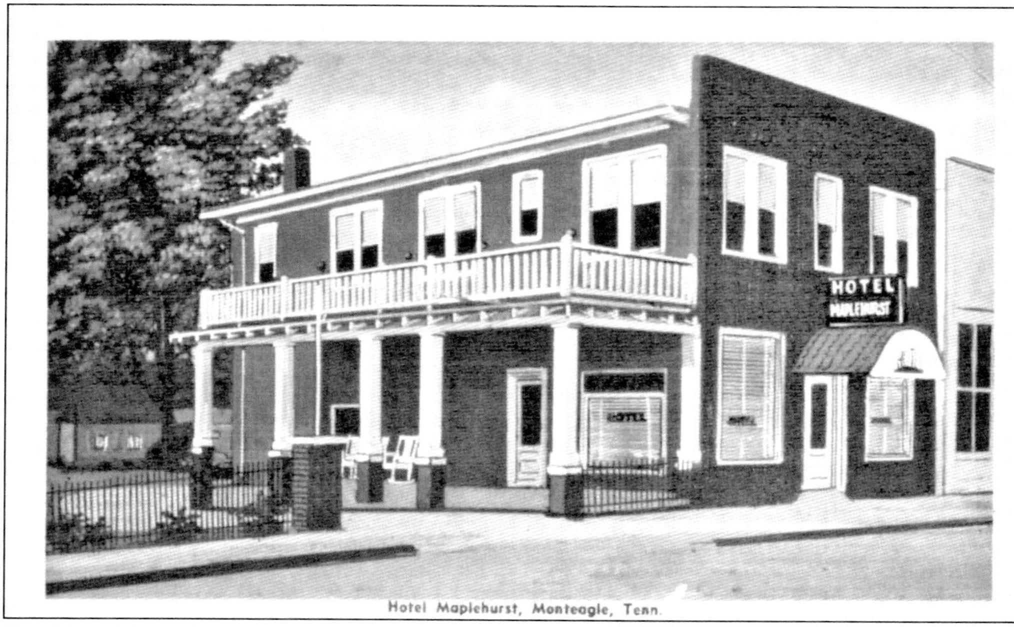

Hotel Maplehurst (once named Brannon Hotel) was across the street from John Harton's Monteagle Hotel. On foggy days, Brannon, dressed as a clown and with rolled-up newspaper in hand, would attempt to wave tourists away from Monteagle Hotel and into Maplehurst. When Mr. and Mrs. W. H. Corn operated the hotel, it was often referred to as "Heartbreak Hotel" because of the numbers of divorced men who lived there. The City Barber Shop was located downstairs.

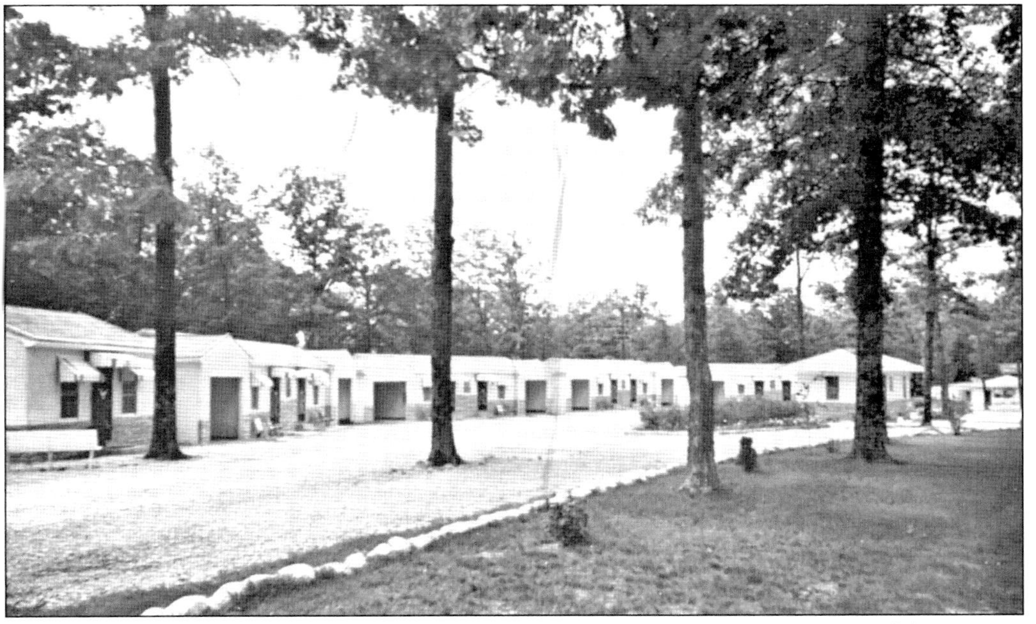

In 2005, this old roadside tourist court is still standing but is vacant and in a state of disrepair. It has 19 units, and all are sided with Crab Orchard stone. The building seen at the extreme right is now Monteagle Auto Parts. Past owners of Oak Terrace Tourist Court include Lee Mitchell's family and Mr. and Mrs. E. L. McFarland.

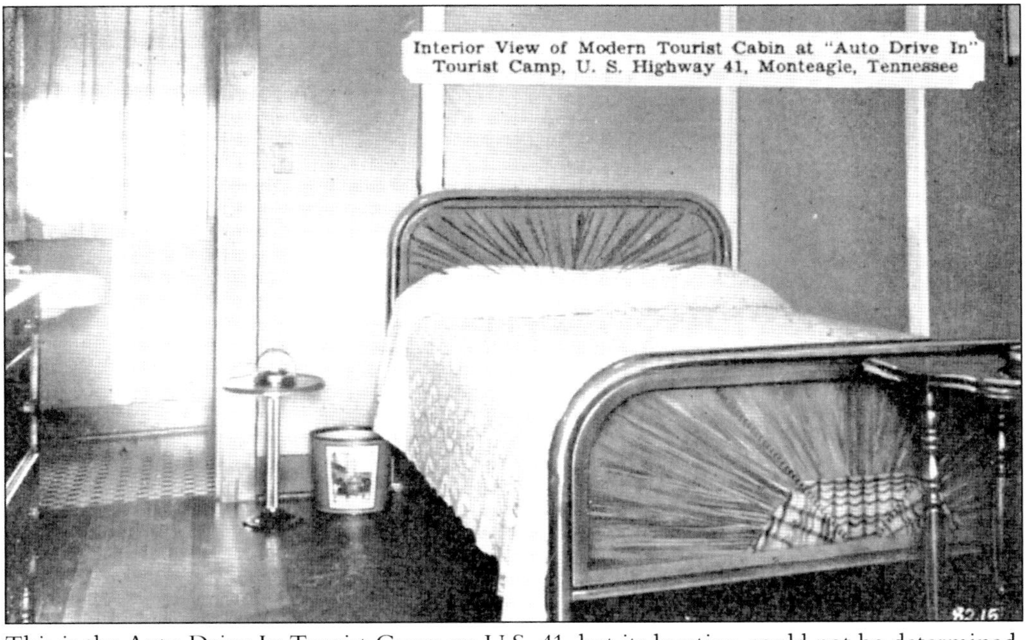

This is the Auto Drive In Tourist Camp on U.S. 41, but its location could not be determined. This interior view gives you a good idea of the "comforts" you would expect in accommodations during the 1930s and 1940s. Ashtrays were in all rooms, as non-smoking accommodations had not been considered.

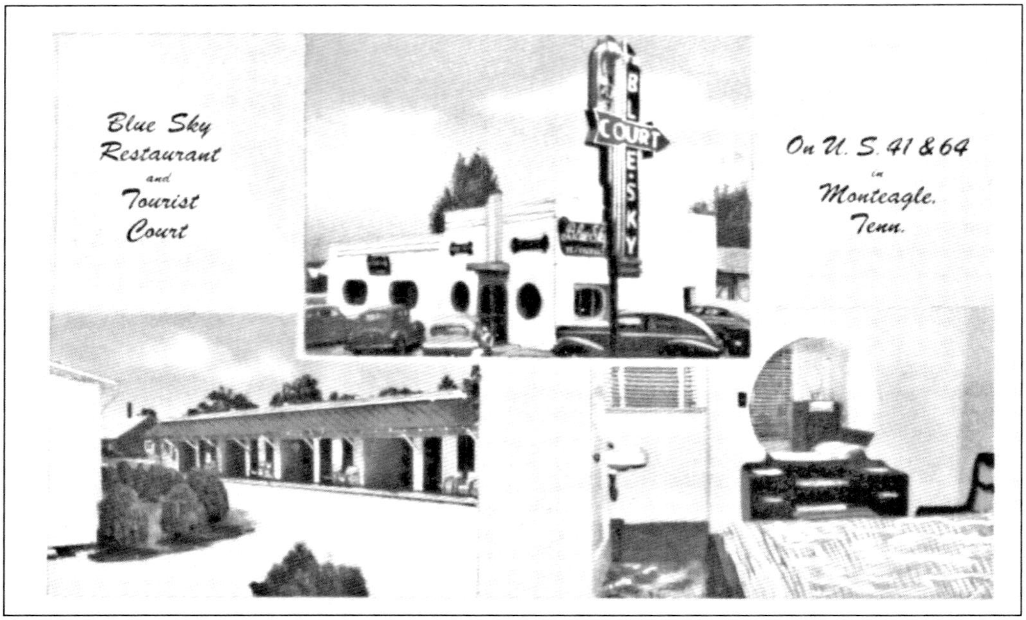

Earlier called Edd's Café, the Blue Sky Restaurant and Tourist Court is gone now but was located approximately where the elementary school and CVS Drugs are today. Clara and Tommy Shoemate opened it. Clara later divorced Tommy to marry a soldier. Whiskey was bootlegged out of the building at bottom left. The Blue Sky sign remained for a number of years after it closed in 1982. It is said the closing was the result of being denied a beer license. Though a block apart and unrelated, Blue Sky and Monteagle Diner burned on same day.

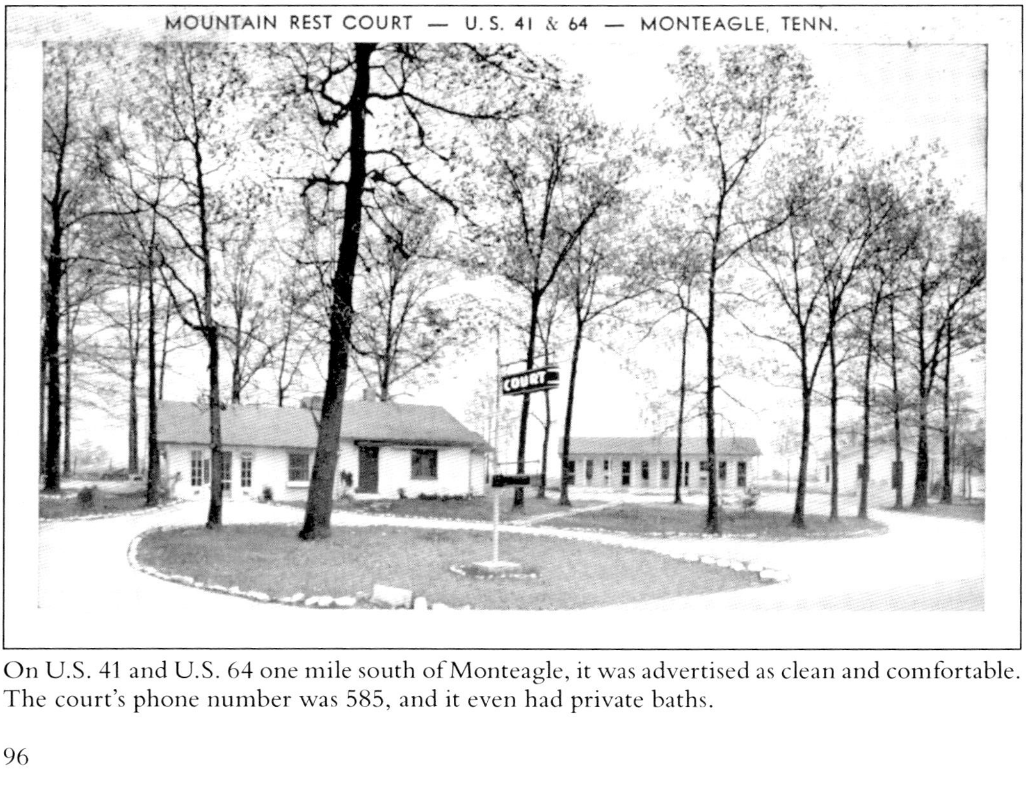

On U.S. 41 and U.S. 64 one mile south of Monteagle, it was advertised as clean and comfortable. The court's phone number was 585, and it even had private baths.

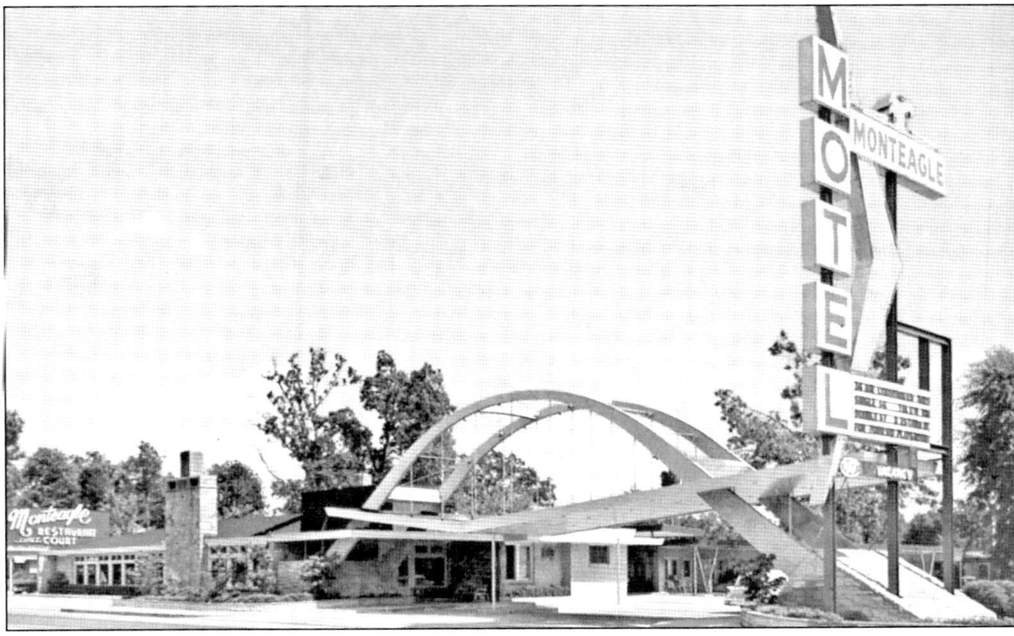

Monteagle Restaurant and Court were built by a "foreigner," a man named Beoncooley. The archway, seen here, was built much later. In 2004, realtor Peter Beasley has the property on the market. It is located at 313 Main Street next to Papa Ron's.

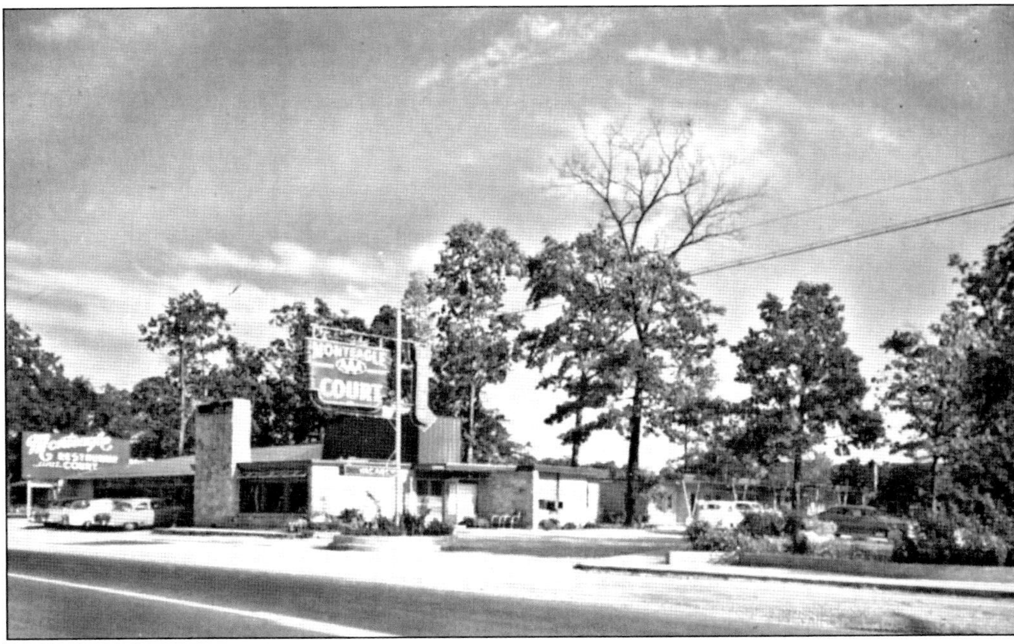

Someone has written on the back of the card that the room was $5.15 and breakfast $1.50. There were 37 luxurious units, and one-stop service was available.

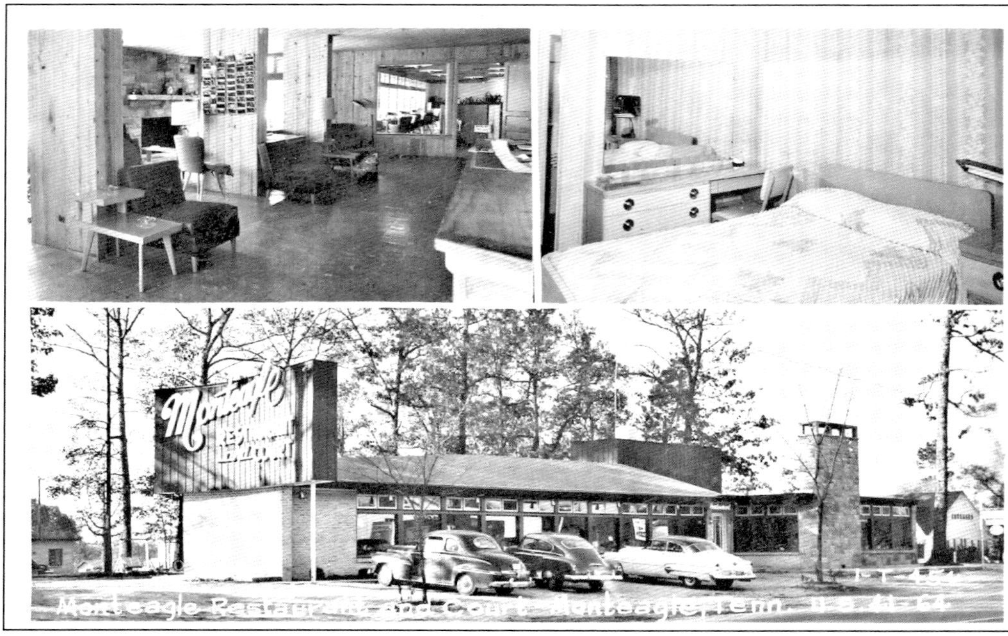

Initially, there were just three little courts. Today there are approximately 40. Opened in 1950, it was owned by Mr. and Mrs. J. M. Colston.

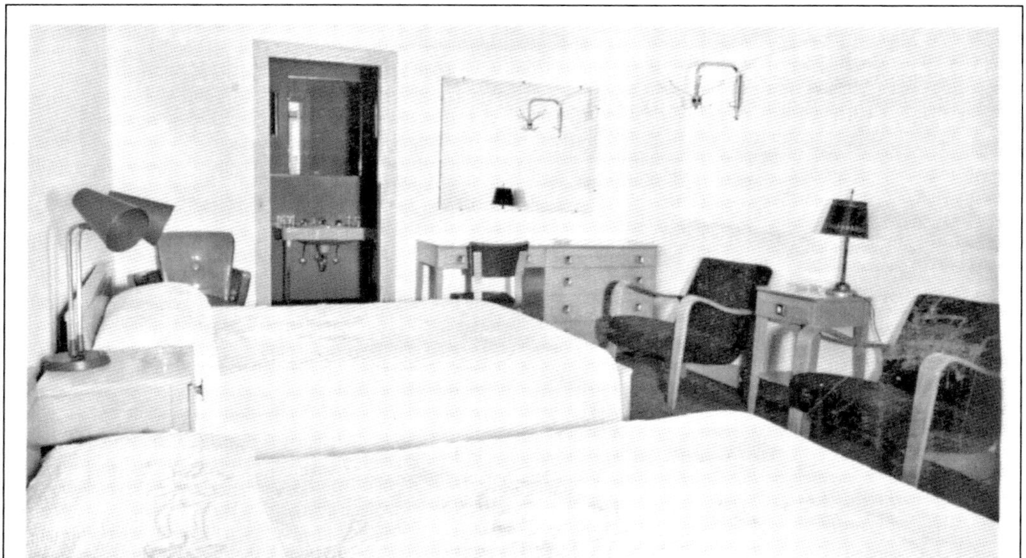

Note the chenille bedspreads and the unusual coat rack on the wall. This is an interior view of the Monteagle Motel.

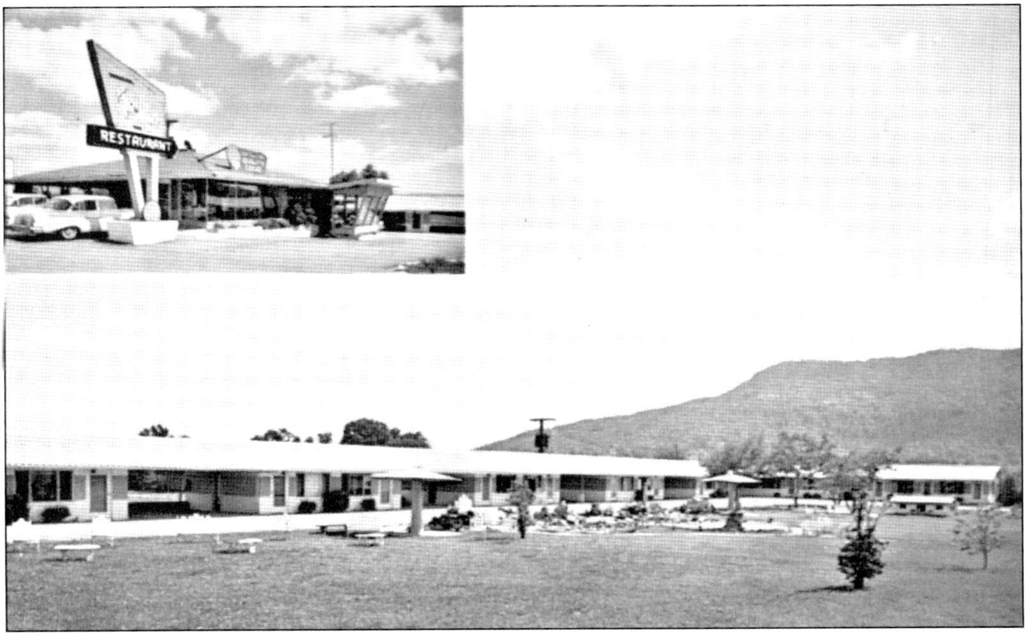

It is believed that Fred Bennett and his wife, Kay, were the first owners of the Ka-Mar (from Kate and Martha) Motel and Restaurant. Mr. and Mrs. Philip Dyer later managed it. The inset photograph is of the restaurant. There is now a McDonalds where it once stood. The mailing address was South Pittsburg, but the business was located at the Kimball Junction.

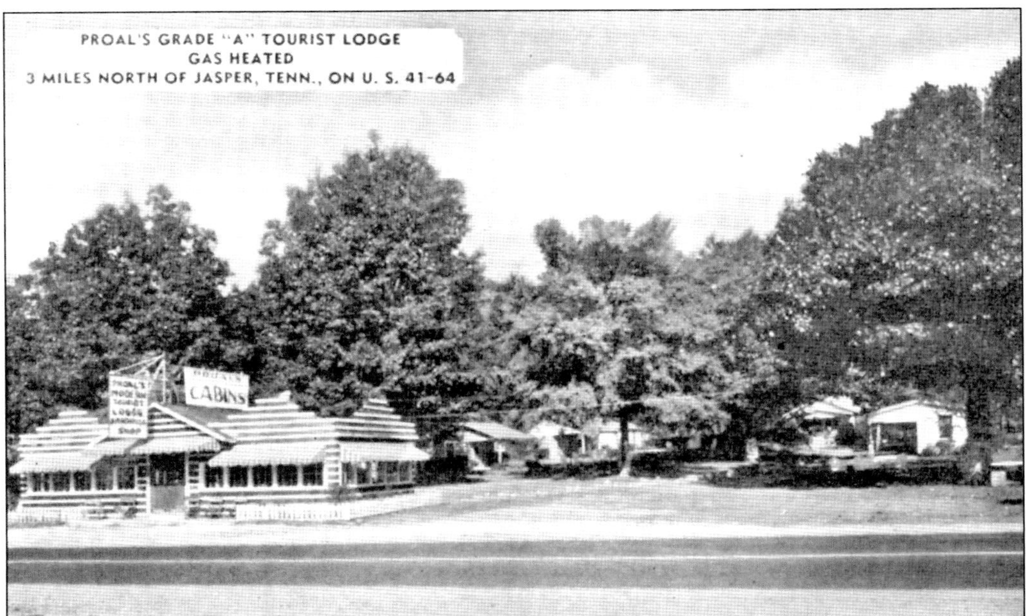

This card was printed in the late 1930s. These mom-and-pop tourist courts were phenomena that lasted, more or less, until in the 1950s. Once Tennessean Kemmons Wilson started "the mother of all Motel Chains—Holiday Inn" near Memphis, these small courts began to disappear. Proals was across the street from where Citizen State Bank is today. Virgil Thomas sold that property.

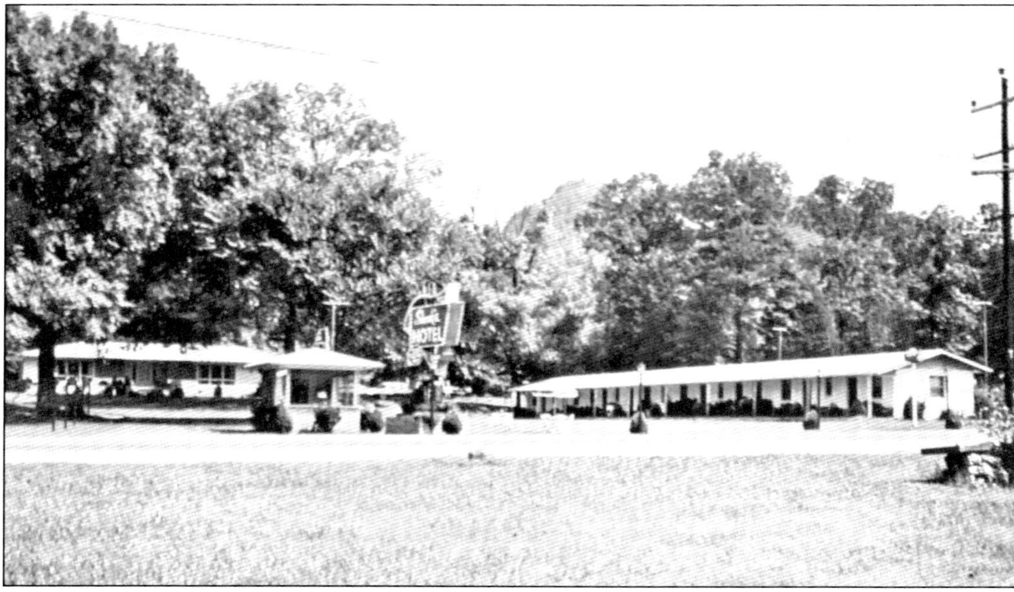

James R. and Mabel Shook built Shook's Motel near where Kimball Office Supply is today. Like Proal's before it, it is gone. Their home was located to the left, and Turney Grocery (built and operated by Leon Eaves) was to the right. There was a television in each cabin, and the telephone number was TE7-6284. This photograph was taken by (Mark) Smith Studio of South Pittsburg, Tennessee.

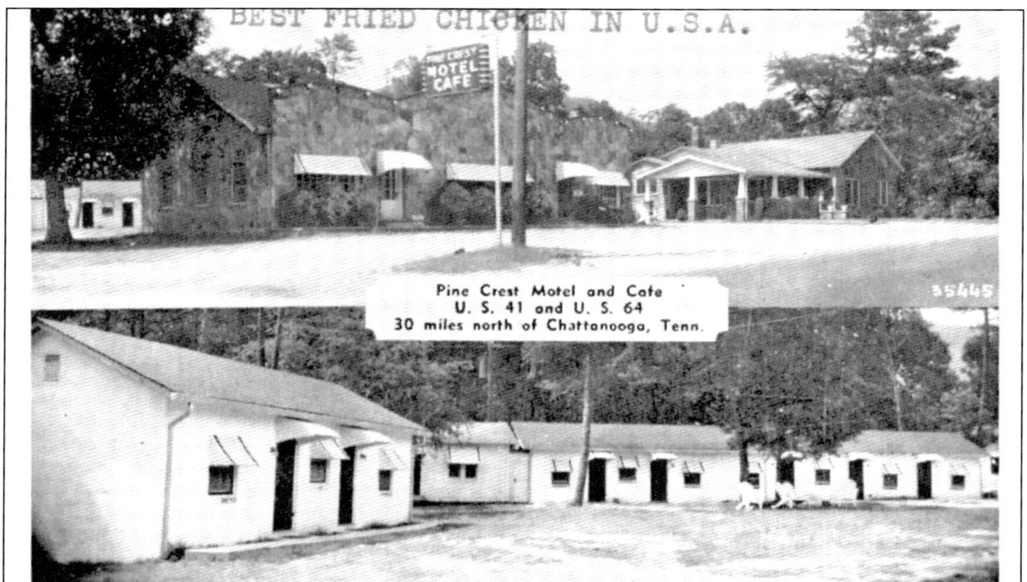

There are many postcards of the Pine Crest Motel and Café, but this appears to be the earliest. The motel and café were built by Charlie Rollins and owned by the colorful A. R. "Buckshot" Walker in the early 1950s. More recent owners were Mr. and Mrs. Lewis Griffith. All the buildings are still there today. The restaurant is now home to Shirley's Styling Center and Tennessee Valley Surveying. The office and motel rooms are now the Creek Side Apartments. It was once the location of the Evening Star Bar, which had a dance hall in the basement.

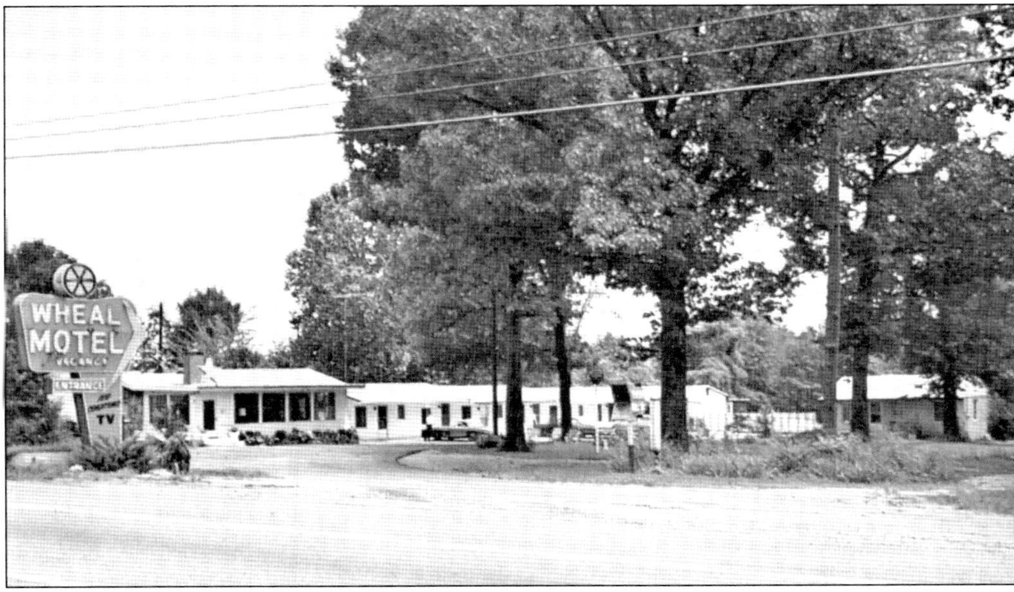

Another Kimball Motel, this belonged to Johnny Wheal and was directly across U.S. 41 from Shook's. There was a restaurant adjacent to the motel property, and the owners boasted of Simmons Beautyrest mattresses in every room. This is a 1970 card.

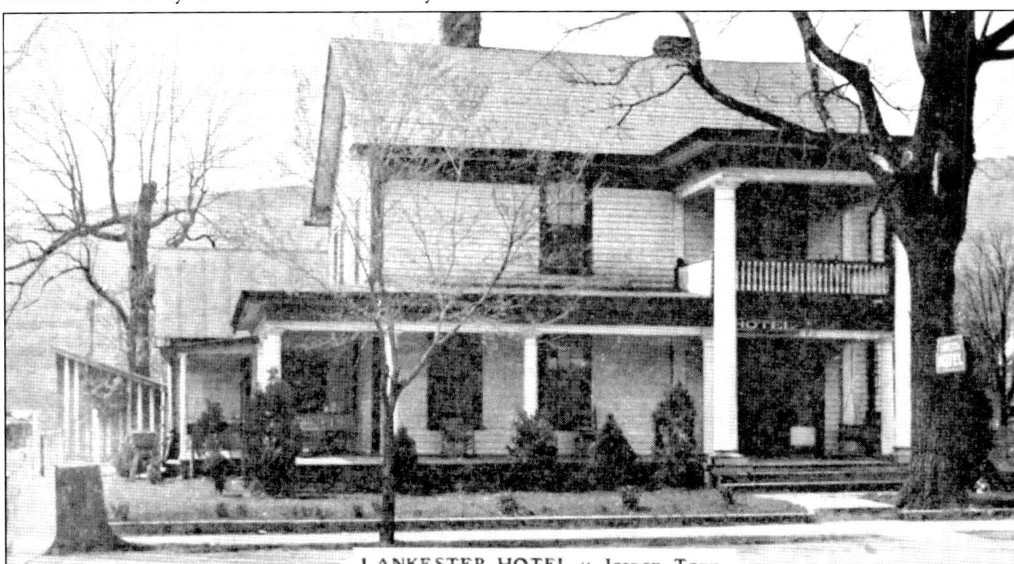

Opened in 1900 and owned by Mr. J. G. Lancaster, "a retired traveling man of fine intelligence and a capable conservationist," it was managed by Albert Lancaster. Guests included John D. Rockefeller and Henry Ford. Mr. Lancaster would often sit on the porch of the hotel and talk with those passing by. Alton "Sticks" Graham ran the hotel for a while. Alton Graham had two brothers. Pete, whose wife was Mava Cabe from Richard City, was a legislator and managed to get a bill passed allowing the sales of fireworks in the county. The third of the brothers was the popular Gob Graham of Jasper. The hotel had a porter and "Dr." Johnson's office. While the "Dr." was very good at healing and quite professional, it turned out he was not licensed.

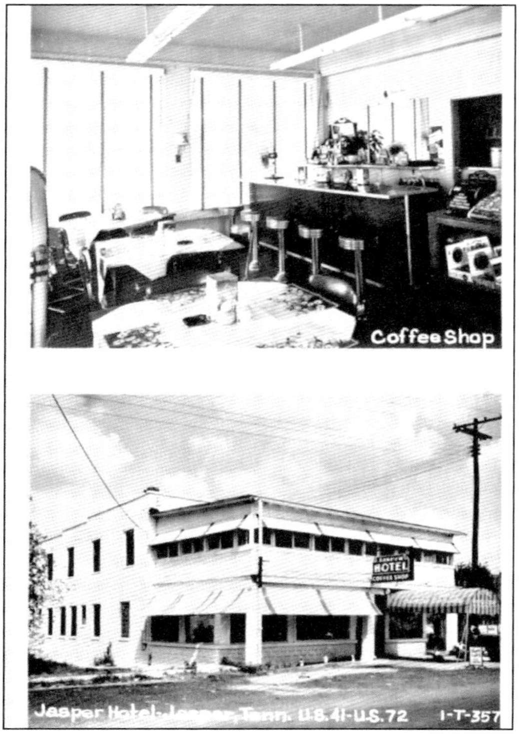

Built by W. G. Phillips, the Jasper Hotel was later owned/operated by "Butterhead" Joyner. The top portion of the card shows the coffee shop located in the hotel. The hotel was just north of the town's only traffic light on U.S. 41. A Rock City Rolodex that provided mileage to other locations can be seen on the counter. The Jasper Hotel was advertised in the *Sequatchie Sun* as early as 1871. Others who operated this business include Charles "Chili" Warren, who, with his family, resided here.

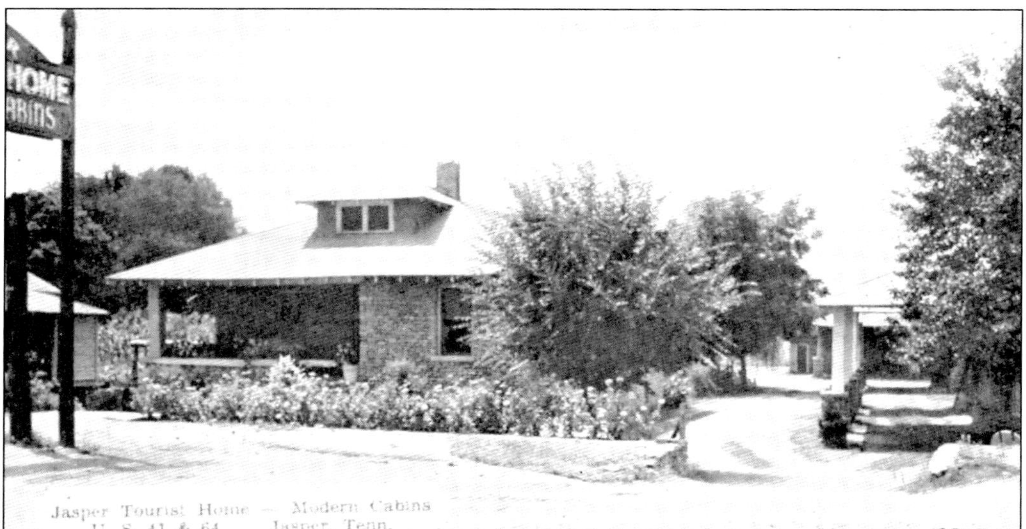

Long known as Shoemate Tourist Court, it was built of river rock by R. C. Shoemate. Shoemate's truck was always filled with river rock. The Clouses purchased the property from Gertrude Ford on June 30, 1950, and eventually sold to Citizen State Bank. There was an Esso service station adjacent to this property. The Clouses are from the Whiteside area, and many still live there. Grover's brother Jim was postmaster at Whiteside. Local attorney Edwin Z. Kelly Jr. is the grandson of Grover Clouse. Spud Parker's grandfather, Isaac Alexander Parker, a Civil War veteran, was married to Lizza Jane Clouse.

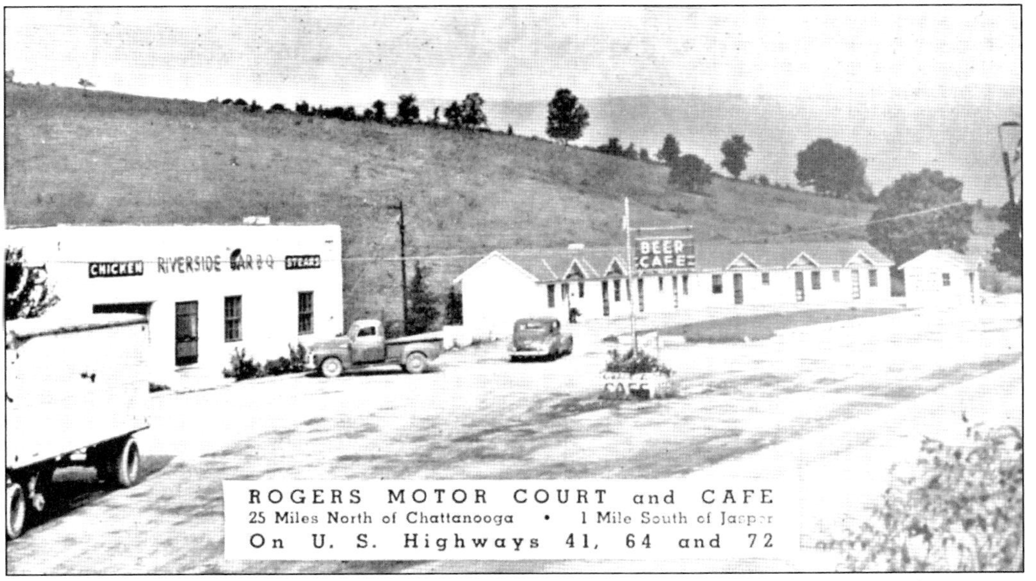

Rogers Motor Court and Restaurant were located on U.S. 41 just north of the Sequatchie River. Owner/operators have included James "Dick Tracy" Rogers Jr. and Howard Wooten (who had to relocate the large building as a result of highway right-of-way). Bobby Forshee owned the court and café for approximately six years before selling it to Stewart Phillips in 2001. Today it is Riverside Apartments, owned by Toby Zigman and managed by Brandy Spinner.

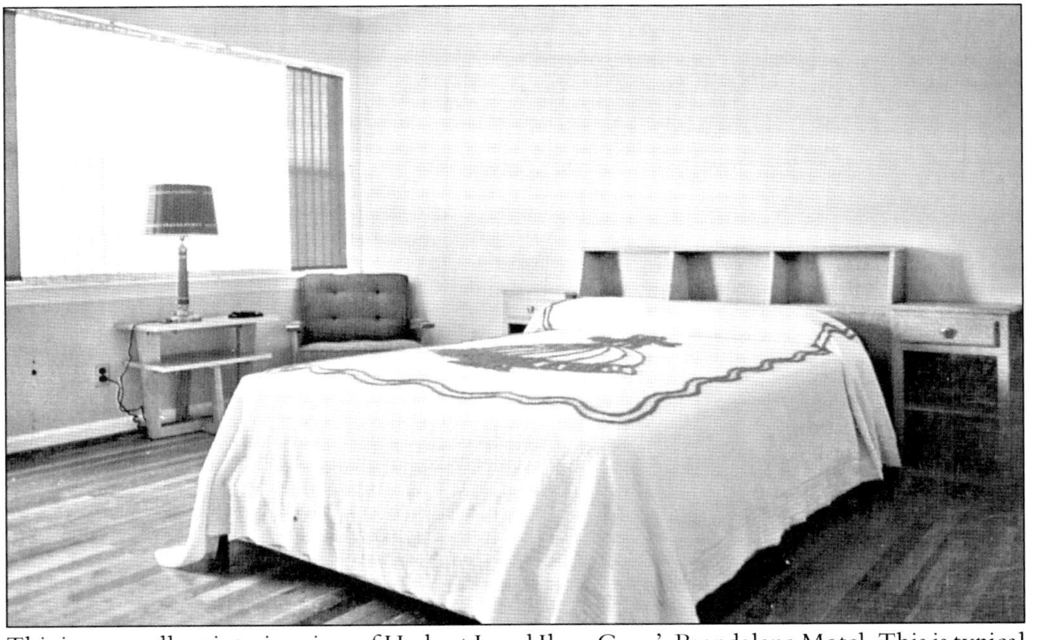

This is an excellent interior view of Herbert J. and Ilene Cross's Brendalene Motel. This is typical of a "modern" motel room in the 1950s, right down to the chenille bedspread. The motel was named for Ilene and her daughter, Brenda. Five miles east of Jasper on U.S. 41, it is thought to be the first motel in Jasper to have a swimming pool. In 2004, the owner is Don Johnson. The Patels, an Indian family, manage it.

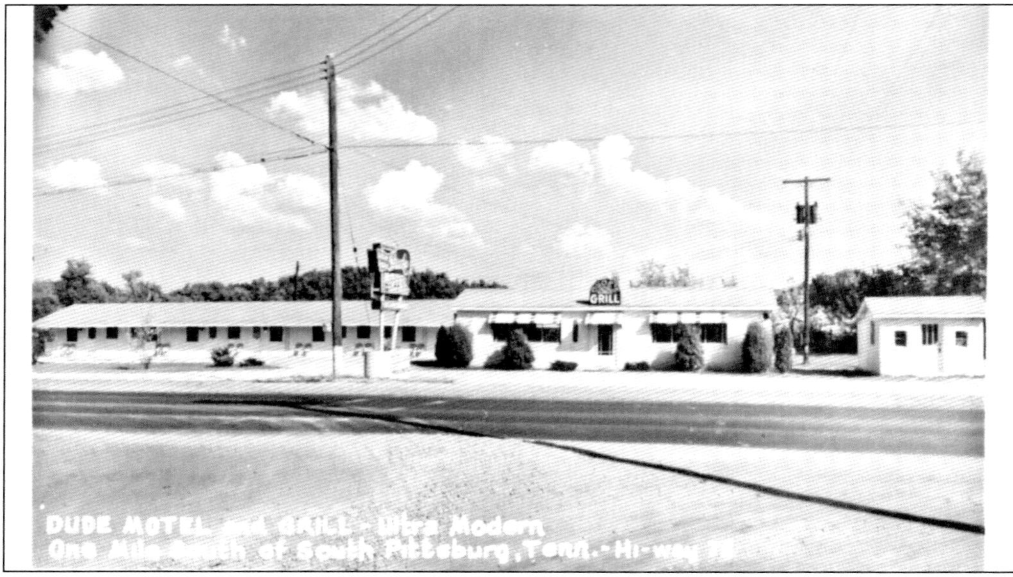

The Dude Motel and Grill was located on Highway 72 at Nineteenth Street (Richard City then, it is South Pittsburg now). In the early 1950s, Dude Matthews (brother of South Pittsburg sheriff Johnny Matthews) won this business in a poker game. Dude also owned the Bama, Jewell, and Maple Hill clubs, as well as other local honky-tonks. Hardy and Ruth Case bought the business in the late 1950s and sold it in the early 1990s. After Hardy's death, Ruth called both the place and herself "Ma Case." Everyone mentioned here is now deceased.

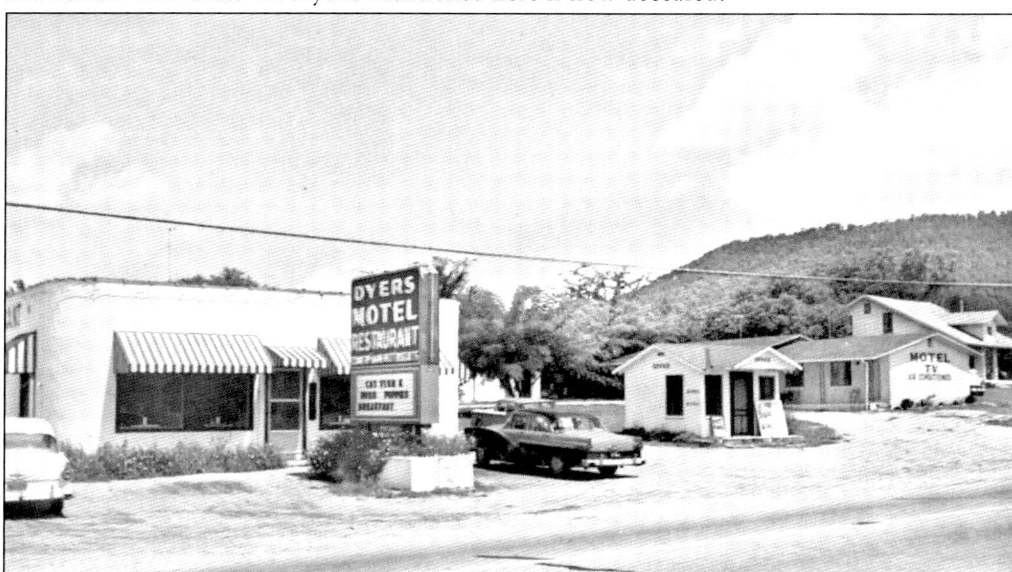

Tom and Sue Dyer were the original owners of this business located just east of the Marion Memorial Bridge in Guild, Tennessee. Once located between the river and where Anchor Inn Bait and Tackle is today, it has been gone for many years. Near here, Coach Johnny Latendress raised the world's largest freshwater pearl, and Lee Cantrell would play hooky after rains to dip boats out for 25¢ each. Much to the surprise of diners, a tractor-trailer once crashed through the wall where the 1956 Ford is parked.

Eight

Roads, Water, and Waterfalls

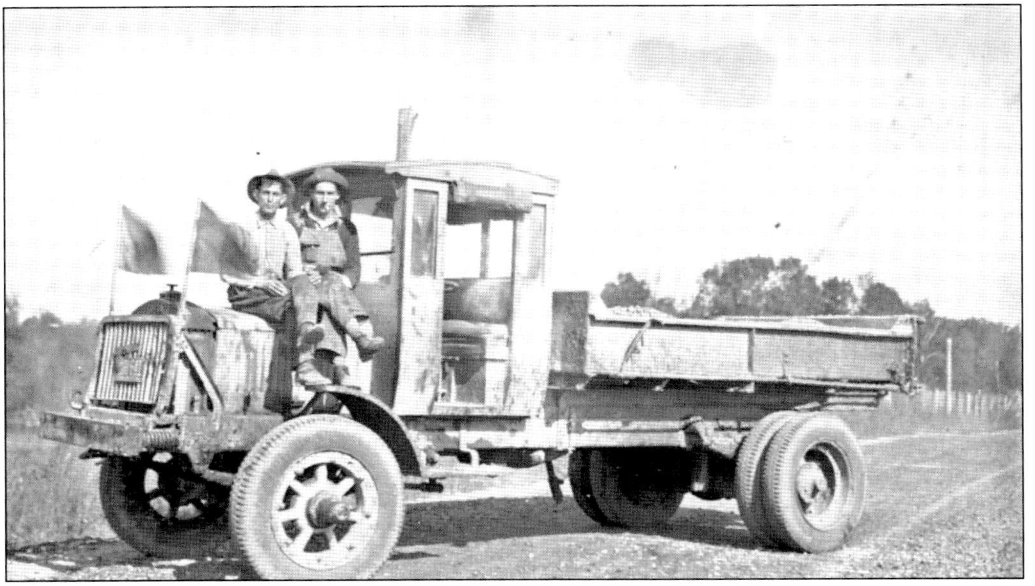

Diamond T, Reo (which stood for R. E. Olds) Speedwagon, and Hug Roadbuilders were popular trucks during the 1920s and 1930s. This one has tandem back wheels and is most likely a one-and-a-half-ton tipper bed. The license plates on the truck are 1929 vintage Tennessee plates. Leonard Morrison of Jasper is on the left, and the other man is unidentified.

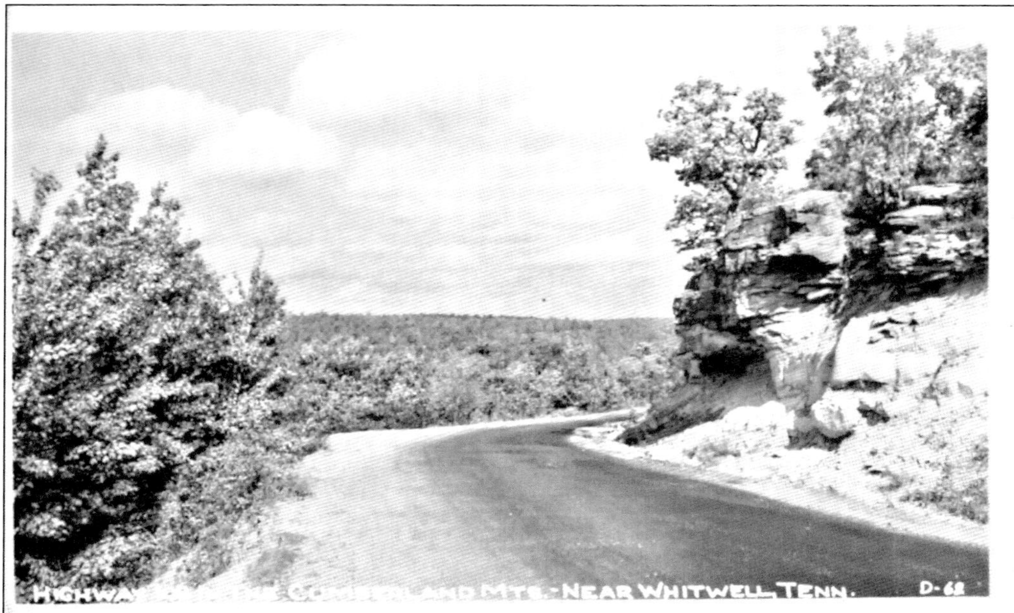

While the writing on the postcard appears to indicate this is Highway 100, it is, in fact, Highway 108. This is on top of the mountain near Mount Olive Road. The renowned stone feature, the 200-foot twin "chimneys," is located near Pocket Creek between Whitwell and Palmer. Beyond the county line, in Gruetli, is where 100 Swiss families settled in 1869. Local resident Terry McBroom has researched the Swiss Colony Cemetery in Gruetli-Laager, Tennessee.

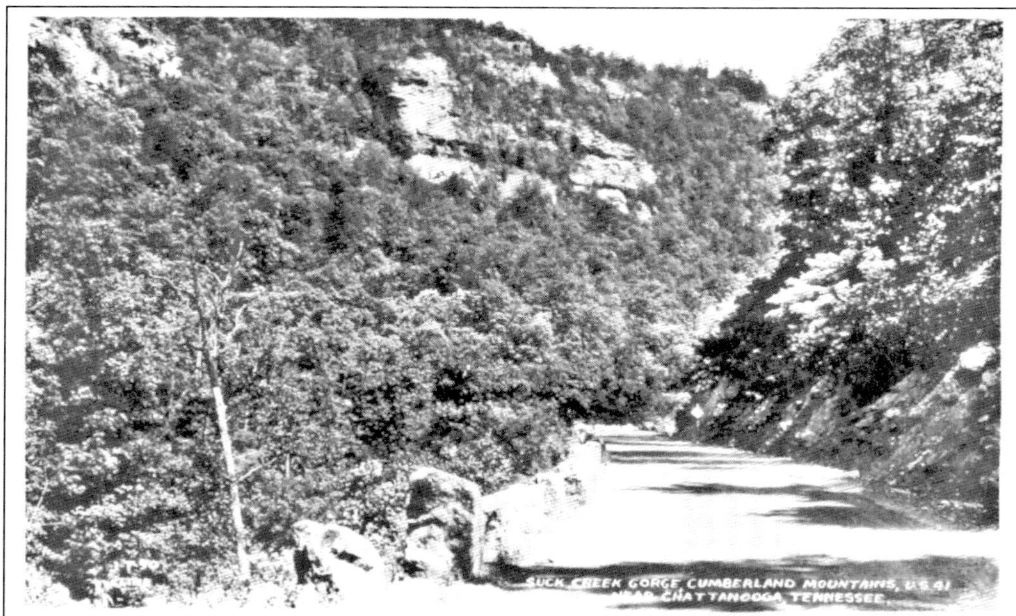

This is on the Walden Ridge section of Cumberland Plateau but does not appear to be U.S. 41. U.S. 41 does not go near Suck Creek Gorge. This is more likely Highway 27 between Powell's Crossroads and Chattanooga, which does go by the Suck Creek Gorge. Lusk is an old name often encountered near Suck Creek (for example, Lusk Point, Lusk Cemetery, and Lusk home).

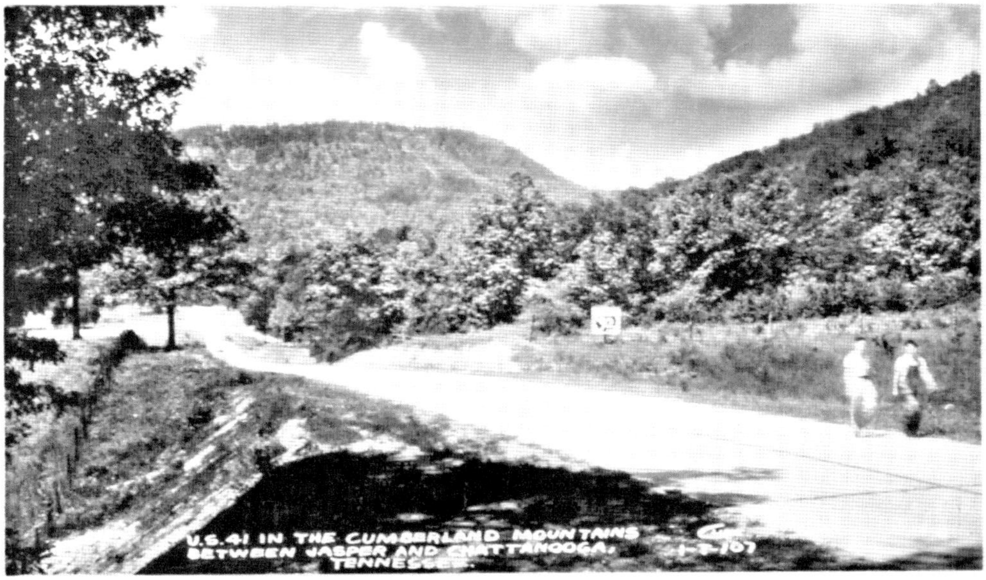

These two barefoot boys are walking (they are on the wrong side of the road to be hitchhiking) toward Guild. Walking and hitchhiking were the two ways most Marion County boys got around prior to the 1950s. The sign is an advertisement for Oertels 92 Lager Beer brewed in Kentucky.

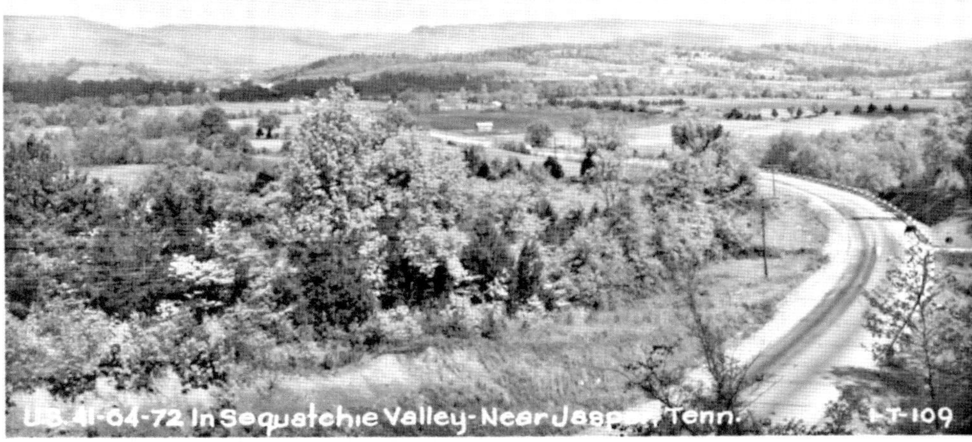

Just east of Jasper near the foot of Anderson's Ridge, cows can be seen alongside and in the road. The Hancock Road bears off to the right just before the barn in the center of the image. A. B. Pemberton built one of the first homes on this road. The Marion County Airport is located between Pleasant Grove Road and the Hancock Road. Castle Rock can be seen in the distance.

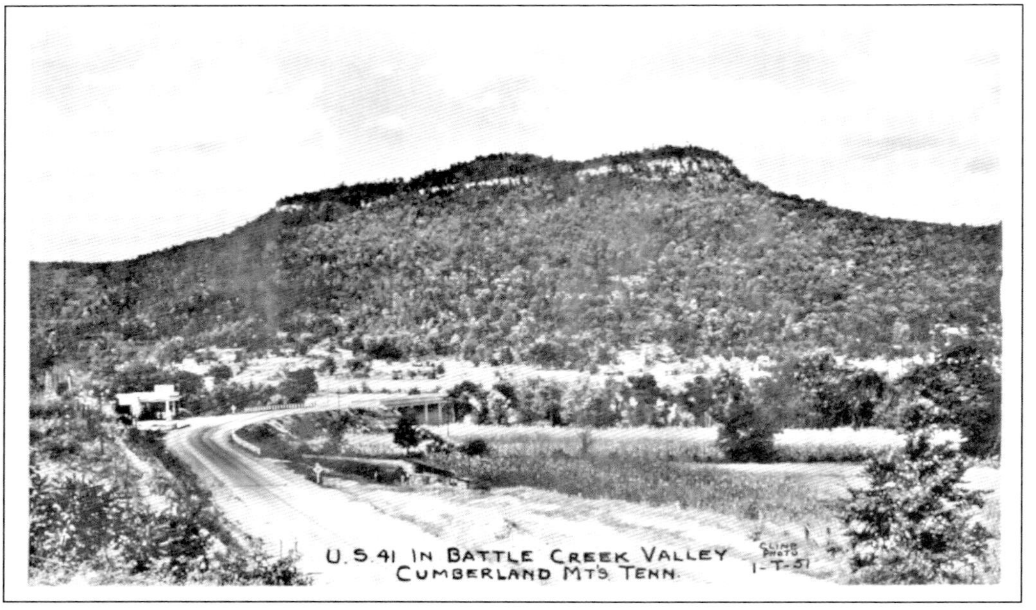

Local photographers often gave too little information to identify a postcard location. This is not U.S. 41. It is Highway 72 between Kimball and South Pittsburg. The service station on the left was owned and operated by Pat Layne. The bridge in the center is now the Pat Layne Memorial Bridge. In the early 1870s, Samuel E. Jones built an experimental blast furnace near here and called it Fiery Gizzard.

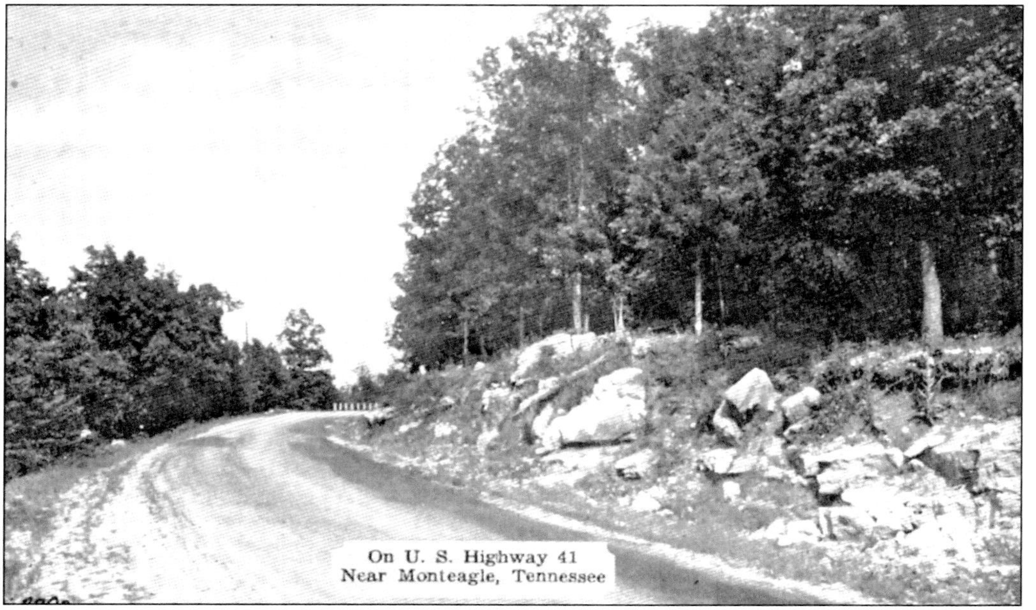

This is a view of "Old 41" near the top of the mountain, coming from the east toward Monteagle. Prior to 1915, there was no state highway department (each county was responsible for its roads), and until 1918, only a wagon road led up the mountain. Local folks often took ashes from their cook stove or fireplace to fill potholes and ensure roads were navigable. In November 1958, blasting for the interstate began on Monteagle Mountain.

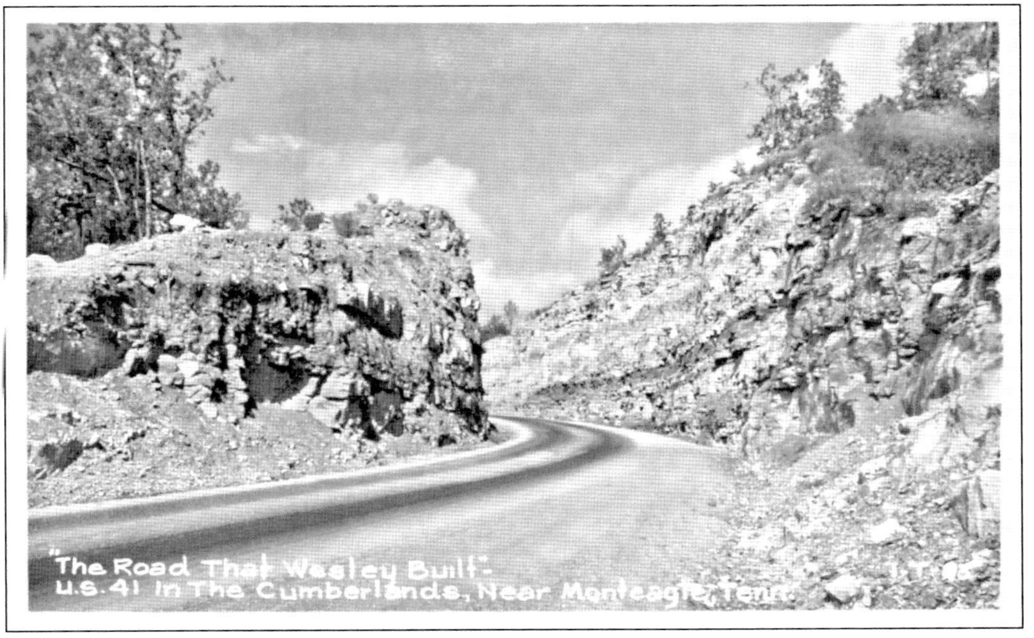

This view is from around 1950, coming up the mountain from Martin Springs toward Monteagle. Other communities on this side of the mountain include Jumpoff, Pinhook, Fiery Gizzard, Comfort, Sweeten's Cove (sometimes referred to as Ketchall), and Star Route.

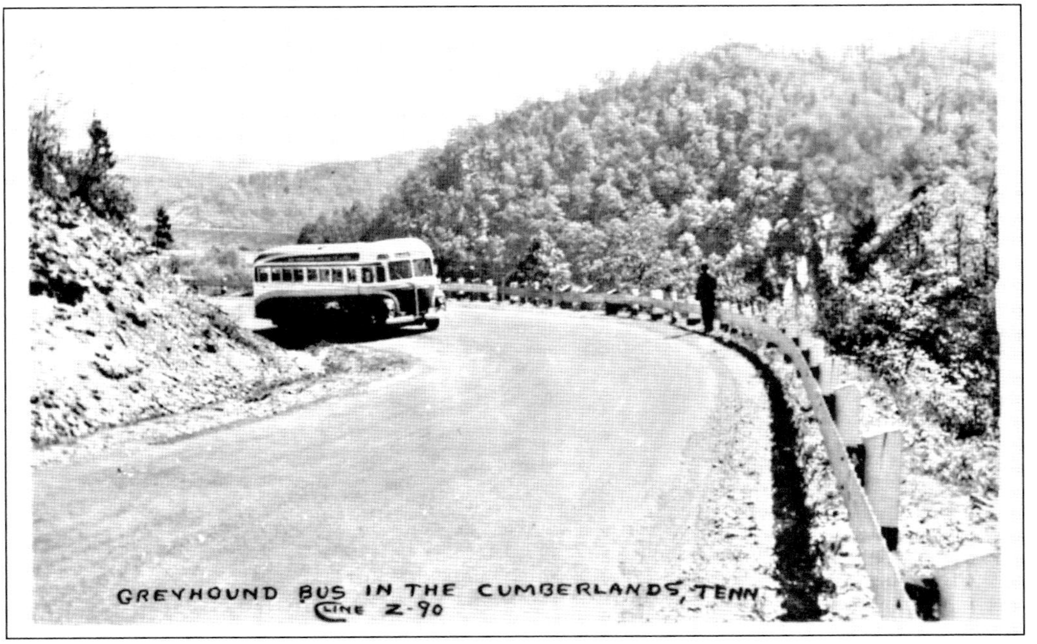

A Greyhound bus is coming up U.S. 41 on the Pelham side of the mountain. Note the man in dark clothing standing on the right side of the road near the center of the postcard. Guardrails were constructed of wood and tin, affording drivers minimum protection. Cars, and particularly trucks, often went through the rails and over the side of the mountain. The message says, "Stayed on top Mt. Eagle [*sic*] last night. Daddy got 2 pr shoes at Rich's."

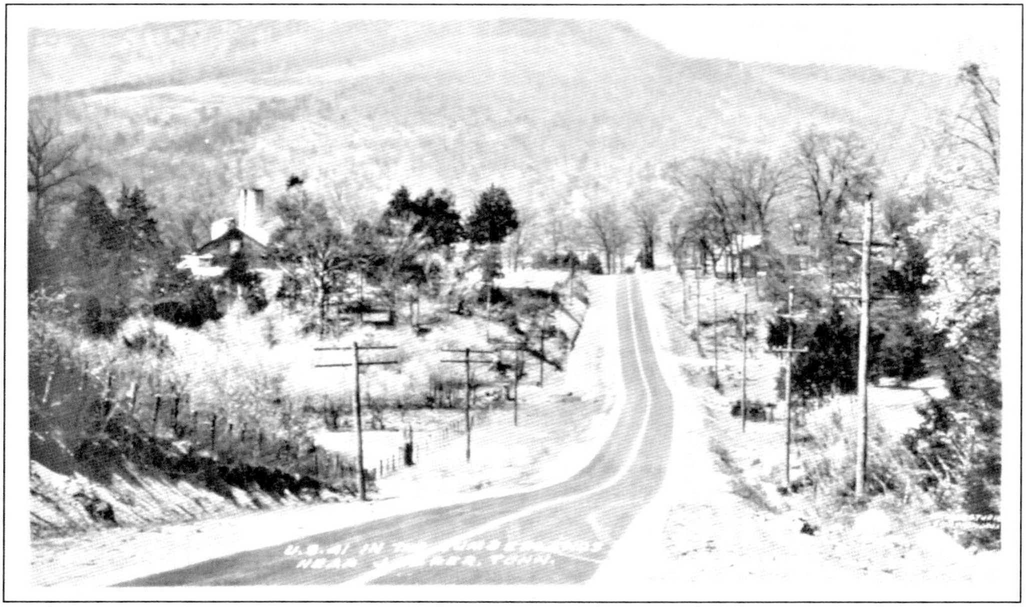

Postmarked Jasper 1934, this is thought to be in the Kimball area. The barn and silos seen on the left are no longer there. Examination under a high-powered magnifying glass reveals the exact location of nondescript views when a sign, license plate, or other clue is found. Occasionally identifying a card defies all efforts, as was the case with this one.

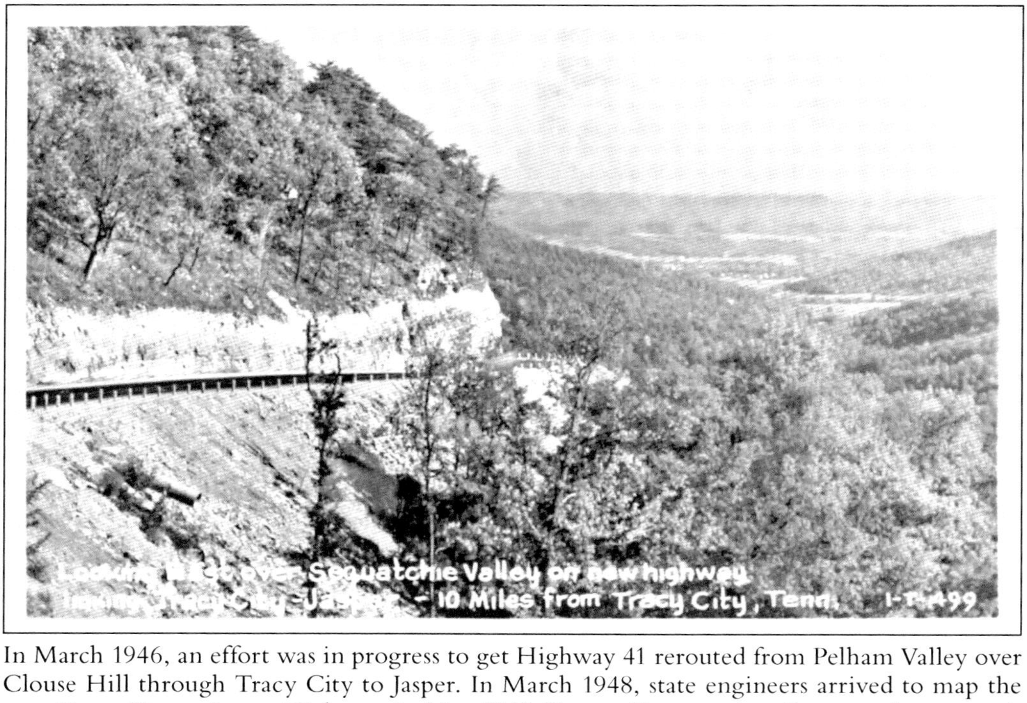

In March 1946, an effort was in progress to get Highway 41 rerouted from Pelham Valley over Clouse Hill through Tracy City to Jasper. In March 1948, state engineers arrived to map the new Tracy City to Jasper Highway. In May 1949, Brown Construction Company began work on the road. The drive up U.S. 41 and Highway 150 from Pryor's Cove past the Big Hill Fire tower, Lick Point, and Oak Grove to Tracy City is breathtaking.

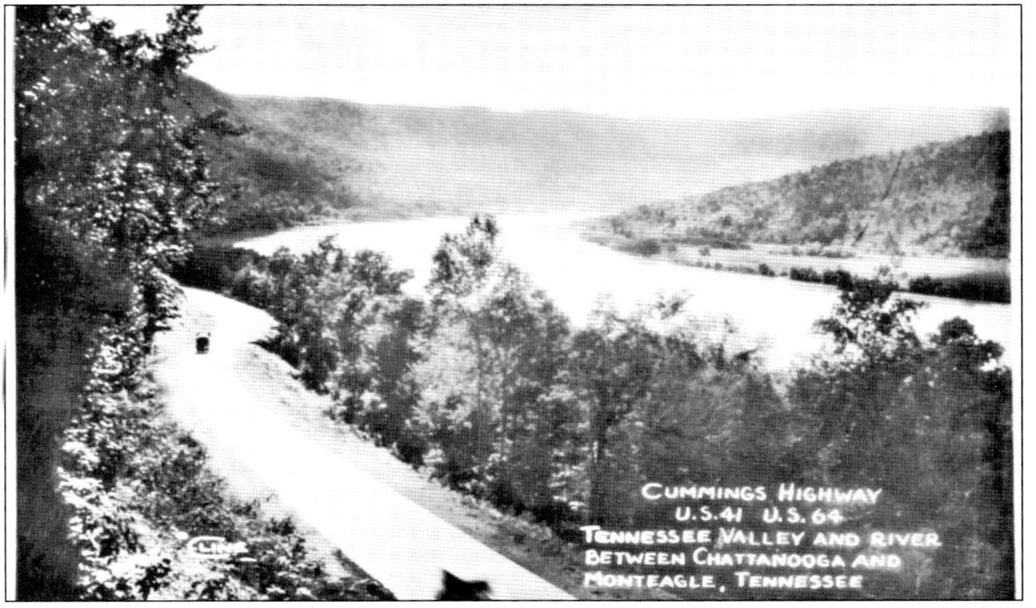

This was taken from the large rock at Sullivan's looking west toward Guild. A crew laying fiber-optic cable destroyed the rock. Randall Sullivan's Store has an impressive collection of photographs of local fishermen and their catches. The Will Cummings Highway, named for the Hamilton County judge who pioneered road building in the early 1900s, extends from Jasper to Chattanooga. The most distant vehicle is a bus with luggage stored on top.

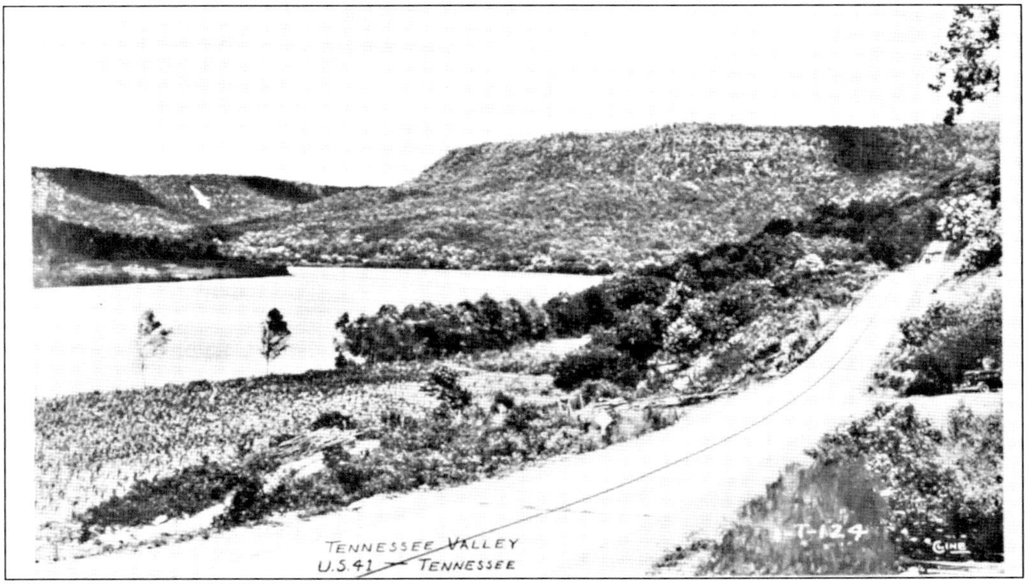

The Sullivans were victims of a rockslide in 1983, when highway workers interfered with natural drainage on the mountain, causing a strip mine filled with water to collapse, bringing tons of water, mud, and boulders down the mountainside. Their home and store were destroyed, and their many antique automobiles were crushed and/or pushed into the Tennessee River. Most were never recovered. Large piles of timber can be seen across the road. This community is the Riverside community.

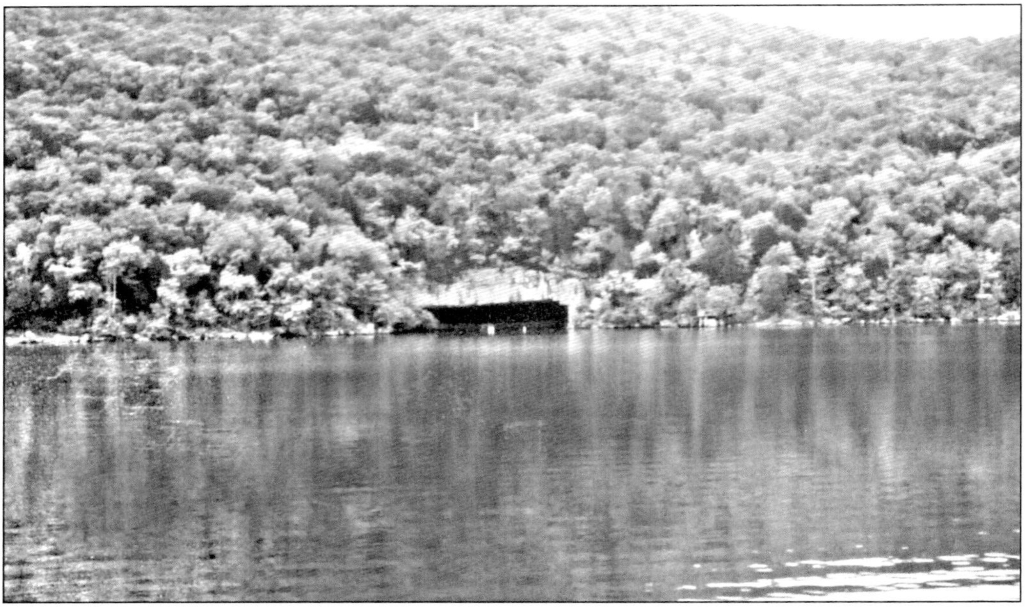

Nickajack Cave was a popular hiding place for the Chickamauga Indians. In 1790, Nick-O-Jack Town (about 40 huts) sprung up directly in front of the cave. In 1823, Pres. James Monroe, Sam Houston, and Andrew Jackson met here, and more than 100 years later, Sheriff Homer Dawson investigated the murder of Louise Holmes in the cave. Johnny Cash once made a suicidal gesture here, and there have been two incredible cave hoaxes related to "lost" cavers. Cars once drove inside the mouth of the cave.

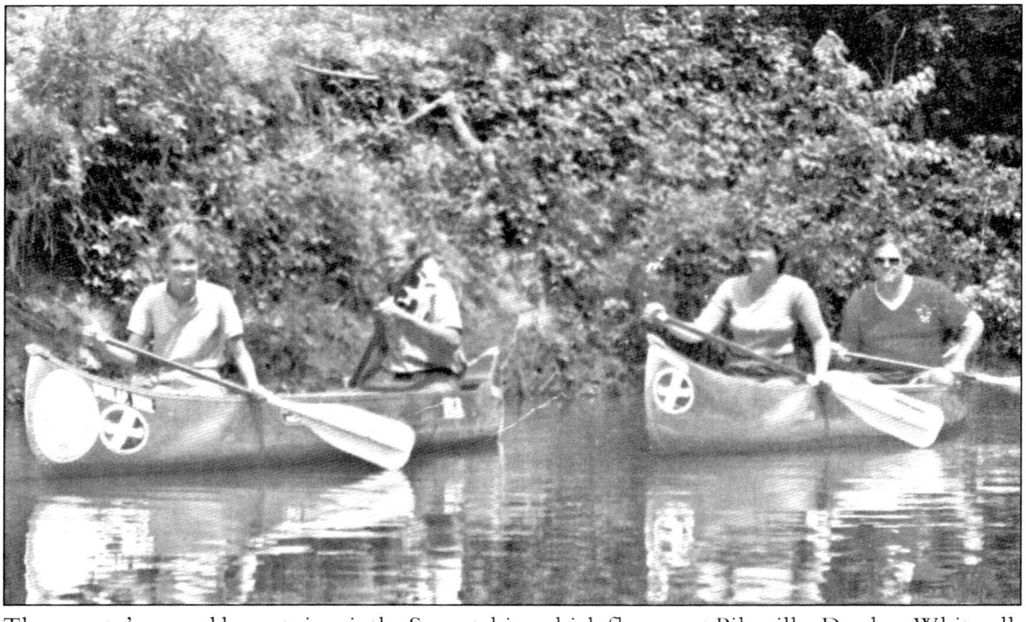

The county's second largest river is the Sequatchie, which flows past Pikeville, Dunlap, Whitwell, and Jasper before emptying into the Tennessee River directly across from New Hope. The American Indian word "sequatchie" means opossum. In the 1950s, Mrs. Kelly Wampler swam alone for miles up and down the Sequatchie River.

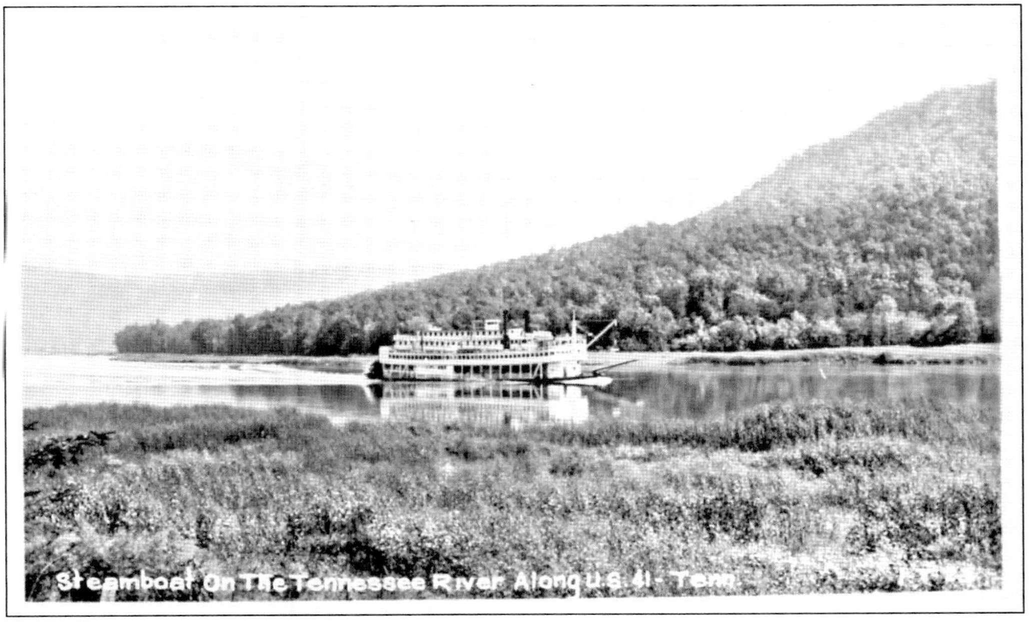

This paddle wheeler, near McNabb's place and TVA Raccoon Mountain Project Shooting Range, is going upstream toward Chattanooga. Highway 41 runs parallel to the river from Guild to Moccasin Bend. This vessel has two stacks that often played havoc with overhead cables and bridges. Few relics remain of the great steamboats, such as the *Chattanooga*, *Paint Rock*, *Dunbar*, *Resaca*, and *Wheeler* that plied the Tennessee River during the 1800s and into the early 1900s.

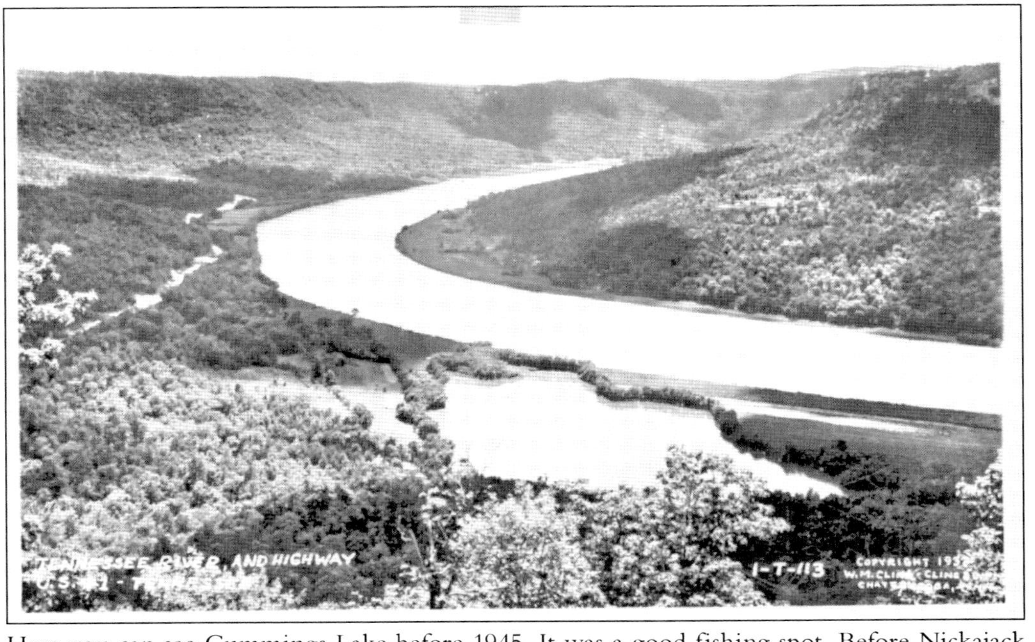

Here you can see Cummings Lake before 1945. It was a good fishing spot. Before Nickajack Dam, there were many like this adjoined by cornfields all along the river. When the TVA flooded this area (50 to 300 feet each side of the river) with shallow water, they became a part of that flood plain.

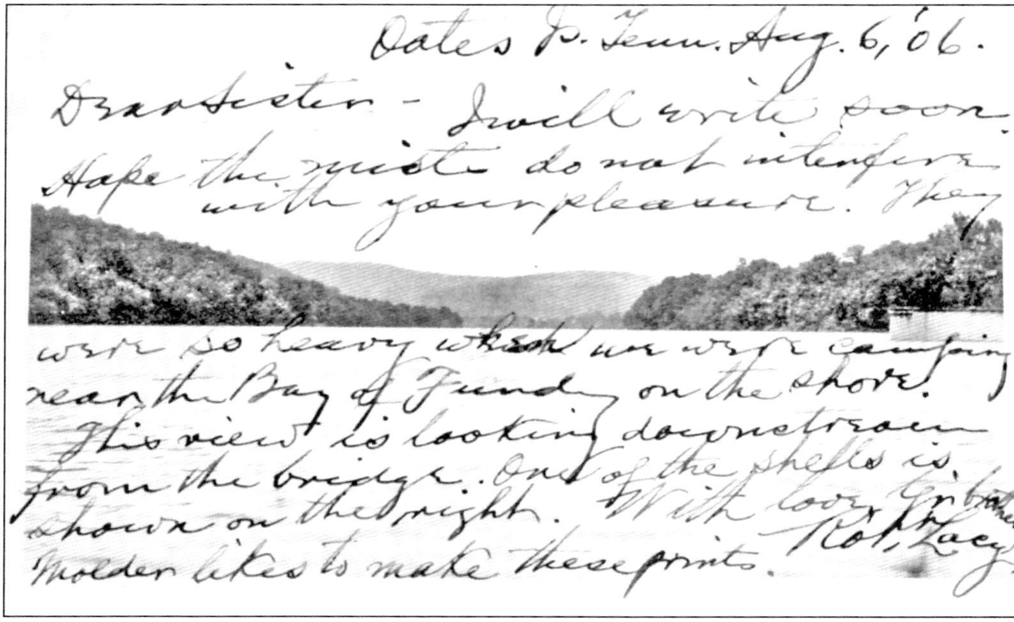

Mailed from Oates Island (in the Mullins Cove area) in 1906, this card shows a view downstream from the bridge with one of the concrete pier "shells" on the right. There are numerous tunnels around this area that were a part of railroad construction. The railroad paid young men to paddle downstream at night and place a lantern on the pier to make it visible to boat captains. They finally blew out the pier and sold the property back to those owning adjoining lands.

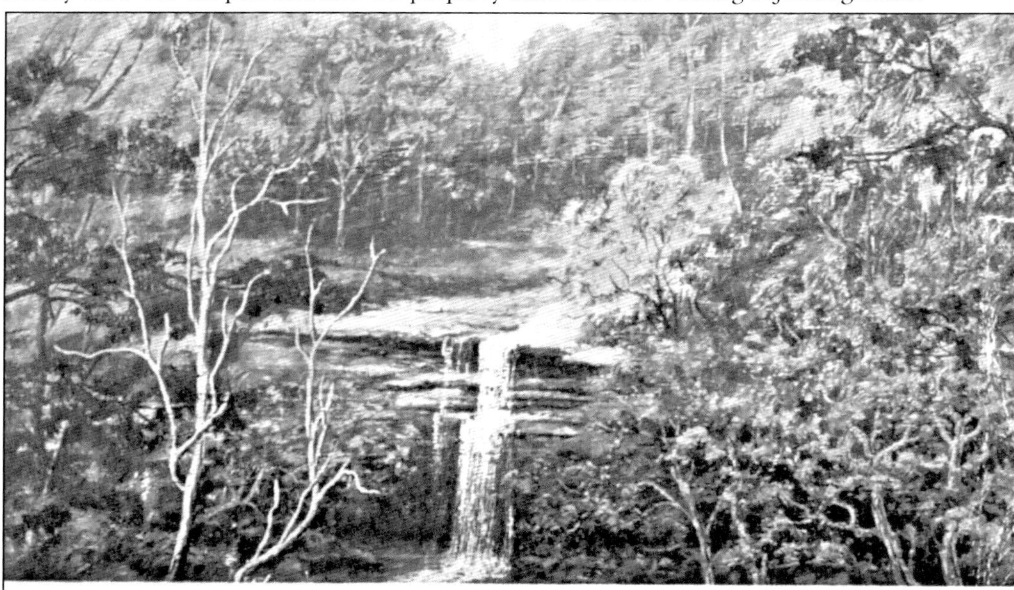

This is a beautiful painting of Monteagle Falls. The 1909 message states, "We have a cozy cottage on the Cumberland Mountains." The author added this card to his collection in 1990 for the price of 25¢. Marvin Runyon, former postmaster general, is a local resident and chair of Friends of Cumberland Mountains.

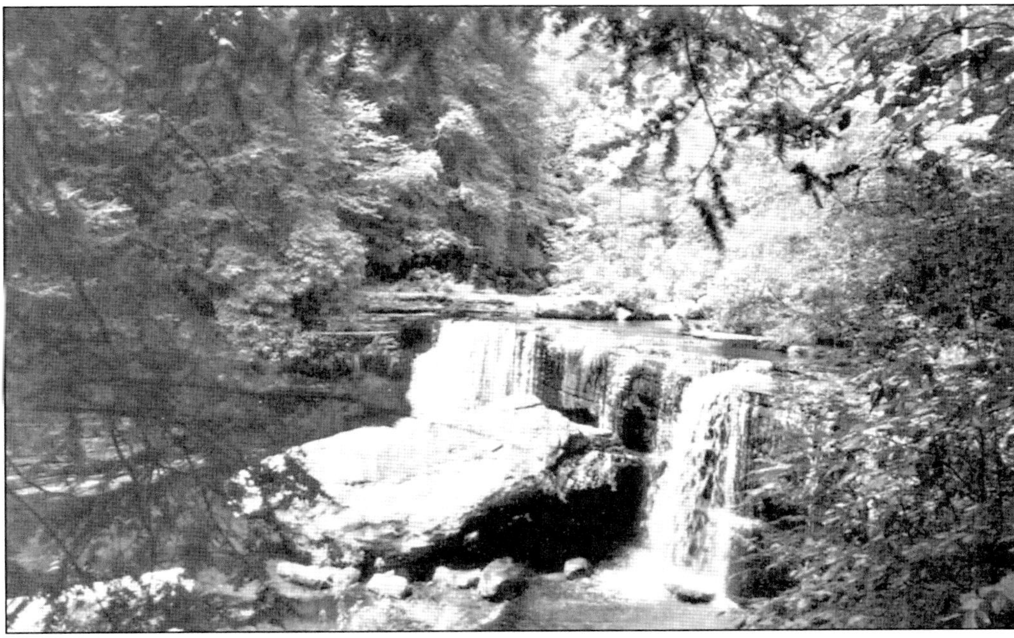

This photograph by Robert Ritchie is of Greeter Falls, one of many mystical waterfalls, located within the South Cumberland Recreation Area. There is a spiral staircase to Lower Greeter Falls. There are unnumbered caves, cascades, and odd stone formations near here.

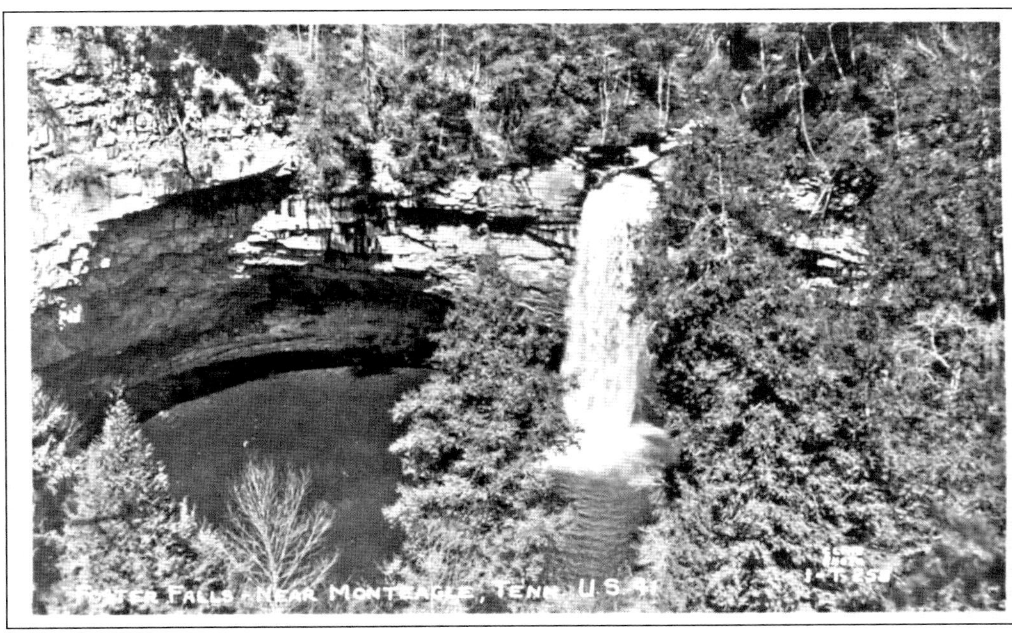

This is a Cline RPPC of Foster Falls between Jasper and Tracy City. At 65 feet, Foster Falls is the highest fall atop the southern part of the Cumberland Plateau. The large pool at the bottom of the falls is perfect for swimming. From time immemorial, this natural fastness has been a refuge and waterhole for wildlife.

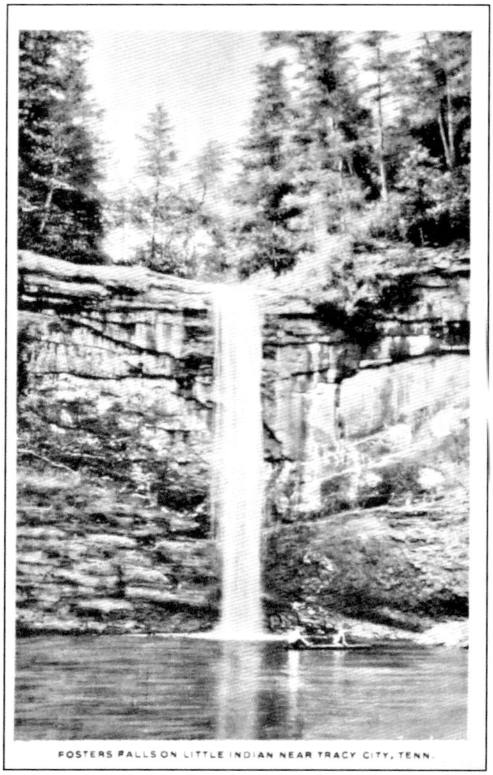

Shown here is a wonderful old sepia card of Foster Falls. Note the two people in what appears to be a flat-bottom or dugout boat. There is a hanging (or swinging) bridge near the falls.

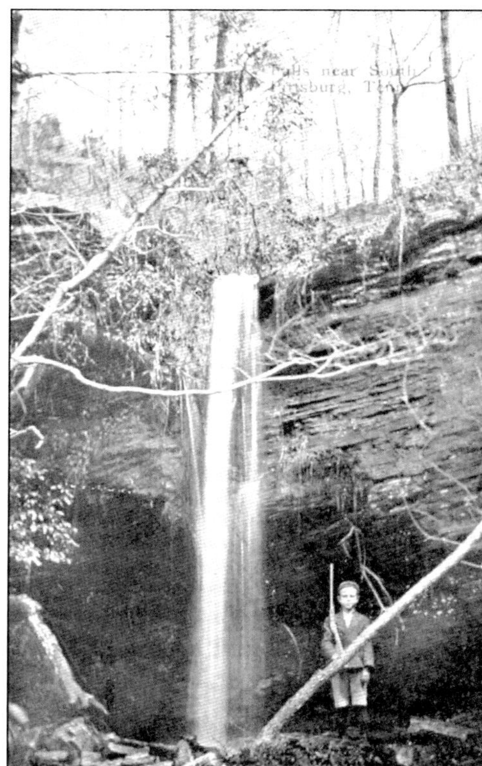

This 1915 card shows a boy and his lever-action rifle. The falls is only identified as being near South Pittsburg.

Nine

MISCELLANEOUS VIEWS

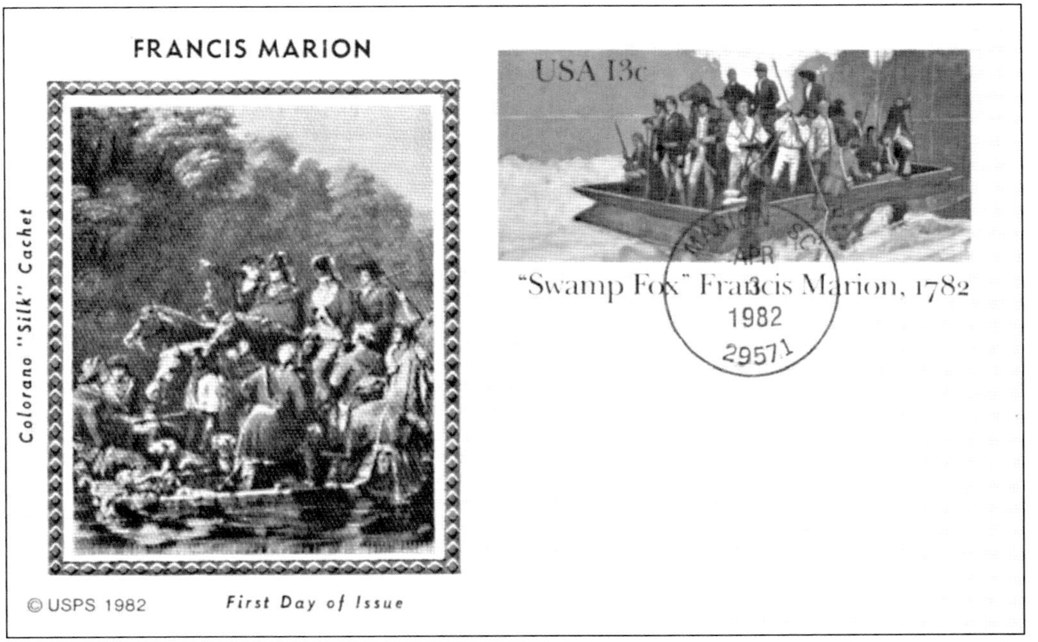

Marion County was named for the Revolutionary hero Sir Francis Marion, widely know as the "Swamp Fox" for his hit-and-run tactics. This 1982 first day cover (FDC) has a beautiful silk cachet of Marion. This is the first day this stamp was sold by the U.S. Postal Service. Cachets began to appear in 1923 and FDCs in 1937.

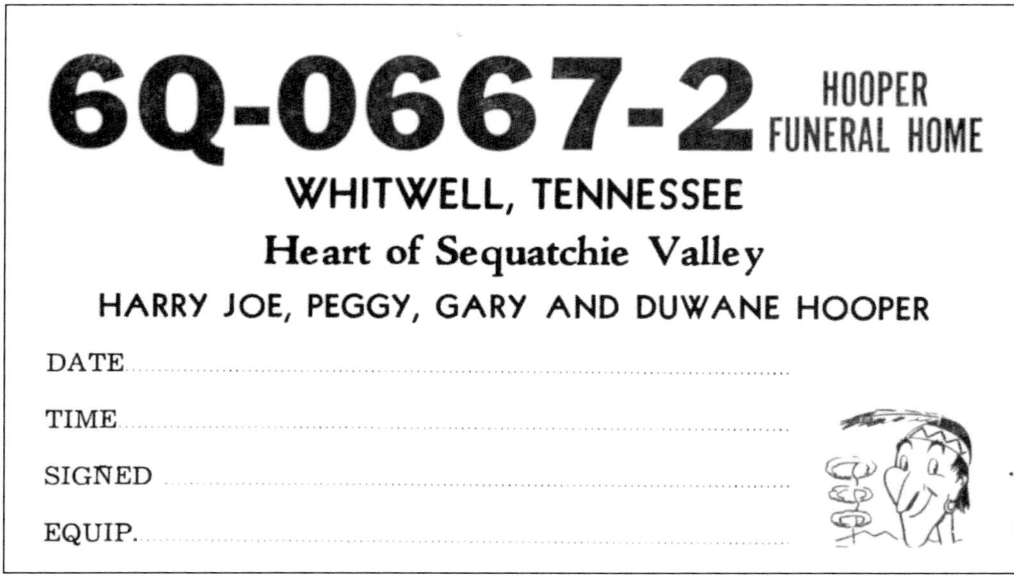

R. G. Putnam of Pikeville started a funeral home in Whitwell in 1939. Frank Henry was the first manager and sold insurance there. Employees from Pikeville did embalming in the Whitwell office. Harry Joe Hooper went to mortuary school in 1951 and bought the funeral home from Jack Putnam in 1962. He changed the name to Hooper Funeral Home. His three sons worked there at various times. The Hoopers were amateur radio operators.

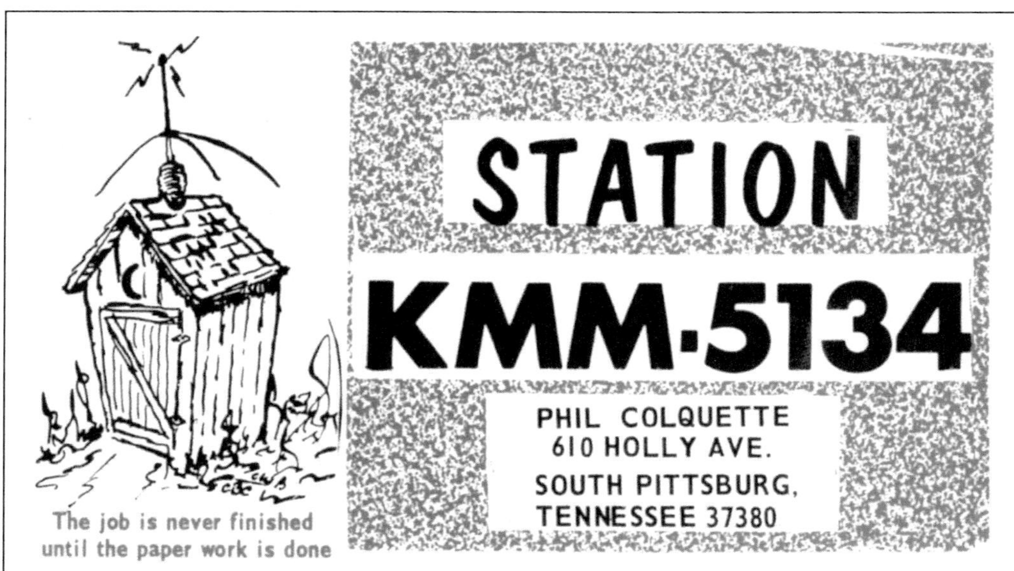

It is interesting that Phil lived on Holly Avenue, as did several other amateur radio operators. Outhouses are a recurring theme on postcards, and there are a number of collectors of the subject.

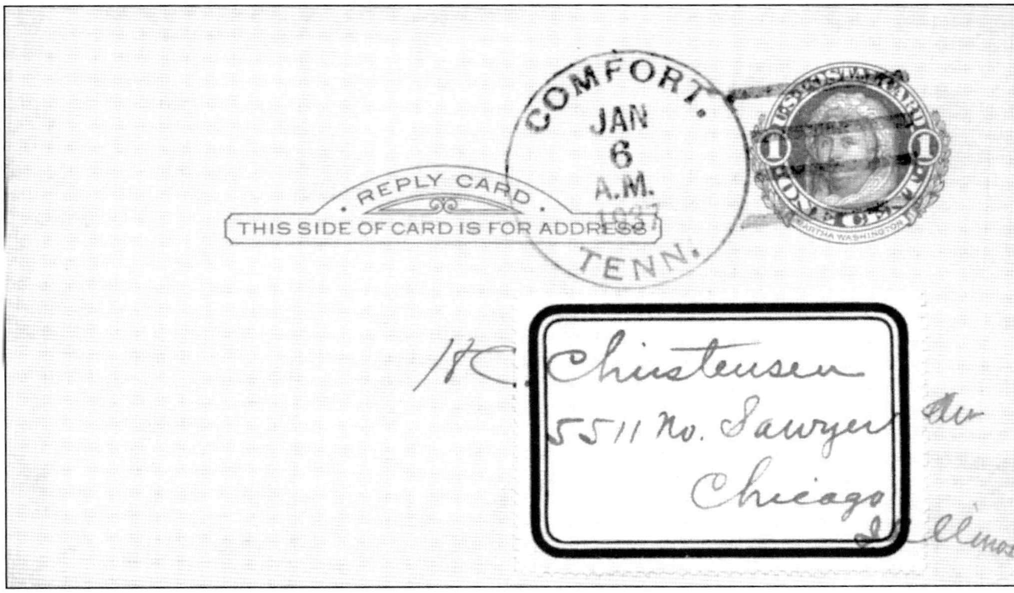

This 1937 postal card was postmarked at the Comfort, Tennessee, post office. Comfort was a community near Battle Creek and home to A. J. Gudger. The Comfort Post Office lasted from 1888 to 1955 and was named for Comfort resident Matilda Tate, who set up the post office in her home 12 miles north of South Pittsburg.

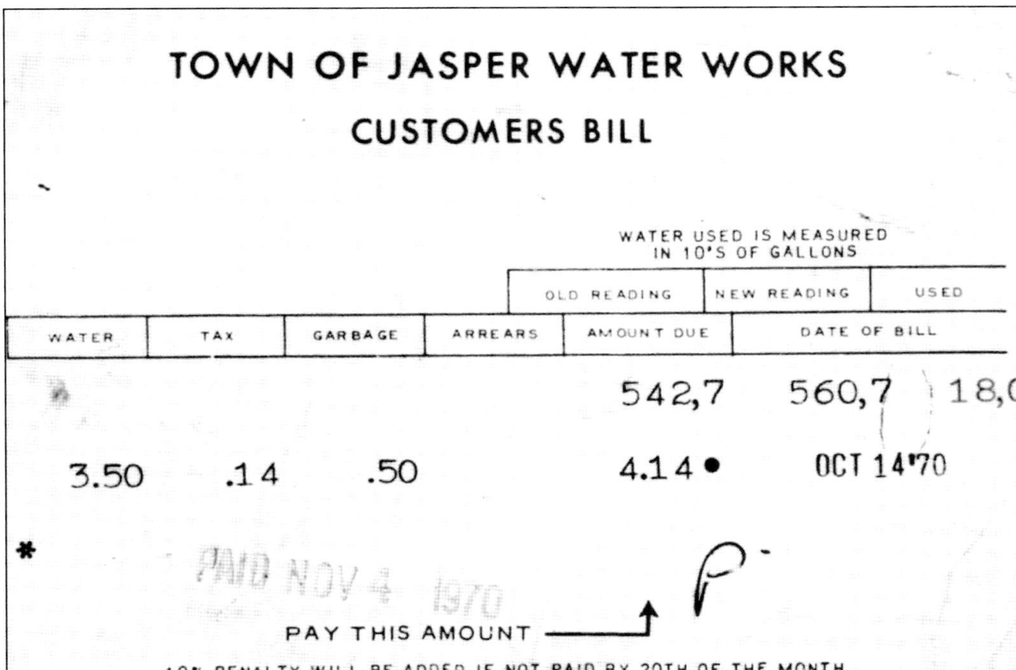

TOWN OF JASPER WATER WORKS

CUSTOMERS BILL

WATER USED IS MEASURED IN 10'S OF GALLONS

OLD READING	NEW READING	USED
542,7	560,7	18,0

WATER	TAX	GARBAGE	ARREARS	AMOUNT DUE	DATE OF BILL
3.50	.14	.50		4.14 •	OCT 14'70

PAID NOV 4 1970

PAY THIS AMOUNT

10% PENALTY WILL BE ADDED IF NOT PAID BY 20TH OF THE MONTH

The town of Jasper Water Works used postal cards to bill customers. Many utility companies do this today. This November 1970 statement was for $3.50. For years, a spring halfway up the mountain has supplied Jasper with water, but at one time, water for the county was pumped directly from the Tennessee River.

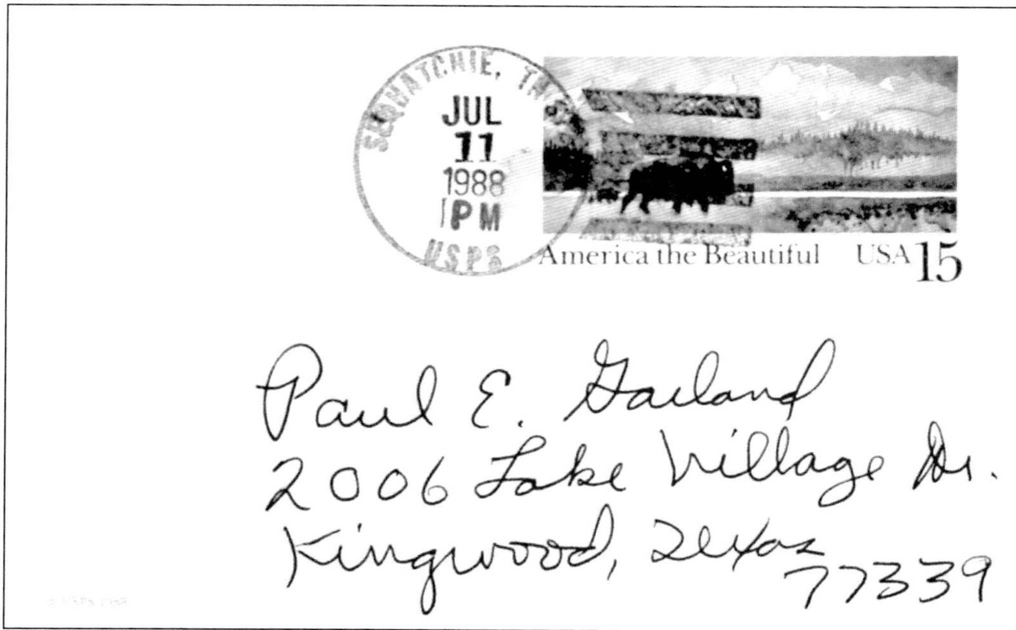

Paul Garland of Lexington, Tennessee, was a postcard and U.S. currency collector. He wrote a number of books on currency and Southern bank notes. In the late 1980s, Paul traveled the state, mailing himself postal cards capturing every postmark and zip code in Tennessee. The author obtained a number of those, such as this one postmarked at Sequatchie (37374). Several years later, Paul's health failed woefully, and he took his own life.

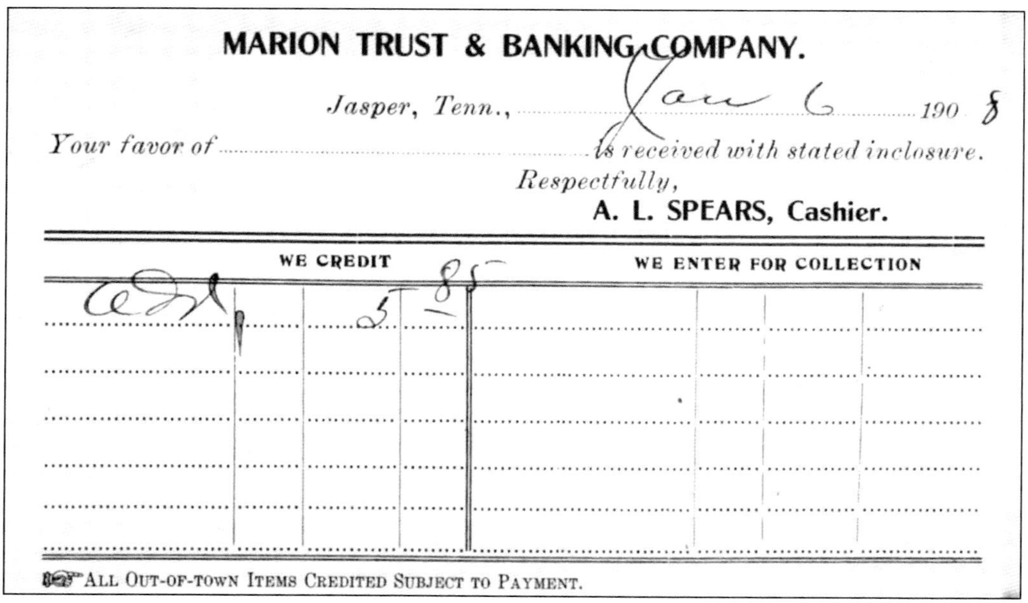

MARION TRUST & BANKING COMPANY.

Jasper, Tenn., Jan 6 *190* 8

Your favor of .... *is received with stated inclosure.*

Respectfully,

A. L. SPEARS, Cashier.

WE CREDIT			WE ENTER FOR COLLECTION			
[illegible]	5	85				

ALL OUT-OF-TOWN ITEMS CREDITED SUBJECT TO PAYMENT.

In 1873, the U.S. Postal Service introduced the penny postal card (government postal with imprinted stamp), allowing preprinted or handwritten messages to be mailed at the reduced rate of 1¢. The bank cashier's position was second only to the bank president at the time.

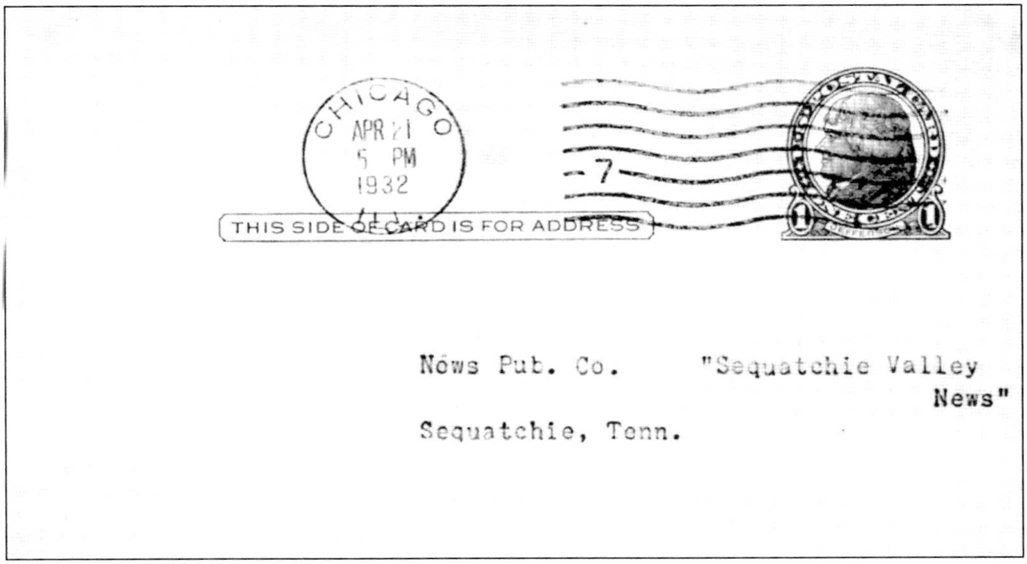

This news source was established in 1891. The back of this card is a printed advertisement for Cooper Black (metal type), Thormod Monsen and Son Inc. of Chicago. W. C. Hill, Roy M. Woodfin, and Roland and Helen Reed served for years as the *Sequatchie Valley News*, *South Pittsburg Hustler*, and *Jasper Journal* editors, respectively.

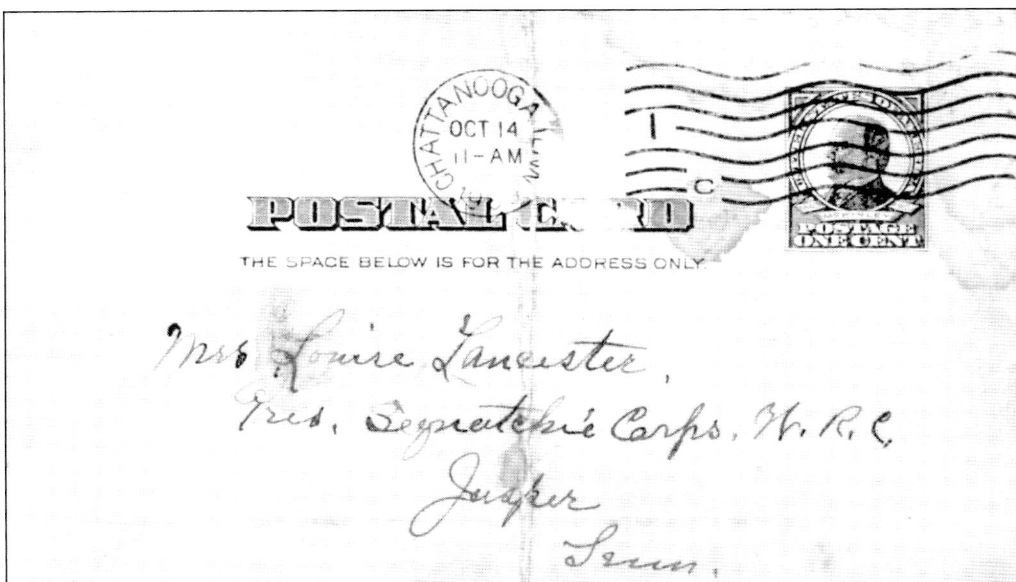

It was the WPA (not the WRC) that built the entire rock fence on Coppinger Cove Road. Postcards remained a communication device of choice into the 1950s. The first telephone exchange in Jasper was not until 1880. In 1914, there were 75 phones in Jasper and, in 1925, a total of 119. Even in the 1950s, many did not have a phone, and most of those who did were on multiple-party lines. Today everyone has cellular phones and e-mail, making the postcard a thing of the past.

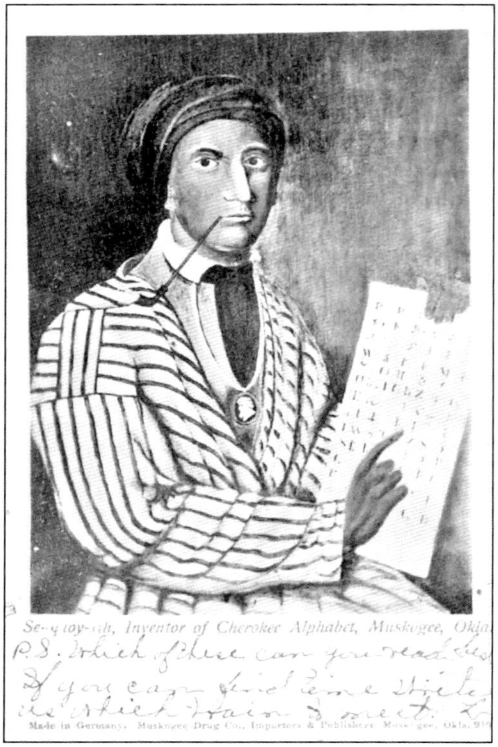

Here Sequoyah (George Gist "Guess") and daughter Ayoka introduce his Cherokee alphabet to the American Indians. He is an ancestor of former MCHS basketball standout Randy Guess, who now lives on Amelia Island. Sequoyah, a cripple for life and a Cherokee of mixed blood, could neither read nor write. In 1835, the Cherokee numbered 16,592, with 1,592 black slaves and 201 whites intermarried with the American Indians.

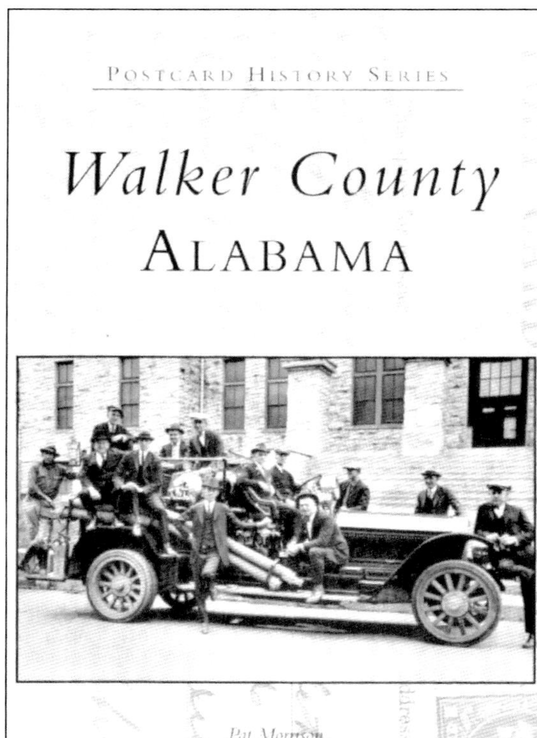

Pat Morrison, a standout football player at MCHS and Middle Tennessee State University, wrote this Walker County, Alabama, book. Pat, oddly enough, was raised in Jasper, Tennessee, and now lives in Jasper, Alabama.

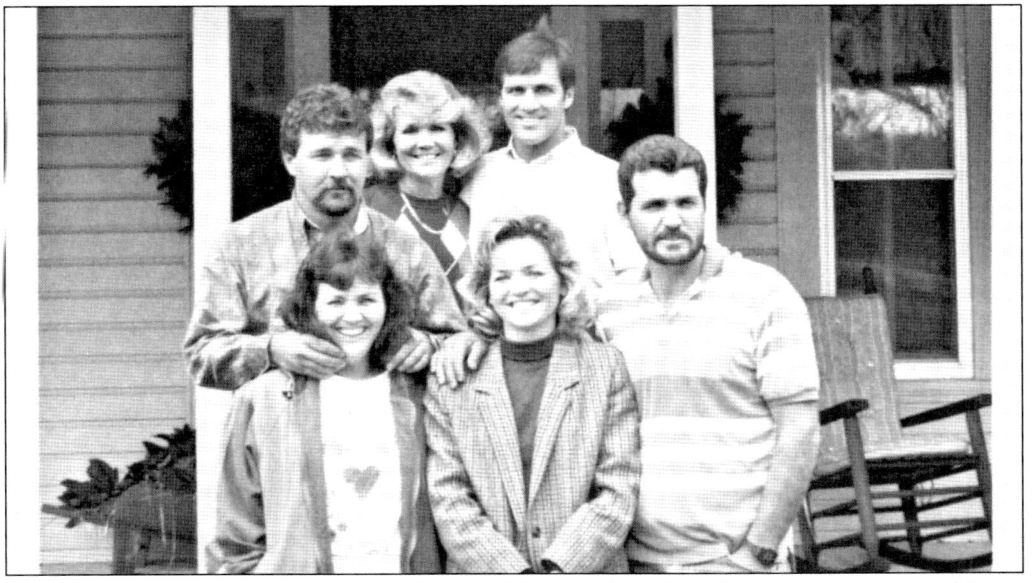

This dilapidated old frame house was the proud home of Frank and Purt Morrison. Frank's son Tom Allen and wife, Faye Morrison, lived in and cared for the home many years after Frank died. Eventually the repeated floods caused them to abandon the home. From left to right in front of the house are (first row) Saredia, Viola, and Shane; (back row) Buck, Evelyn, and Alabama. All are Morrisons, and all but Evelyn attended schools in Marion County.

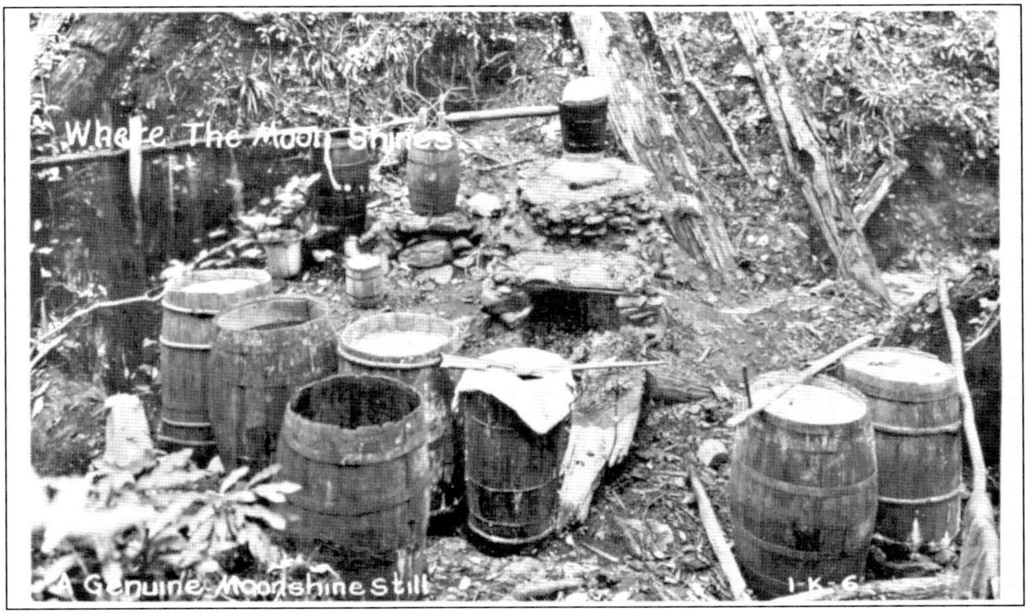

Moonshine stills were commonplace in Marion County, where good water and remoteness presented ideal conditions for them, and they earned the area the reputation as the "moonshine capital." During the Prohibition era, the business of smuggling whiskey out of the valley and off the mountains became scandalously big and complex. Before Prohibition, most moonshine was made for family and friends. Some was distilled for socialization and some for medicinal purposes. Many Marion County bootleggers felt if it was their corn, then they could eat it—or drink it.

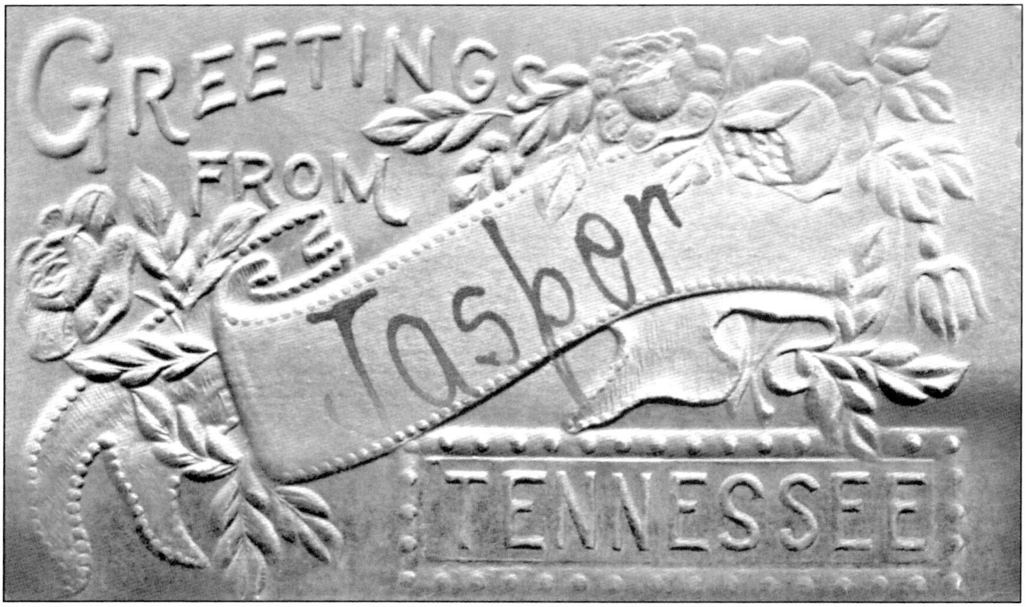

Embossed cards, popular in the early 1900s, were fragile and did not survive well. This card was printed around 1905. The word "Tennessee" is embossed, and "Jasper" is written with a glittery type of paint. In postcard circles, the term "Golden Age of Postcards" is often used. It refers to the time when the best quality and greatest quantity of postcards were created. The period of time for this has not been narrowly defined but generally is accepted to be from around 1898 to 1920.

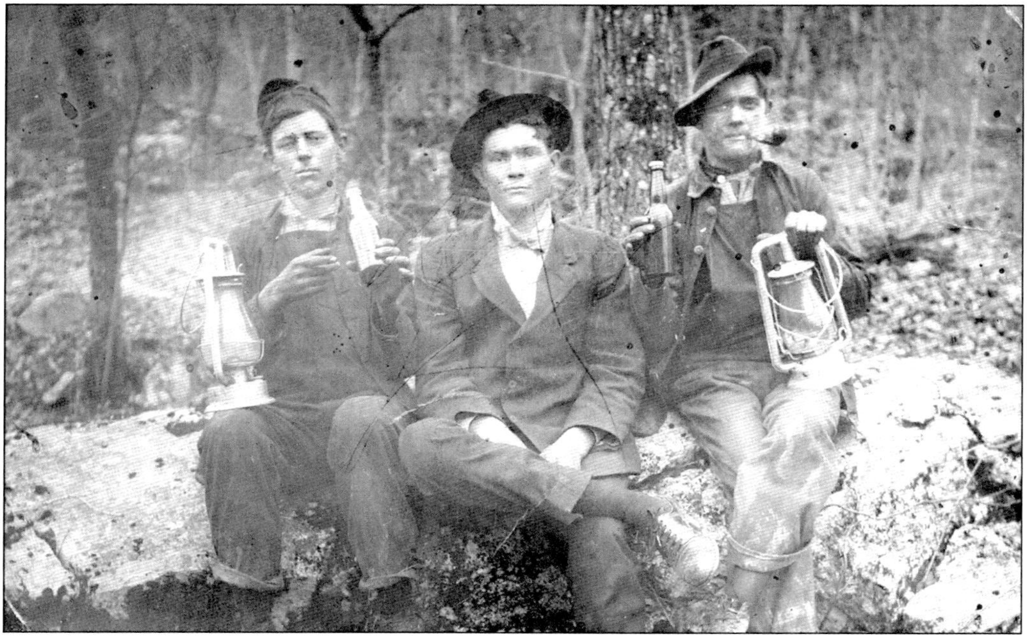

From left to right are Frank Fox, George "Foots" Jones, and Milton Jones, all of Jasper. It appears the threesome, all descendants of good stock, have been coon hunting and carried along beverages to ward off the chill of night. Foots, blessed with athleticism, is reputed to have hit the longest homerun ever hit in Jasper. This postcard appeared in the *Jasper Journal* on November 26, 1996.

Here is a group of Jasper residents. From left to right, they are George David Jones, Dora Thorne Jones Henderson, Arthur Milton Jones, and Katherine Viola Jones (standing in front), the daughter of George. Conspicuously missing in this RPPC, taken about 1920, is the other Jones brother, James "Tince" Brownlow Jones.

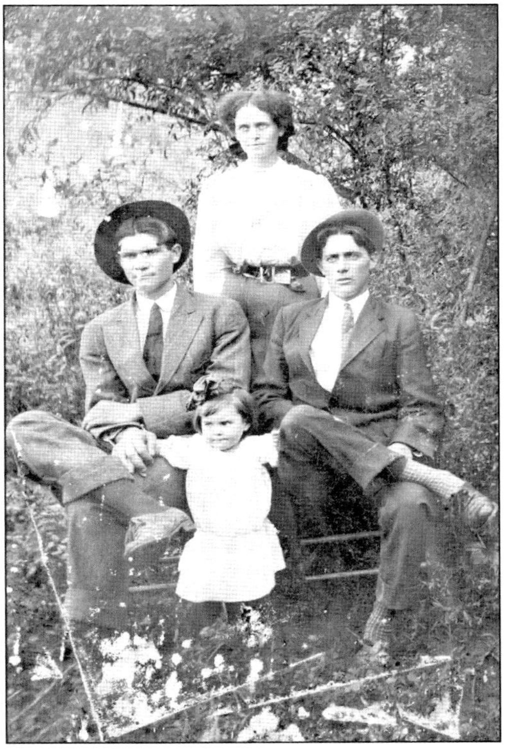

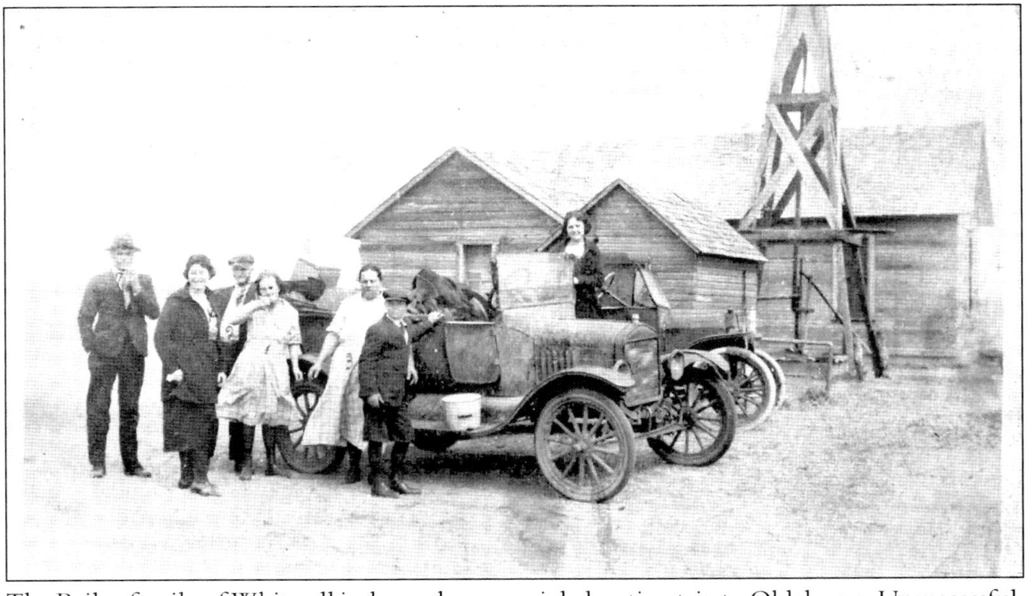

The Bailey family of Whitwell is shown here on a job-hunting trip to Oklahoma. Unsuccessful, they returned to Whitwell. From left to right are James Henry Bailey, Ester Burnett Bailey (daughter of Dr. Elijah Burnett), James Henry Bailey Jr., Luna Lenora Bailey, Fred Bailey, and an unidentified Bailey girl thought to be a daughter or daughter-in-law. Ester sent this to her sister Laura Morrison back in Whitwell saying, "We sure are a long way from Whitwell and are having our bucket dinner."

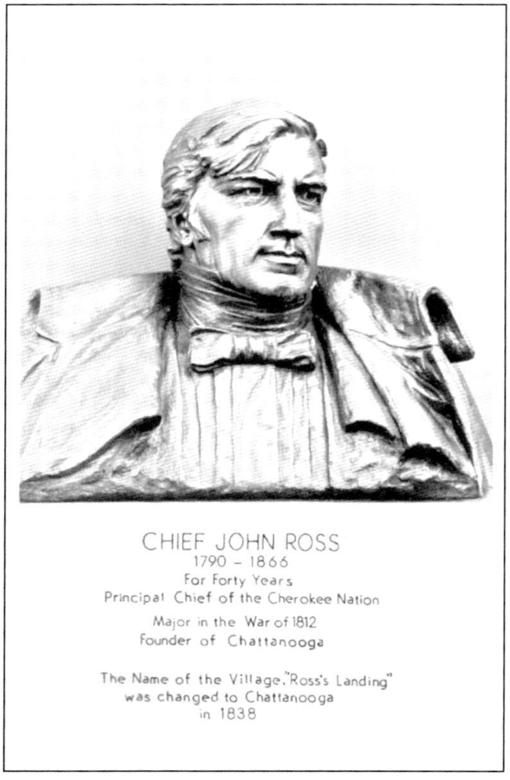

Chief John Ross lived from 1790 until 1866. Belle Kinney sculpted this, and the Chattanooga Women's Press Club sponsored the related programs. Ross was the principal chief of the Cherokee Tribe during the American Indian removals. The reader can find more information, paintings, and other things related to the Cherokee in Oklahoma than in Tennessee.

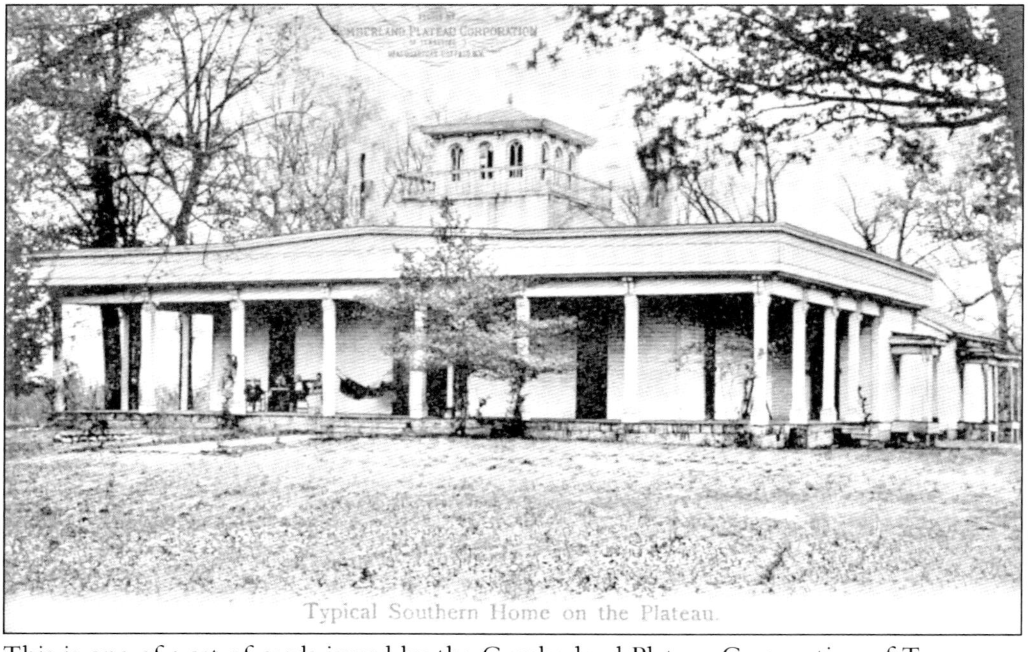

This is one of a set of cards issued by the Cumberland Plateau Corporation of Tennessee, headquartered in Buffalo, New York. Most cards from this set are postmarked 1906. This was not typical of homes on the mountains in 1906.

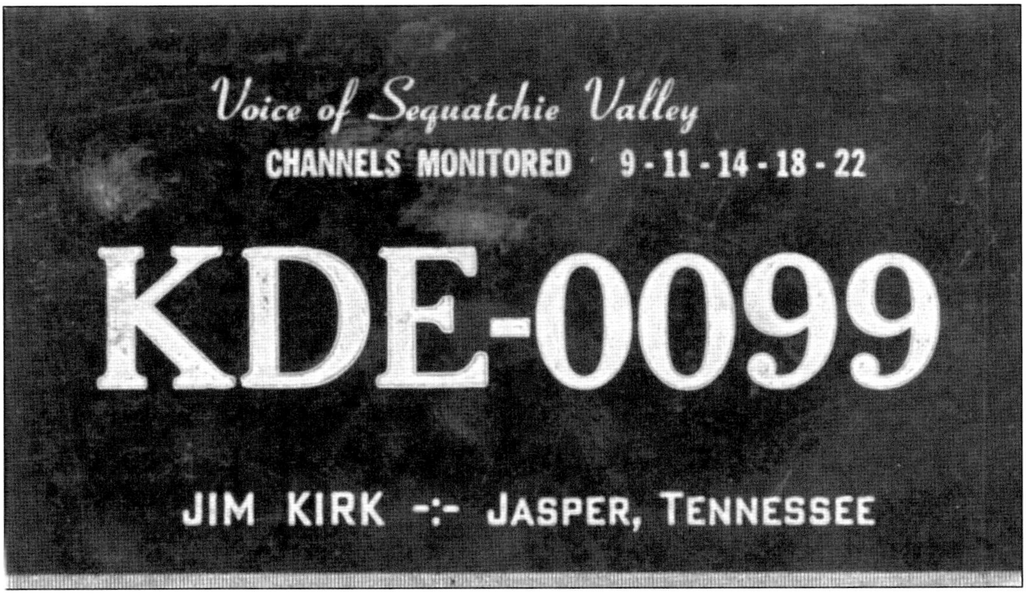

Jim Kirk was the oldest child of Charlie and Polly Kirk. He served as vice-mayor in Jasper and was a county commissioner. Jim died recently, and his family still resides in Jasper.

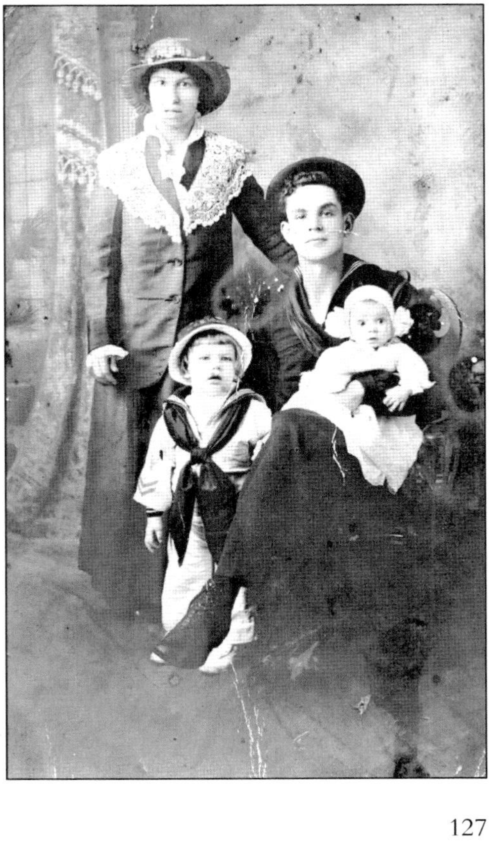

Around 1907, Joseph Daniel Morrison was in the navy. This RPPC shows his wife, Louisa, and sons, Joseph (Buck) and Daniel (Little Dan, sitting). Little Dan would leave Jasper to become a career navy man, attorney, and entrepreneur. He and half brother Chester were business partners throughout their adult lives. In trouble with the law over business, Chester "purportedly took the rap" for Dan and went to prison. Afterwards they relocated to the Altamonte Springs area of Florida, purchased part of a railroad company, and became uncommonly successful.

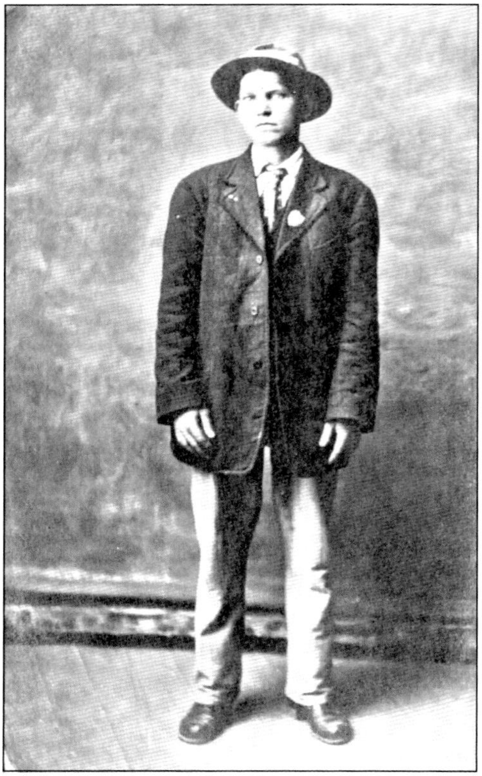

"Snapshot" was originally an expression referring to hunters firing with no forethought when flushing birds. The term migrated to photography when Eastman produced Kodak #1 in 1888 and coined the slogan, "You press the button, we do the rest." To serious photographers, "snapshot photographer" was a title of ridicule. This is a fine "snapshot" of Potsy Jones, who was a cousin to Jasper, Tense, Riley, and George Jones (not "The Possum").

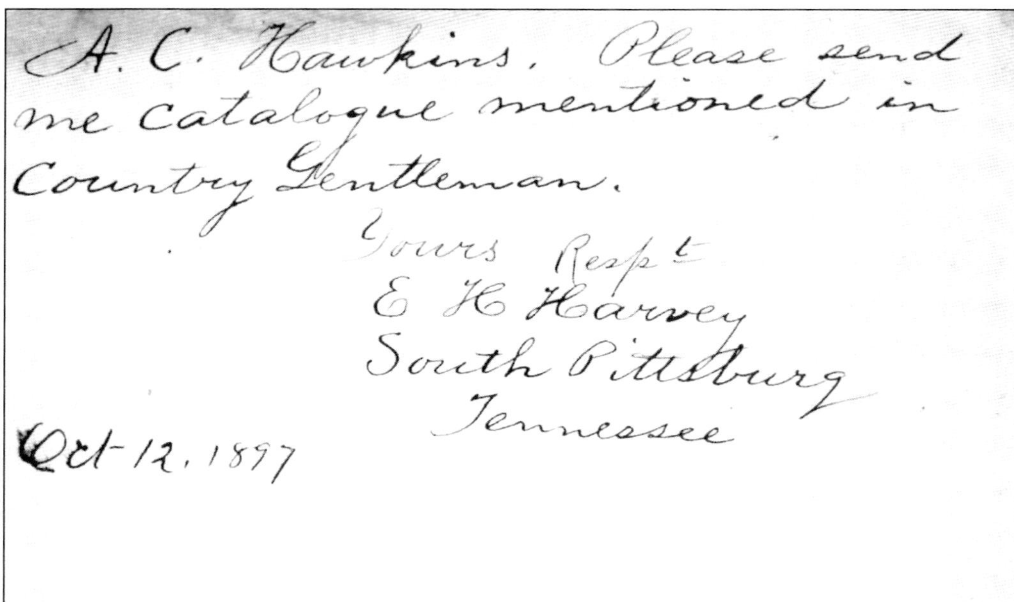

A. C. Hawkins. Please send
me catalogue mentioned in
Country Gentleman.
Yours Resp t
E H Harvey
South Pittsburg
Tennessee
Oct-12, 1897

This 1¢ postal card was sent to A. C. Hawkins, Box 100, Lancaster, Massachusetts.